ASSESSING READING 1: THEORY AND PRACTICE

Assessing reading ability is regarded all over the English-speaking world as one of the most important ways of monitoring educational standards, and there is ongoing controversy as to the best way of assessing reading and when and how this should be done.

This book, along with its companion volume *Assessing Reading 2: Changing Practice in Classrooms*, was originally conceived as the major outcome from an international seminar on reading assessment held in England. It focuses particularly on theoretical and methodological issues, though with a clear series of links to practices in assessment, especially state and national approaches to classroom-based assessment in the USA, the UK and Australia, at both primary and secondary levels.

Chapters offer new perspectives on the theories that underlie the development and interpretation of reading assessments, national assessments and classroom-based assessment, challenging readers to think in different ways.

Colin Harrison is Professor of Literary Studies in Education at the University of Nottingham and **Terry Salinger** is a Senior Research Analyst at the American Institutes for Research, Washington DC.

i

ASSESSING READING 1: THEORY AND PRACTICE

International Perspectives on Reading Assessment

Edited by Colin Harrison and Terry Salinger

London and New York

First published 1998
by Routledge
11 New Fetter Lane, London EC4P 4EE

Simultaneously published in the USA and Canada
by Routledge
29 West 35th Street, New York, NY 10001

© 1998 Colin Harrison and Terry Salinger, selection and editorial matter;
Individual chapters © their contributors

Typeset in Garamond by Florencetype Limited, Stoodleigh, Devon

Printed and bound in Great Britain by Creative Print
and Design (Wales), Ebbw Vale

British Library Cataloguing in Publication Data
A catalogue record for this book is available from the British Library

Library of Congress Cataloguing in Publication Data
Assessing reading: international perspectives on reading assessment/
edited by Colin Harrison and Terry Salinger.
p.   cm.
Contents: 1. Theory and practice.
ISBN 0–415–14893–6 (v. 1). – ISBN 0–415–14894–4 (v. 1: pbk.)
1. Reading–Ability testing. 2. Educational tests and measurements.
I. Harrison, Colin, 1945–   . II. Salinger, Terry S.
LB1050.46.A847   1996
428.4'076–dc21   97–14699
CIP

ISBN   0–415–14893–6
0–415–14894–4 (pbk)

CONTENTS

FIGURES

CONTRIBUTORS

Donna E. Alvermann	National Reading Research Center, University of Georgia, USA
Mary Bailey	University of Nottingham School of Education, England
Paul Brock	New South Wales Department of Training and Education Co-ordination, Australia
Greg Brooks	National Foundation for Educational Research, England
Jay Campbell	Educational Testing Service, Princeton, New Jersey, USA
Michelle Commeyras	National Reading Research Center, University of Georgia, USA
Lizanne DeStefano	University of Illinois at Urbana-Champaign, USA
Alan Dewar	Dukeries Community College, Nottinghamshire, England
Beverly Falk	National Center for Restructuring Education, Schools, and Teaching, Teachers' College, Columbia University, New York, USA
Georgia Earnest García	University of Illinois at Urbana-Champaign, USA
Colin Harrison	University of Nottingham School of Education, England
Louise Hayward	St Andrew's College, Glasgow, Scotland
James Hoffman	University of Texas, USA
Sue Horner	Schools Curriculum and Assessment Authority, England
P. David Pearson	Michigan State University, USA
Nancy Roser	University of Texas, USA
Terry Salinger	American Institutes for Research, Washington DC, USA
Ernie Spencer	Scottish Office Education and Industry Department
Denis Vincent	University of East London, England
Jo Worthy	University of Texas, USA

INTRODUCTION

Colin Harrison and Terry Salinger

The New Paradigms in Reading Assessment Seminar

This book, and its companion volume *Assessing Reading 2: Changing Practice in Classrooms*, were originally conceived as the major outcomes from an invited international seminar on reading assessment held in England in 1995. The seminar had been proposed for two main reasons. First, at the time of the seminar, the assessment of reading in England and Wales was in turmoil. The government had taken over reading assessment, but it had dismissed a number of groups which were originally funded to write national tests, and recruited others whose efforts were not fully implemented due to a national boycott of tests by teachers. There was an urgent concern within the UK that government initiatives on assessment did not so absorb the attention and energy of those concerned with reading assessment that a vacuum would be created in relation to a broader consideration of principles, theory and practice. Second, a similar pattern of national anxieties over standards and reassessment of approaches to testing was evident in other countries, and within those countries many significant changes and innovations were under way.

In Australia and in Scotland, innovative practices were being introduced within national curriculum assessment, and in the USA literacy professionals had begun the search for new paradigms within which to address the urgent issues of assessment, both within the National Reading Research Center initiatives and the National Standards project, and within the wider reading assessment community. The seminar, which was titled *New Paradigms in Reading Assessment*, sought to set up an international forum for pooling information on these initiatives in reading assessment, to bring together the work of internationally recognized academics in the reading field in order to share information in this rapidly expanding area, to advance and clarify theories of reading assessment, to locate areas for new research initiatives, to reduce duplication of effort, and to disseminate evidence of reliability, validity and utility for potential users in other professional contexts.

The chapters in this book have developed significantly since they were given as papers at the original NPRA seminar, and in all cases have been revised, updated and rewritten to achieve two further goals, namely to provide a much more coherent volume on the key theoretical and practical issues in reading assessment in the English-speaking world than would accrue simply from a collection of conference papers, but also to take account of seminal developments in assessment practice which have occurred since 1995.

The following were the original participants in the seminar (affiliation at the time of participation in parentheses):

Donna Alvermann, University of Georgia (co-director, National Reading Research Center, USA)

Ingolv Austad (Deputy director, Norwegian national reading assessment project)

Greg Brooks (Editor, *Journal of Research in Reading*; senior researcher, NFER, UK)

Martin Coles (Senior Lecturer in Education, University of Nottingham)

John D'Arcy (Principal Officer for Research and Development, Northern Ireland CCEA)

Graham Frater (former Staff Inspector of English, Department for Education, UK)

Cathy Givens (National Primary Centre, University of Northumbria, UK)

Colin Harrison (Reader in Education, University of Nottingham)

Louise Hayward (National Development Officer, 5–14 assessment, Scottish Office Education Dept)

James Hoffmann (senior researcher, NRRC, University of Texas-Austin)

Sue Horner (Professional Officer, Schools Curriculum and Assessment Authority)

Rhonda Jenkins (former chair of publications, Australian Reading Association; nominee of the Australian government)

P. David Pearson (Dean, College of Education, University of Illinois at Urbana-Champaign, USA)

Terry Salinger (Director of Research, International Reading Association, Delaware, USA)

Ernie Spencer (Staff Inspector for English, Scottish Office Education Department)

Denis Vincent (East London University, director 1989–91 of a Key Stage 3 SCAA assessment project)

Alastair West (Inspector, London Borough of Redbridge; vice-chair of NATE)

Funding was secured from the National Literacy Trust and from the Educational and Social Research Council to subsidize travel and accommodation costs of the seminar, and this support is gratefully acknowledged. As is normal with this type of seminar, a small number of less experienced participants were invited to contribute, so that the seminar could fulfil a professional development role for future leaders in the field. These were two Heads of English in comprehensive schools in the Midlands, Alan Dewar and Dr Mary Bailey (both from Nottinghamshire), and two overseas doctoral students specializing in reading at the University of Nottingham, Ismail Ahmad (Malaysia) and Lia Maka (Tonga). Administrative arrangements for the seminar were ably managed by Sue Content.

To provide a book which charts key theoretical and practical issues in reading assessment in three continents is extraordinarily difficult, not only because the culture of assessment varies greatly between countries, but also because the discourse of assessment varies so greatly. Yet it is imperative that we learn from each other's theory and practice, in order to avoid duplication of effort, and, if possible, duplication of error. To do this, however, the editors felt that it would be necessary to have each chapter edited twice, from a national and an international perspective, where necessary cross-referencing and rewriting to make the argument clearer to colleagues from a different assessment culture and discourse community. This process has taken time, but the editors were fortunate in having authors who cooperated fully and cheerfully in this enterprise, and it is the hope of both authors and editors that this process will have been successful in producing a volume which advances theory and practice in its field in three continents.

The content and structure of this book

The scope of the book is broad. Chapters such as those by Harrison, Bailey and Dewar, by Pearson, DeStefano and García, and by Alvermann and Commeyras offer new perspectives on the theories that underlie the development and interpretation of reading assessments. They challenge readers to think about assessment in different ways, to stretch their own paradigms on what aspects of literacy can and should be measured and on how to accomplish this complex goal. For example, Pearson and his colleagues ask what is perhaps the most important question of all: can we really measure reading with these new approaches? Another way of thinking about this question is to wonder what we really are measuring when we think we are assessing students' interactions with text. Harrison, Bailey and Dewar propose a definition of 'responsive assessment' and offer guidelines for this approach that then reappear in numerous other chapters. Alvermann and Commeyras draw upon feminist theory as they ponder new paradigms for reading assessment.

Issues of national assessment are considered next. Chapters by Brock, by Horner and by Salinger and Campbell demonstrate the challenges inherent in developing large scale national assessments. Whether or not they are tied to a mandated national curriculum, tests designed to provide a 'nation's report card' take many different forms. These tests are often contentious, always closely scrutinized, and are generally highly politicized. The chapters by Brooks and Vincent aim to problematize the issues surrounding national assessments and to offer opposing views on test content or measurement theory, raising intelligent questions about the Key Stage assessments discussed by Horner.

Classroom-based assessments are the focus in the final four chapters. Hayward and Spencer discuss efforts in Scotland to develop a nation-wide system of classroom-based diagnostic assessments that encourage teachers to 'take a closer look' at students' literacy development. This metaphor of taking a closer look is echoed in chapters by Falk and by Hoffman. Falk describes how teachers in New York City have successfully implemented a British assessment method, the Primary Language Record, in their efforts to take a closer look at students and to teach reading more effectively. Hoffman reports the initial stages of a project in which teachers in Texas collaborated with university faculty to develop an alternative to standardized testing for young learners, and Salinger describes a study of teachers who had been implementing a similar early literacy assessment system for almost ten years. A clear emphasis on teachers as the appropriate agents of assessment pervades all these chapters.

Assessing Reading: Changing Practice in Classrooms

Many of the issues which are addressed in the present book are developed further in the companion volume to this one, *Assessing Reading 2: Changing Practice in Classrooms*, which also has an international editorial team: Martin Coles of England and Rhonda Jenkins of Australia. Many of the original seminar participants report additional classroom-based explorations of new approaches to reading assessment, and offer a wide range of illustrations of alternative assessments, including portfolio assessment, diagnostic assessment, self-assessment and reading interviews. The authors also continue the discussion of such important issues as how alternative approaches to assessment might be integrated into the curriculum, and how these approaches may be used to serve the information needs at state or national level.

Part I

THEORIES AND ASSUMPTIONS UNDERPINNING READING ASSESSMENT

1

RESPONSIVE READING ASSESSMENT

Is postmodern assessment of reading possible?

Colin Harrison, Mary Bailey and Alan Dewar

Introduction

This chapter presents some suggestions concerning a postmodern approach to reading assessment, and in the light of this analysis goes on to outline the principles which might underpin an approach to what we call 'responsive' reading assessment. We suggest a number of possible practical frameworks within which responsive reading assessment might be put into practice.

The chapter develops the analysis in the following ways. First, the case for offering a postmodern analysis is argued, then Lyotard's definition of postmodernism as *incredulity towards metanarrative* is examined to cast light on a key aspect of a postmodern position on reading assessment – a mistrust of traditional 'scientific' approaches to reading research. We then offer an account of some postmodern positions in literary theory, which are important since they introduce a mistrust of authoritarian notions of meaning in a text and place a different interpretation on the role of the reader in determining meaning. These analyses lead to two sets of implications for assessment, some of which derive directly from a consideration of the nature of authority in scientific enquiry, some of which are correlatives which have evolved as postmodern positions from literary theory. Finally, an attempt is made to examine the ways in which it might be possible to develop procedures for collecting information on response which are compatible with the implications of a postmodern approach, taking into account problems related to the inaccessibility of reading processes.

Why national approaches to reading assessment are likely to be conservative

The assessment of reading tends to be conservative, and the more central-ized the assessment arrangements, the more conservative those arrangements tend to be. States and governments often regard national performance in reading as an indicator of the effectiveness of the educational system, and take the view that assessment is too important a matter to be left in the hands of teachers. A national agency, such as the Schools Curriculum and Assessment Authority (SCAA), which controls curriculum and assessment arrangements for England and Wales, can seek opinions from whomever it wishes to consult, but teachers' organizations may have no direct right to representation. So far as the assessment of reading is concerned, neither the National Association for the Teaching of English (NATE), nor the United Kingdom Reading Association has any right of representation or participation on the committees at SCAA which decide on how testing is to be organized and implemented.

Such a situation contributed to a national boycott by teachers of the government's tests in 1993, when test instruments which had been devel-oped by agencies commissioned by SCAA were taken by less than 2 per cent of the target school population. The boycott, which had widespread support from school governors and the public, was staged because of concerns related to validity, and in protest at the lack of piloting and advance notice given in relation to the tests, which were due to be admin-istered in May 1993 to test students' performance in relation to national curriculum goals.

The central goals of policies related to the testing of reading in England during this period were determined by the then Secretary of State for Education, Kenneth Clarke, who, in a meeting with representatives of literacy associations (Clarke, 1991) declared, 'Anyone can tell whether or not a child can read, in five minutes', and 'What we need are quick pencil-and-paper tests, not tests that drag on over a month.' The results of this policy are still being felt, as agencies have tried to make the best of awkwardly constrained test-development remits based on Kenneth Clarke's principles, which have not overlapped at all satisfactorily with the national curriculum that they were meant to assess.

There are a number of reasons why reading assessment is likely to develop in a conservative manner. First, as we have just indicated, national or state-level approaches to assessment are likely to put faith in traditional 'pencil and paper' procedures, on the assumption that they have worked in the past and are therefore more likely than novel procedures to work well in the future. Second, politicians generally hope to find evidence of changes over time, either (if there are improvements) to demonstrate the effectiveness of their policies or (if there is a decline) to demonstrate that teachers are failing and that new policies are necessary. It is difficult enough under any circumstances to demonstrate unequivocally that reading standards have changed (Stedman and Kaestle, 1987; Cato and Whetton, 1991), but if evidence of change is sought, this would imply a conservative approach to testing, with incremental and evolutionary change to tests which have enough in common to enable valid comparisons to be made over time. In such a climate, if test development agencies wish to remain in business, they have to bid for contracts to continue incremental development of traditional tests, and radical alternatives are unlikely to find acceptability.

The need for a fundamental rethinking of reading assessment

There are, however, good reasons for undertaking a fundamental rethinking of reading assessment: in England and Wales, the government has introduced a National Curriculum within which reading is to be assessed separately from speaking and listening, and separately from writing. As one of us has argued elsewhere (Harrison, 1994), this separation of reading as an assessment area poses a challenge which we have hardly begun to meet. This challenge is one to which we shall devote some attention in the present chapter, because in our view it demands careful consideration.

But there are other reasons for rethinking reading assessment, which are related to much wider changes at the societal level. These changes have affected our views of the nature of epistemology in general, of the nature of scientific knowledge and methodology in particular, and have affected literary theory, particularly in relation to the problem of how we decide on a text's 'meaning'. In short, what we are suggesting is that it is important to consider the challenges posed by postmodernism. This is not the place to attempt (even if it were possible) a comprehensive account of postmodernism, but we will offer a partial account, especially as the concept relates to reading assessment. We will suggest that two important aspects of postmodernism, namely (a) a rethinking of the nature of scientific enquiry and (b) a rethinking of the concept of meaning in text, have very significant implications for reading assessment.

There are pressing reasons for undertaking such an analysis. 'Postmodernism' is not a philosophical movement which we can choose whether or not to adopt. It is a term for the state of our culture. As the French philosopher Jean-François Lyotard has expressed the matter, postmodernism: 'has altered the game rules for science, literature and the arts' (1984, xxiii). The condition of our society and culture is 'postmodern', and our task is therefore not so much a matter of deciding whether or not to accept a 'postmodern' position as to try to understand its implications, and to decide how to act on them.

Postmodernism and scientific enquiry

In his essay, *The Postmodern Condition*, Lyotard (1984, xxiv) defined post-modernism as an 'incredulity towards metanarratives'. By the word 'metanarratives', Lyotard was referring to the grand socio-historical narra-tives, one of which portrays science as a dispassionate march towards objectivity, and it is such grand narratives which postmodernism calls into question. A postmodern account of science would note the many ways in which science has had to reinvent its own rules – in post-Newtonian physics, in metamathematics and in quantum theory, for example – as a result of which many scientists have become incredulous towards superor-dinate concepts such as 'truth', 'scientific accuracy', 'objectivity' and 'expert'. These new systems of thinking have replaced a single notion of 'science' with a more flexible one: the single metanarrative has been replaced by a series of locally applicable discourses, and the scientist's role is to select from these as appropriate.

The postmodern condition implies a repositioning of the scientist as a philosopher, rather than an 'expert'. An expert 'knows what he (*sic*) knows and what he does not know' (Lyotard, 1984, xxv). A philosopher, on the other hand, does not. The expert concludes; the philosopher questions. Following Wittgenstein, and using his theory of 'language games', Lyotard argues that in science, as in philosophy, we must accept a multivalent solu-tion: we will find ourselves using a range of language games, each of which has its own discourse rules. Each language game produces its own strand of narrative, which is locally coherent and which generates new under-standings. Postmodernism presents us with the need to deal with the fact that we already inhabit a society in which the old rules and authority of metanarratives, including those of science, have changed.

How does all this relate to reading assessment? Very directly, since we can apply the argument to the question of which models or paradigms of assessment should be accepted as valid by the authorities (scientific or governmental). Traditional models (those of the 'metanarrative') are those which emphasize efficiency, performance and improvement, not of indi-viduals directly, but of the state. Assessment is a 'modernist' project: a project which focuses on 'improvement' at the system level, rather than at the individual. In the case of reading assessment, the 'metanarrative' involves large-scale national testing of skills and knowledge, using norm-referenced procedures. Within such an approach, testing would be part of a national programme for not only educational but also economic improvement.

A postmodern view, by contrast, calls into question the validity and authority of such national testing programmes. It questions the extent to which it is valid to assume that it is even possible to test reading attain-ment on a national scale, and it would certainly question the assumption that test data can present an 'objective' picture of reading standards, given that so many subjective decisions have to be made to produce national test results. Of course, such questioning is not new, it has been increasingly prevalent over the past fifteen years, but it is important to note that an incredulity towards the metanarrative of national testing has come, not only from classroom teachers, but from within the community of 'experts'. Or to be more precise, the 'experts' have become 'philosophers'. It is from among national leaders in the field of assessment, experts in statistics, measurement and test construction, that incredulity towards the metanarratives of traditional national assessment has been given its most powerful expression (see, for example, Choppin, 1981; Gipps and Goldstein, 1983; Stedman and Kaestle, 1987; Cato and Whetton, 1991; Gipps, 1994). It is important to observe that the central claim of these commentators is not that the approaches advocated by the UK government in recent years are damaging to children or school systems (though this may indeed be the case), but rather that they simply do not work, that they do not deliver valid and reliable data on reading attainment at national levels which could be used to make well-informed decisions about changes in reading attainment over time.

Where does all this leave us? A postmodern analysis would lead to three specific implications: that we acknowledge the potential of local system solutions if global system solutions are difficult or impossible to achieve; that we acknowledge the importance of the individual subject, given that the concept of 'objectivity' has to be recognized as problematic; that we acknowledge the importance of accepting as valid a range of methodologies, given that it is no longer possible to bow to the authority of a single, grand scientific metanarrative. These principles – of local rather than global, of emphasizing the subjective rather than the objective, and of valuing a range of methodological discourses – appear to have a good deal of potential in reading assessment, and we shall go on to explore their potential later in this chapter.

Postmodernism and literary theory

The traditional view of reading assessment has given great prominence to one method of testing, the reading comprehension test. In the previous section, our analysis of postmodernism has focused on its implications for the 'scientific' or methodological part of reading assessment, i.e. the 'test'. But postmodernism also has much to contribute to the other part of assessment, namely our notions of 'comprehension', particularly in relation to the concept of 'meaning'. Postmodernism has brought about a fundamental rethinking of the nature of authority in a number of fields, of which science is one, and it has also brought about a number of parallel seismic shifts in the field of literary theory. A full perspective on the relationship of literary theory to notions of assessment is beyond the scope of this book, but we shall indicate some initial points of reference in this chapter, and some parts of our argument are developed in Donna Alvermann's chapter on gender and assessment. One useful way into postmodern literary theories is through the writing of Mikhail Bakhtin (Medvedev and Bakhtin, 1978; Bakhtin, 1973).

Bakhtin's topics ranged widely, but one constant theme was a challenge to the notion of a 'monologic' concept of meaning. Instead of a fixed or passive notion of meaning, Bakhtin emphasized its 'dialogic' nature, and argued that language was a series of acts of communication, each of which takes place in a unique social, cultural and ideological context. One clear implication of this position is that 'meaning' is not something to be regarded as immutable. The 'meaning' of a word is not fixed, because 'meaning' is a social as well as a linguistic phenomenon, as a result of which it varies subtly within each context of production and interpretation. Bakhtin's view of the concept of meaning as dynamic rather than static also extended to literature. He argued that not just words but whole texts were 'dialogic'. Dostoevsky's novels, for example, are not 'monologic', like those of Tolstoy. They do not offer a single, unified authorial view of the world. Dostoevsky's novels, suggested Bakhtin, introduce and celebrate a 'polyphonic' range of points of view, expressed through the various characters, and between which the author does not adjudicate. Instead, the reader is faced with the difficult task of struggling to come to an active, personal and individual interpretation of meaning, and to engage in a personal search for unification.

The conception of meaning in literary text as something uniquely determined by each reader, and the view that there is no act of reading which is not also a 're-writing', are now widely accepted postmodern positions. As Eagleton (1983, p. 74) has pointed out, in recent years there has been a marked shift of attention in literary theory away from the author (the focus of nineteenth-century criticism) and the text (the focus of structuralist criticism in the early and middle years of the twentieth century), towards the most underprivileged of the trio, the reader. Eagleton's account of the new focus on the reader develops from a description of phenomenology and hermeneutics in the early twentieth century into an explanation of reception theory and the work of Wolfgang Iser. Iser (1978) argued that the process of reading is a dynamic one, to which readers bring personal experiences and social and cognitive schemata, in which predictions, assumptions and inferences are constantly made, developed, challenged and negated. Iser's reception theory positions readers as central and active collaborators in making meaning, whose habits of interpretation are challenged and disconfirmed by reading, a process which leads to new insights and understandings, not only of the text, but also of themselves. Iser's theory goes further than Bakhtin's, in suggesting that the text is unfinished without the reader's contribution to making meaning: it is the reader who, in partnership with the author, fills the 'hermeneutic gap' in the text, bringing to it his or her own experience and understanding, and resolving the conflicts and indeterminacies which the author leaves unresolved.

Perhaps the most extreme challenge to any notion of stability in meaning and interpretation – a notion which is essential if we are to retain any hope that it is possible to assess response to reading with any validity – is that posed by the literary theories of Jacques Derrida. Derrida's *Of Grammatology* (1976) proposed a theory of 'deconstruction' of texts which was so radical that it seemed to imply not only the 'death of the author' as determiner of meaning, but to threaten the death of meaning itself. According to Derrida, the reader's role is not to discover meaning, but to produce it: to dismantle (*déconstruire*) the text and rebuild it another way. Derrida uses the metaphor of *bricoleur* to describe the reader's role. The reader is a handyman or do-it-yourself enthusiast, for whom the words of a text, the signifiers, are no more than tools to be used in deconstructing, not constructing, the text. Traditional accounts of reading, argues Derrida (1976, p. 158) imply no more than a respectful 'doubling', a concept of reading which has only protected, and never opened up, a text. He denies that the search for meaning can be so banal as a simple 'logocentric' transfer of consciousness from the 'transcendental subject' (the author) to the 'subject' (the reader). For Derrida, written texts are the site of an endless series of possibilities, oppositions and indeterminacies. Deciding on a text's meaning under these circumstances is not possible – the reader can do no more than look for traces of meaning, and contemplate the text's geological strata during the unending fall into the abyss of possible deferred meanings.

We would argue that the positions from literary theory outlined above are postmodern in their overthrowing of traditional notions of authority in text and meaning, in similar ways to those outlined in our account of some postmodern positions in science. As was the case with our account of postmodernism in science, we want to suggest that three broad implications follow from our analysis. The first is that we acknowledge that we need to recognize a polysemic concept of meaning; the second is that we acknowledge a privileging of the role of the reader; the third, related to the first two, is that we acknowledge a diminution of the role of the author, or to express it the other way, a diminution of the authority of the text. We shall defer a fuller consideration of the implications for reading assessment of these points until later in this chapter, but it is clear already that, just as postmodern theories of reading pose serious challenges to traditional models of teaching English (see, for example, the seminal analyses of Rosenblatt, 1985, Eagleton, 1983, and Beach, 1994) a reassessment of the concept of meaning, of the role of the reader and of the authority in text raise enormous questions about the nature of reading assessment, particularly in its traditional forms.

What is responsive assessment?

We intend to use the term 'responsive assessment' to refer to assessment practices that take account of the postmodern nature of assessment. Responsive assessment, as we see it, would need to be responsive to the changes which we have described in scientific thought and methodology, and would also need to take account of developments in literary theory. In this sense, therefore, responsive assessment of reading leads not only to new methodologies, but to a new emphasis on the reader. We are not suggesting that our recommendations are novel; nearly everything we would advocate has been tried and is being developed by other groups, somewhere in the English-speaking world, and many are reported in this book and its companion volume. What we feel is important, however, is to make a connection between the principles we are outlining and these new approaches to assessment.

The imperatives for responsive assessment, as outlined in the sections earlier, were the following:

1 We need to acknowledge the potential of local system solutions if global system solutions are difficult or impossible to achieve.
2 We need to acknowledge the importance of the individual subject, given that the concept of 'objectivity' has to be recognized as problematic.
3 We need to acknowledge the importance of accepting as valid a range of methodologies.
4 We need to acknowledge the need to recognize a polysemic concept of meaning.
5 We need to acknowledge a privileging of the role of the reader.
6 We need to acknowledge a diminution of the authority of the author and of the text.

Let us now consider these in a little more detail. As we have already suggested, many assessment specialists have questioned the feasibility of monitoring national changes in reading ability over time. This incredulity towards the metanarrative of national reading statistics may surprise non-specialists, but it is no surprise to most reading specialists. Monitoring reading ability at national levels is not as straightforward as monitoring stock exchange activity. The reasons for this are easy to see, but difficult to take account of. Testing over time makes the assumption that the test populations are broadly similar, and this may not be the case if, as in the UK, over a period of years there are significant demographic changes – changes in the birth rate, population movements and so on. These changes make it difficult to meet the criterion of population stability. Another crucial fact is that both language and culture change over time.

One well-known reading test in the UK included the sentence 'The milkman's horse got lost in the fog.' This is not a difficult sentence for an adult to read, but for a beginning reader who has never heard of a 'milkman's horse', it would be a much more difficult sentence to read than would have been the case when the test was written. Some statisticians believe that there are adequate mathematical procedures for dealing with such problems, but at least as many do not, and within the UK government's own Assessment of Performance Unit the consensus view was that there remain fundamental difficulties in reliably monitoring changes in national reading performance over time (APU, 1983, 124).

Of course, if governments demand test data, teachers and researchers must choose either civil disobedience or an attempt to make the best of a bad job. In England and Wales, both strategies have been tried, and currently teachers are required to administer classroom tests whose aim is to place every student in the aged seven, eleven or fourteen group at one of eight 'levels' of reading ability. The following is a sample level description:

> In reading and discussing a range of texts, pupils identify different layers of meaning and comment on their significance and effect. They give personal responses to literary texts, referring to aspects of language, structure and themes in justifying their views. They summarise a range of information from different sources.

What is it to be able to accomplish what is described here? Many teachers would argue that an average 11-year-old can do all these things, given appropriate texts and contexts, and yet this is a description of the National Curriculum Attainment Target at Level 6, which is deemed to be more challenging than the level of reading attainment achieved by most 14-year-olds. In any event, most assessment specialists would argue that it is difficult or impossible to judge reliably whether or not a student has or has not achieved what is described here, since the Level 6 description contains (depending on how you analyse the paragraph) between ten and twelve implied tasks which are to be carried out on unspecified material and achieved at unspecified levels. As a basis for gaining reliable information about national attainment levels in reading, such a broad global statement is impractical.

However, in considering our first imperative, which is to look for local system solutions if global system solutions are difficult or impossible to achieve, there are a number of ways forward. If the level description is interpreted as a focus for curriculum activity at a local level, rather than as a national benchmark which has or has not been achieved, there are many useful approaches open to the teacher. First, if the emphasis is switched to the classroom, and to curriculum-focused assessment practices, this statement could supply a guide to a whole reading programme. If, instead of attempting to reduce the whole of a student's reading achievement to a single level, and an attempt is made to avoid oversimplification, assessment can begin to serve two essential purposes which national assessment programmes usually ignore – the assessment evidence can be of value to the teacher, and it can be of direct value to the student.

Next, if we consider the second imperative, that of recognizing the importance of the subjective, and consider what it might be to make a virtue of this, we can connect an emphasis on classroom-based assessment with a privileging of three types of assessment which tend to be marginalized within national assessment programmes, namely teacher assessment, self-assessment and peer assessment. In our view, the process of investigating what it might be to explore these forms of assessment has only just begun, but the authors of the chapters in this book and its companion volume are among those who are beginning the exploration. The challenge of shifting the emphasis and responsibility for assessment towards the teacher and, even more significantly, towards the reader is the following: a postmodern perspective implies a complete rethinking of the assumptions and power relations underpinning assessment, and it will take courage and imagination to undertake this and argue for it. As Lather (1986), quoted by Tierney (1994, 1180) puts it: 'Emancipatory knowledge increases awareness of the contradictions hidden or distorted by everyday understandings, and in doing so it directs attention to the possibilities for the social transformation inherent in the present configuration of social processes.' Putting an increased emphasis on teacher assessment is important because it offers the possibility of making much better use of assessment information to guide instruction and assist the development of individuals, as the Scottish 'Diagnostic Procedures' and 'Next Steps' projects, for example, make clear. These are discussed in the chapter in this book by Louise Hayward and Ernie Spencer. We recognize that many decades of externally administered tests of reading have made many teachers feel deskilled in the area of reading assessment, but we would argue that teachers are the adults who are potentially in the best position to make a contribution to assessment processes, and most likely to be able to put the information which comes from assessment to good use. In England and Wales, teachers of English in secondary schools have had more positive experiences of being given responsibility for making 'high stakes' assessments over a number of years, and these experiences have given this group of teachers both confidence and expertise in making judgments about students' reading and writing achievement in a wide range of contexts.

Giving serious attention to self- and peer assessment, however, is potentially even more powerful than teacher assessment, since it implies a shift of perspective from the student as the object of assessment to the subject, the controlling agent. Denny Taylor's 'student advocacy model' of assessment (1993) is one of the approaches which attempts to recognize this radical shift, but, as with many innovations, it is not without its precedents. Twenty years ago, Terry Phillips (1971) was filming teacherless small groups of 9-year-olds discussing children's literature, and recording the sort of evidence that is currently being considered as part of a student self- and peer-assessment approach. We would certainly want to suggest that it will be enormously important to develop a wide body of information on self- and peer assessment in the near future, and to put in place mechanisms for sharing the information. To attempt this is not without risk, however. As teachers, we tend to teach students what it is to be able, and what it is to be a failure, and as a result, children's self-assessments are socialized (Johnson, 1994). Students, like teachers, will need support if their own contribution to assessment is to be truly emancipatory, but studies such as that of Almasi (1995) into peer-led discussion of literature suggest that this can be done, and that information can be obtained which captures much of the richness and complexity of decentralized participation structures.

The third imperative from our postmodern analysis was that we acknowledge the importance of making choices from among methodologies. A postmodern analysis suggests that a single model of theory and methodology can no longer suffice. In science for example, the traditional Newtonian rules do not apply at the quantum mechanics level, and other equations, methodologies and theories, some of which are incompatible with those of Newtonian physics, have had to be devised. In the social sciences, there has been a parallel explosion of new methodologies, though we are some way short of consensus on whether some of these are mutually exclusive, nor is there consensus on the principles for selecting relevant methodologies for different research tasks. We would wish to suggest that in seeking to make principled choices among methodologies, a context-sensitive and responsive approach to assessment is called for.

It is appropriate to acknowledge at this point that in using the adjective 'responsive', we are echoing the use of the term in the literature on curriculum evaluation, especially in the influential definition of 'responsive evaluation' put forward by Robert Stake (1979). To be more accurate, Stake did not so much define responsive evaluation as to state its principles; by its nature, responsive evaluation is not fully defined in advance – it remains open and untidy. Stake's paper was important in the USA and Europe in encouraging the notion that in evaluating a curriculum the traditional 'preordinate' model of evaluation, one in which every stage of an evaluation is planned in advance, should be only one of a range of approaches. He surprised some traditionalists by suggesting that evaluations should not only draw upon a range of methodologies, but that these should be negotiated with the participants. This notion of adopting a negotiated and context-related choice of evaluation practices is one which we would very strongly advocate in reading assessment. Stake's responsive evaluation began with talking: the evaluator was to talk with all participants in the evaluation – sponsors who were funding the work, programme staff, those

11

who would be the audience for the evaluation, and so on – in order to discover their purposes and concerns before deciding upon information needs and the methodologies to meet those needs. In Stake's view, it was essential to avoid premature closure in deciding upon what was important and what should be reported; instead, he advocated that the evaluator should spend much more time than was formerly the case observing what was happening in classrooms, and seeking to portray this, in a continuous process of renegotiating the key issues, and matching these to the needs of the different groups involved. He argued for the need to accept complexity in portrayal, and to accept uncertainty and the representation of multiple realities. In a memorable sentence, he summed up his view of the problem of data reduction: 'Oversimplification obfuscates.'

In endorsing Stake's overall approach, therefore, we would argue not only for accepting the need for methodological diversity, but also for the principles of assessment being negotiated with all the participants. Such negotiated decisions might relate to the contexts within which assessments occur, the nature of the assessment procedures, the format and structure of assessment reports, the nature of what is to be considered as evidence, and the final content of any report which is to be shared with a wider audience. The issue of evidence is a crucial one. Understandably, it is usually teachers and other assessment specialists who decide what is to be counted as evidence; it is relatively unusual for students to make those decisions. We would argue both that students should be involved in deciding what evidence of their response to reading is to be recorded, and that the range of evidence should be broadened. Stake suggested that all of the following were possible sources of evidence in portraying an educational experience: playscripts, logs, scrapbooks, narratives, maps, graphs, taped conversations, photographs, role-playing, interviews and displays. Stake does not rule out traditional tests; he simply argues that such data are insensitive to so much of what is educationally important, especially in relation to the purposes behind what is being taught. We would also add that we accept that the term 'evidence' is problematic, in that it carries legal and judgmental connotations; we continue to use the term, but have sympathy with teachers who prefer the less judgemental term 'information'.

The approach outlined in the previous paragraph has not been widely adopted in assessment in schools, and yet there are already many degree courses in universities on which all these approaches are used, in negotiation with the students. The model is not, therefore, one which is impractical; the issues in implementing such a model are about power rather than feasibility. However, it would be naive to imagine that it would be a trivial matter to introduce such a model into reading assessment within school systems. As Johnson (1994, 12) expressed it, in a seminal paper on reading assessment as social practice: 'assessment, more than any other domain of education is resisting movement away from technological thinking'.

The final three imperatives for responsive assessment were those derived from literary theory. The first of these was the need to take account of a polysemic concept of meaning. The most immediate result of challenging a 'monologic' concept of meaning is to question the appropriateness of traditional, multiple-choice comprehension tests, in which a single 'correct' answer is the only one considered acceptable. However, as Beck points out, in the introduction to the International Reading Association's excellent book on authentic reading assessment (Valencia, Hiebert and Afflerbach, 1994, p. v), eliminating multiple-choice tests does not guarantee that one is improving assessment. Moving towards a polysemic model of meaning is likely to be uncomfortable for assessment specialists, since it appears to introduce both unreliability and subjectivity. The postmodern response to such a charge would be to argue that reliability can be manufactured artificially in comprehension tests, but at the cost of penalizing any creativity in response. One could also add that there is subjectivity in all assessment procedures, but that to seek to accept open-ended responses is to place a value on the reader's subjectivity, rather than privileging that of the test constructor. The challenge is to seek ways in which to position subjectivity as valuable rather than as an irritant.

In our view, the issue of seeking to value the subjective is one of the greatest challenges facing those working to develop responsive reading assessment practices. Portfolio assessment approaches seek to place greater value on authentic tasks and on the reader, though it is certainly possible to use the term 'portfolio assessment' for what is little more than a standardized, narrowly conceived reading test, but with testing spread out over a week and retained by the student in a folder, rather than conducted in an hour and retained by the teacher. Attempts to increase the authenticity of the tasks which form the basis of reading assessment have been very important, however, and some of these are reported in this book. Equally important, in our view, is the need to attempt to capture the authenticity of response to reading which takes place within a task, and to obtain evidence of the transactions which form the reader's response. Tierney (1994, 1174) puts this challenge clearly: 'Our goal is to track the nature of the readers' and writers' involvement as they create, inhabit and maneuver [sic] within the text worlds they create.'

Such a stance is directly implied by our second imperative from literary theory, namely the privileging of the role of the reader. There are already many ways in which reading assessment has begun to take greater account of a reader's response: there has been a clear parallel development of theories in reader response and approaches such as the twenty years' work on children's transactions with text initiated by Ken and Yetta Goodman (see Goodman and Goodman, 1994, and Goodman, 1994, for an overview). The Primary Language Record, originally created within the Inner London Educational Authority, has also been an influential framework for recording and valuing developmental aspects of the reading of students in primary education, and Beverley Falk's chapter in this volume gives an account of its use in an American context. Such approaches are flexible, and meet one of Stake's key criteria in that they are able to capture unanticipated outcomes. It is usual to describe such approaches as the kind which emphasize process rather than product. We would certainly advocate this emphasis, but would describe it somewhat differently: our goal is to treat the process as the product, and the challenge is to explore new ways of capturing the reader's interactions and processes, and of retaining them as products.

In our chapter in the companion volume to this one, we present some evidence of our attempts to capture, through interviews, evidence of readers' interactions with text. Naturally we recognize that such approaches are problematic, not least because of the socially constructed nature of a teacher–student relationship. Nevertheless, we want to suggest that interviews offer a basis for exploration which is potentially fruitful, for a number of reasons: interviews can be open-ended and dynamic; taped data can be stored, retained and played back later for comparison and discussion; many attempts to obtain responses to reading require the student to write, and taping frees the student from this constraint; tape recording offers the potential for a teacherless context for collecting evidence, over which a student or group of students can have some authority and sense of ownership. One Australian approach to reading assessment which lists dozens of types of evidence which might be admissible as what the authors call 'signs of achievement' is that of McGregor and Meirs (1991). These authors offer plenty of illustration to support their claim that such an approach opens up assessment and yet retains rigour. Like us, they too find the term 'responsive assessment' a useful one to describe the central thrust of their approach. Paul Brock's chapter in this book develops the argument that such approaches can be linked into national assessment practice.

In focusing on the reader's response, we are also very attracted by the arguments of Dole and her co-authors (1991) concerning the potential value of focusing on readers' active reading strategies, rather than having a conceptualization of reading comprehension as a set of passive 'subskills'. In an important article, these authors argued for a view of reading as interactive and constructive, and for pedagogy which instantiated such a perspective. Dole and her co-authors do not go on to deal with the problems of assessment, though it seems clear that an active model of reading comprehension based on flexible strategies is likely to pose some assessment challenges. Nevertheless, since active reading strategies are likely to use consciously controlled metacognitive awareness, there would seem to be opportunities for capturing such processes through the recording of interview or protocol evidence. In reviewing the research, Dole *et al.* report that such data can be gathered from children in the early years of schooling, and refute suggestions that evidence of complex inference can only be gathered from older students.

14

Afflerbach (1995) offers rich evidence of a comprehensive attempt to capture the texture of readers' active strategies and responses in his paper on the 'engaged assessment of engaged readers'. Afflerbach's model presents reading as a cognitive and social activity which involves prior knowledge, motivation and planning as well as the actual reading of a text, and views these factors as dynamic, not static. He describes assessment practices which have high 'ecological validity' as well as meeting many of the criteria we have outlined as necessary for responsive assessment, and is one of the few approaches which recognizes the importance of providing information for diverse audiences and different purposes. Afflerbach's engaged assessment places value on both teacher assessment and self-assessment, but also recognizes that both groups are likely to benefit from support in becoming more skilled and more confident in making sound judgments.

Our final imperative, derived from a consideration of literary theory, was the need to acknowledge a diminution of the authority of the author and of the text. In many respects, the emphasis in the previous paragraphs on a dynamic model of the reader as meaning-maker begins to achieve this, since it presents the reader as taking a dominant role in the construction of meaning, rather than as a passive receiver of a message transmitted by the author. The emphasis, in terms of literary theory, is on opening up texts for exploration rather than protecting them. Readings 'against the grain' of a text are increasingly accepted in school English courses, so for example, a feminist reading of a novel such as *Wuthering Heights* would be much more acceptable today than it would have been fifteen years ago. In looking for areas where texts are opened up rather than protected, it might be more profitable to consider the influence of media studies courses than literature courses. By their nature, media studies courses are likely to problematize notions of authority in relation to both authorship and a range of media texts, and in both schools and universities such courses have been innovative in introducing assessment approaches which reflect their postmodern genesis.

One other area in the reading curriculum in schools which most certainly has the potential to reflect postmodern influences is that of directed reading activities, of the type known in the USA as DRTA and in the UK as DARTs (Directed Activities Related to Texts; Lunzer and Gardner, 1984). These reading activities were the focus of a national cross-curricular project in the UK, and while its influence certainly did not reach all schools, the project's work in both English and content-area subjects was significant in developing a range of practical approaches to opening up texts for dialogue and debate. The approaches included a number of text deletion activities developed from cloze procedure, text segmentation, diagramming of text structure, text prediction and the sequencing of randomly reordered paragraphs of text. Clearly all of these approaches involve the reader in active reflection on or reconstruction of texts, and in this sense position readers alongside the originator of the text as co-authors. Furthermore, the DARTs activities place great emphasis on peer collaboration and discussion. Activities such as cloze were seen by Lunzer and Gardner as little more than passive traditional tests unless the reader completed these cooperatively, with the active hypothesis formation, dialogue and engagement which were possible in small group work. We would wish to suggest that having students engage in DARTs activities most certainly meets the demands of our final imperative, but also offers a great deal of potential evidence which could be incorporated into responsive assessment practices.

Six principles of responsive assessment

The six imperatives derived from postmodern perspectives lead us to six broad principles which should underpin responsive assessment. We list them below, together with some of the ways in which responsive assessment might be put into action.

- *First, in responsive assessment, the emphasis is switched to the classroom,* and to curriculum practices; at this point assessment can begin to serve two essential purposes which national programmes usually ignore – assessment evidence can be of direct value to the teacher, and it can be of direct value to the student.
- *Second, responsive assessment calls for increased emphasis on teacher assessment, self-assessment and peer assessment.* We would suggest that it will be enormously important to develop a wide body of information, not only on teacher assessment, but on self- and peer assessment, and to put in place mechanisms for sharing the information.
- *Third, responsive assessment of reading should not only draw upon a range of methodologies, but should be negotiated with the participants.* Students should be involved in deciding what evidence of their response to reading is to be recorded, and that range of evidence should be broadened to include, for example, playscripts, logs, scrapbooks, narratives, maps, graphs, taped conversations, photographs, role-playing, interviews and displays.
- *Fourth, it is important to increase the authenticity of the tasks which form the basis of reading assessment.* Equally important, however, is the need to attempt to capture the authenticity of response to reading which takes place within a task, and to obtain evidence of the transactions which form the reader's response.
- *Fifth, it is important to take greater account of a reader's response.* We suggest that interviews offer a basis for exploration of response which is potentially fruitful, for a number of reasons: interviews can be open-ended and dynamic; taped data can be stored, retained and played back later for comparison and discussion; tape recording offers the

potential for a teacherless context for collecting evidence, over which a student or group of students can have some authority and sense of ownership.

- *Sixth, responsive assessment of reading should acknowledge a diminution of the authority of the author and of the text.* In our view, tasks which involve the reader in active reflection on texts, with the active hypothesis formation, dialogue and engagement which are possible in small group work, offer great potential for achieving this final goal, which positions the reader in a central and powerful role as an active and purposeful user of texts and creator of meaning.

The elusiveness of reading processes

As one of us has argued elsewhere (Harrison, 1994), the fact that so much work has been carried out already on reading assessment can at least partially blind us to one important fact – namely that it is extraordinarily difficult to get at what happens when a person is reading. We often use the term 'reading comprehension' as if it refers to a dichotomous knowledge state: a student either does, or does not, understand a certain passage or text. This is far from the case. It might be more helpful to begin from the much more radical position of suggesting that there is no such thing as 'reading comprehension'. To give due weight to the dynamic nature of the reading process one might suggest the following: that reading is an interactive process, as a result of which the knowledge state of the reader changes perhaps four times a second (once for each fixation). A reader understands a text not so much in the manner of 'understanding' the significance of an exit sign, but more in the manner of understanding *The Times Concise Atlas of the World*, or as one understands New York City. In other words, understanding is dynamic, fluid, socially and culturally located, and it acquires temporary stability only in goal-related and purposive contexts, which may have little to do with the understandings which are generated in other contexts.

Given the plasticity and elusiveness of reading processes, and while acknowledging that many of the approaches we have suggested as part of responsive assessment are seeking to overcome this problem, there are some final challenges we would wish to bear in mind, which are borrowed from the earlier paper:

1 We need to be aware of the fluidity and inaccessibility of reading processes.
2 We need to be aware of the inevitable intrusiveness of assessment in relation to reading and the reading process, and that any method of evoking or making assessable a reader's response is likely to change that response, in both social and cognitive dimensions.

3   We need to be aware that responding in writing to what has been read requires a double transformation, from reading response into verbal discourse, and then into written form, and in the light of this we should consider methods of eliciting responses to reading which do not disadvantage those who are not fluent writers.

It is our view that in seeking to develop responsive assessment practices, it would be important to keep these final points in mind, in order to remain continually aware of the cognitive and sociocultural filters through which the reader's response has to pass before it becomes accessible to others.

Is postmodern assessment of reading possible?

Can there be such a thing as postmodern national assessment? The answer is clearly 'No' – and 'Yes'. 'No', because national assessment implies a 'modern' and not a 'postmodern' philosophy, a positivist and traditional 'scientific' approach, which can be attempted, but which will fail. 'Postmodern' large-scale, national assessment, therefore, is a contradiction in terms. Even if 'postmodern' local, subjective and responsive solutions are attempted, to aggregate them will be fruitless and will fail. Furthermore, from a societal point of view, one must recognize that if the superordinate bureaucracy is coercive, the operation of the assessment apparatus is likely to be coercive. Its effects will be those of the 'modern' project, even if it attempts to use 'postmodern' practices. From this point of view, therefore, the major tasks facing assessment specialists go far beyond that of convincing bureaucrats that traditional 'benchmark' testing is ineffectual. The tasks facing us include convincing both bureaucrats and teachers themselves that every experienced teacher is indeed an assessment specialist, convincing students that they too can become assessment specialists, and convincing bureaucrats that even a five-day portfolio task may not provide an authentic and valid basis for reading assessment.

However, postmodernism is not independent of modernism. Postmodern and modern discourses will continue to coexist. 'Postmodern' is simply a description of the condition of our society which makes certain points about an overthrow of tradition that has already occurred. In the reading field, this has certain implications, some of which we have attempted to point out. The 'Yes', therefore is about the fact that what will take place, whatever a government's project might be, will be 'postmodern'. The decisions before us relate to the extent to which we acknowledge the postmodern condition, and the extent to which we advocate for changes in assessment practices in order to take account of this condition. It is our hope that the approaches we have grouped under the term 'responsive assessment' make some contribution to mapping the changes which are needed. Our map is incomplete. That's fine: a map must be incomplete, by its nature, but what we hope is that it will have some utility in charting the territory of assessment in a manner which includes some fresh perspectives, and which enables some new routes to be explored.

References

Afflerbach, P. (1995) 'Engaged assessment of engaged readers'. In Linda Baker, Peter Afflerbach and David Reinking (eds) *Developing Engaged Readers in Home and School Communities*. Hillsdale, NJ: Lawrence Earlbaum Associates, 191–214.

Almasi, J. F. (1995) 'The nature of fourth graders' sociocultural conflicts in peer-led and teacher-led discussions of literature'. *Reading Research Quarterly*, 30(3): 314–51.

Assessment of Performance Unit (1993) 'Language Performance in Schools: Secondary Survey Report No. 2'. London: Department of Education and Science.

Bailey, Mary (1993) 'Children's Response to Fiction'. M.Ed. dissertation, University of Nottingham.

Bakhtin, M. (1973) *Problems of Dostoevsky's Poetics*, (trans. R. W. Rotsel). Ann Arbor, MI: Ardis.

Beach, R. (1994) 'Adopting multiple stances in conducting literacy research'. In Robert B. Ruddell, Martha Rapp Ruddell and Harry Singer (eds) *Theoretical Models and Processes of Reading* (4th edn). Newark, DE: International Reading Association, 1203–19.

Cato, V. and Whetton, C. (1991) *An Enquiry into LEA Evidence on Standards of Reading of Seven-year-old Children*. London: Department of Education and Science .

Choppin, Bruce (1981) 'Is education getting better?'. *British Educational Research Journal*, 7(1): 3–16.

Clarke, Kenneth (1991) 'Personal communication': meeting at the Department of Education and Science with representatives of UKRA, NATE, the Book Trust and the Association of Advisers and Inspectors for English, 11 February 1991.

Derrida, J. (1976) *Of Grammatology*, (trans. G. C. Spivac). Baltimore, MD: Johns Hopkins University Press.

Dole, J. A., Duffy, G. G., Roehler, L. R. and Pearson, P. D. (1991) 'Moving from the old to the new: research on reading comprehension instruction'. *Review of Educational Research*, 61(3): 239–64.

Eagleton, Terry (1983) *Literary Theory*. Oxford: Basil Blackwell.

Gipps, C. V. (1994) *Beyond Testing*. London: Falmer Press.

Gipps, C. V. and Goldstein, H. (1983) *Monitoring Children: an Evaluation of the Assessment of Performance Unit*. London: Heinemann Educational Books.

Goodman, K. (1994) 'Reading, writing and written texts: a transactional psycholinguistic view'. In Robert B. Ruddell, Martha Rapp Ruddell and Harry Singer (eds) *Theoretical Models and Processes of Reading* (4th edn). Newark, DE: International Reading Association, 1093–130.

Goodman, Y. M. and Goodman, K. S. (1994) 'To err is human: learning about language processes by analyzing miscues'. In Robert B. Ruddell, Martha Rapp Ruddell and Harry Singer (eds) *Theoretical Models and Processes of Reading* (4th edn). Newark, DE: International Reading Association, 104–23.

Harrison, C. (1994) 'The assessment of response to reading: developing a post-modern perspective'. In Andrew Goodwyn (ed.) *English and Ability*. London: David Foulton, 66–89.

Iser, Wolfgang (1978) *The Act of Reading: a Theory of Aesthetic Response*. Baltimore, MD: Johns Hopkins University Press.

Johnson, P. (1994) 'Assessment as social practice'. In D. J. Leu and C. K. Kinzer (eds) *Examining Central Issues in Literacy Research, Theory and Practice*. Chicago: National Reading Conference, 11–23.

Lather, P. (1986) 'Research as praxis'. *Harvard Educational Review*, 56(3): 257–77.

Lunzer, Eric and Gardner, Keith (1984) *Learning from the Written Word*. Edinburgh: Oliver and Boyd.

Lyotard, Jean-François (1984) *The Postmodern Condition: A Report on Knowledge*. (trans. from the French by Geoff Bennington and Brian Massumi). Manchester: Manchester University Press.

McGregor, R. and Meirs, M. (1991) *Telling the Whole Story*. Hawthorne, Victoria: Australian Council for Educational Research.

Medvedev, P. N. and Bakhtin, M. (1978) *The Formal Method in Literary Scholarship*, (trans. A. J. Wehrle). Baltimore: Johns Hopkins University Press.

Phillips, T. (1971). 'Poetry in the Primary School'. *English in Education*, 5(3): 15–62.

Protherough, Robert (1983) *Developing a Response to Fiction*. Milton Keynes: Open University Press.

Rosenblatt, L. M. (1970) *Literature as Exploration*. London: Heinemann Educational Books.

Selden, R. (1985) *A Reader's Guide to Contemporary Literary Theory*. Brighton: The Harvester Press.

Stake, R. E. (1979) 'Program evaluation, particularly responsive evaluation'. In W. B. Dockrell and D. Hamilton (eds) *Rethinking Educational Research*. London: Hodder and Stoughton.

Stedman, L. C. and Kaestle, C. F. (1987) 'Literacy and reading performance in the United States, from 1880 to the present'. *Reading Research Quarterly*, 22, 8–46.

Taylor, D. (1993) 'Assessing the complexity of students' learning: A student advocacy model of Instructional assessment'. In *From the Child's Point of View*. Portsmouth, NH: Heinemann.

Tierney, R. J. (1994) 'Dissention, tensions, and the models of literacy'. In Robert B. Ruddell, Martha Rapp Ruddell and Harry Singer (eds) *Theoretical Models and Processes of Reading* (4th edn). Newark, DE: International Reading Association, 1162–82.

Valencia, S., Hiebert, E. H. and Afflerbach, P. P. (eds) (1994) *Authentic Reading Assessment: Practices and Possibilities*. Newark, DE: International Reading Association.

2

TEN DILEMMAS OF
PERFORMANCE ASSESSMENT

P. David Pearson, Lizanne DeStefano and
Georgia Earnest García

This essay is a deliberate critique of performance assessment, especially as
it has unfolded as an alternative to standardized testing within the English
language arts, and even more particularly as it has been championed as an
alternative to conventional reading assessment. Our experience in trying
to build and evaluate various approaches to performance assessment has
spawned this critique. Each of us has served, in some circumstances, as
an advocate of performance assessment and as a critic of conventional
assessment practices. In other circumstances, we have served as critics of
performance assessment and advocates for conventional assessment, especially when those circumstances involved issues of budget, time limitations, the content domain, the nature of the inferences to be drawn and
the audience for the assessment (e.g., Pearson and DeStefano, 1993a,
1993b, 1993c, 1993d; DeStefano, Pearson, and Afflerbach, 1996; García,
1991, 1994; García and Pearson, 1991; García and Pearson, 1994; Valencia
and Pearson, 1987). We offer this critical commentary not in an attempt
to discredit performance assessment, but to hold it to the highest of
conceptual, ethical, psychometric and utilitarian standards. We truly want
performance assessment to succeed. But we want it to succeed because it
has met the challenge of high standards, rather than because we have decided
to overlook its blemishes in a blind quest for something better than we are
currently using.

There is good reason for the educational community to be concerned
about assessment in general. Assessments have assumed a larger and more
central role in almost every aspect of schooling than ever before (Resnick
and Resnick, 1992), although the effects of tests on teaching and learning
have been questioned by some (Shepard, 1989). In the minds of many
who want to reform education, it seems to be a linchpin in their plat-
form. The New Standards Project (Simmons and Resnick, 1993), the
National Board for Professional Teaching Standards (1994), the Coalition

of Essential Schools (Sizer, 1992), several states in the United States (Valencia, Pearson, Peters, and Wixson, 1989), and several countries throughout the world have all created new and different assessments as a leading component in their reform initiatives. During Bill Clinton's presidency, the United States government entered the fray; Goals 2000 and the reauthorization of the Elementary and Secondary Education Act (the major US programme for compensatory education), explicitly privileged content and performance standards and accompanying assessments by requiring that states develop and hold themselves accountable to both in return for the receipt of federal dollars (Smith, Cianci and Levin, 1996; Smith and O'Day, 1991).

The time has come to conduct an honest and thorough examination of the issues we have to address if performance assessment is to gain an important place in the array of assessments educators use to make decisions of consequence about individuals and groups in today's highly politicized educational milieux. We attempt to accomplish this critical feat by discussing a set of dilemmas related to our concerns about whether reading can actually be measured by performance assessments and whether these measurements are useful for a variety of purposes. We use the label 'dilemmas' because the problems we will outline do not lend themselves to clear solutions, as at least a few problems do; instead, the routines one might use to manage them are as likely to raise new problems as they are to solve the apparent one.

We have organized the dilemmas according to four loosely constructed themes. The first three dilemmas address the problems presented by the very nature of performance assessment: its representation of the construct of reading, the purposeful inclusion of conative and affective factors, and its social nature. Dilemmas Four to Six raise issues about the usefulness of the information gained through performance assessment: public and professional acceptance of standards as reference points, instructional utility and implications for professional development. The Seventh dilemma examines the need to hold performance assessment itself to some measurement standards, either traditional or newly established. The final trio of dilemmas highlight the political and societal implications of performance assessment: the public nature of its content and standards, equity issues related to its use in a diverse society and monitoring and accountability issues.

As we raise each dilemma or problem, we have attempted to follow a format that entails an explication and exemplification of the dilemma, some suggestions for dealing with it, and some suggestions for research initiatives that students of performance assessment might consider as they plan to help us, as a profession, research our way out of that particular dilemma.

Theme 1: The nature of performance assessment

Dilemma 1: How do we examine the relationship between an assessment and its underlying cognitive domain?

The case of reading assessment Years ago (see, for example, Thorndike, 1917), when we first realized that understanding what we read was a legitimate index of reading accomplishment, we started to measure reading comprehension with indirect indices, such as open-ended and multiple-choice questions. We settled on indirect measures largely because we knew we could not observe 'the real thing' – comprehension as it takes place on-line during the process of reading. In a very real sense, the history of reading assessment has been a history of developing the best possible artifacts or products from which to *draw inferences about* what must have been going on during the act of comprehension. We never really see either the clicks or the clunks of comprehension directly; we only infer them from distant indices.

The important question is whether, by moving to performance assessments, we are moving closer to the on-line process of comprehension or even further away from it. With performance assessments offering multiple opportunities for the inclusion of multiple texts, multi-media formats, collaborative responses and problem solving, and a heavy burden on writing, it is hard to argue that we are very close to observing and documenting the process of comprehension itself. Here is the dilemma: on the one hand, performance tasks reflect authentic literacy activities and goals – the kind of integrated, challenging activities students ought to be engaged in if they are to demonstrate their ability to apply reading and writing to everyday problems. On the other hand, we can question whether judgements about performance on these tasks really measure reading. Are they simply an index of the uses to which reading (or perhaps more accurately, the residue or outcomes of reading) can be put when they are complemented by a host of other media and activities?

We know much too little about the impact of task characteristics and response format on the quality and validity of judgements we make about individual students to answer these questions. Intuition would tell us that there are many students, for example, for whom the requirement of writing responses creates a stumbling block that yields a gross underestimate of their comprehension. Even when task writers try to escape the boundaries of conventional writing by encouraging students to use semantic webs or visual displays, they do not fully achieve their goals. Even in these formats, the student for whom writing is difficult is still at a decided disadvantage. As we have pointed out (García and Pearson, 1994), the matter of response format is all the more problematic in the case of second language learners, where not only writing but also language dominance comes into play. For example, when Spanish bilingual students are permitted to respond to English texts in Spanish rather than English, they receive higher scores on a range of tests (see García and Pearson, 1994, for a summary of this work).

An obvious way to address this dilemma would be to examine systematically the relationship among task characteristics, response formats and judgements of performance. Through controlled administrations of carefully constructed assessments, it would be possible to identify the relative impact of task characteristics, such as group discussion, video presentation, and various oral and written response formats, on the scores assigned to student performance. However, while such an analysis would elucidate, in terms of portioning out the score variance, how complex tasks affect student response, it does not really get at the more central construct validity issue of how well the assessment represents the domain of reading.

The more general question of domain representation This issue can be examined conceptually as well as psychometrically, and when it is, the question becomes one of judging the validity of different conceptualizations of the domain under consideration, in this case, reading accomplishment. It is a question of infrastructure and representation – determining the components of the domain and their interrelations. How validly does the assessment in question measure the cognitive domain underlying its construction and use? This would not be an issue if there were only one, or even a small number of commonly held conceptualizations of reading accomplishments. Nor would it be an issue if our measurement tools could easily distinguish among empirically valid and invalid conceptualizations. Alas, neither assumption holds for reading as for most domains of human performance. The complexity of the act of reading, along with the seemingly inevitable covariation among its hypothesized components, renders the statistical evaluation of competing models quite complex, often baffling even the statistical dexterity of our most sophisticated multivariate and factor analytic approaches.

These conceptual shortcomings ultimately devolve into epistemological and ethical issues, as performance is subjected to judgements and action in the form of decisions about certification, mastery, or future curriculum events. And here the interpretive and the realist perspectives on research and evaluation meet head on. Those who take a naive realist perspective tend to view the mapping of performance onto standards and eventual judgements about competence as a transparent set of operations: tasks are designed to measure certain phenomena, and if experts and practitioners agree that they measure them, then they do. Students who do well on particular tasks exhibit high levels of accomplishment in the domain measured; those who do not do well, exhibit low levels. But those who take a more interpretive perspective (see Moss, 1994, 1996; Delandshere and Petrosky, 1994), view the mapping problem as much more complex and indeterminate. Students do not always interpret the tasks we provide in the way we might have intended.

To ground this contrast in a real example, take the case of the early versions of the National Board of Professional Teaching Standards (NBPTS) Early Adolescent English Language Arts assessment for Board Certification. One of the tasks required teachers to submit a portfolio entry (actually a video plus commentary) to document their ability to engage students in discussions of literature (NBPTS, 1993). An assumption is made, in the realist view, that levels of performance on video index expertise in leading literature discussions. But the interpretivist might argue that even though that task may have been designed to elicit evidence about accomplishment of a standard about teaching literature, particular candidates may decline the invitation to use that task to offer such evidence – not because they cannot meet it, but because they interpret the task differently. Ironically, in their completion of the post reading discussion entry, candidates may provide very useful and insightful evidence about some other standards, such as sensitivity to individual differences or appreciation of multicultural perspectives. Conversely, they may provide evidence of meeting the literature standard on another task, itself designed to elicit evidence about other standards; for example, an exercise about how to diagnose student learning might permit a teacher to reveal deep knowledge about how to engage students in literature.

To further complicate the matter, test-takers are not the only group involved in interpretation of performance assessments. Applications of standards and scoring criteria are subject to individual interpretation, thus introducing another threat to construct validity. Once tasks are completed, judges are likely to disagree about the nature, quality and extent of evidence provided by particular individuals and particular tasks. Even if one judge concludes that a particular task yields evidence about standard X, other judges may disagree, thinking that it provides evidence of other standards or that other tasks provide better evidence about standard X. We will elaborate on the roles played by interpretation and judgement when we discuss reliability and generalizability issues in Dilemma 7, but presented here, they raise the issue of 'What construct are we measuring anyway?' The one intended by the assessment developers, the test takers, or the judges?

Research possibilities This is an area in which some useful and important research could be conducted without great expense. We need to examine carefully the process of creating and evaluating performance assessments and portfolios, particularly the manner in which: (a) tasks are selected to represent particular domains, such as reading; (b) test-takers interpret what is being asked of them and how it will be evaluated; and (c) scorers assign value to different sorts of evidence provided by different entries or tasks.

At the heart of this research agenda is a need for traditional construct validity studies in which the constructs to be measured are operationalized and explicitly linked to the content of the assessment and its scoring criteria or standards. Coherence at this level is not enough, however. It is also necessary to demonstrate relationships between the construct as measured and other constructs or outcomes. For example, do judgements of a student's reading accomplishment on performance tasks correlate with teacher's judgement of accomplishment? With performance on other tasks or measures of reading? With general academic success or real world self-sufficiency? While proponents of performance assessment hold that the authentic nature of the tasks attests to their validity as measures of reading, a collection of 'authentic' tasks may fall short in terms of representing the broad domain of reading. It is impossible to know whether the domain is adequately represented without studies of this kind.

Think-aloud procedures could be useful for understanding how participants perceive the tasks and the standards used to judge their responses or work (Ericsson and Simon, 1984; Garner, 1987). By asking students to tell us the decisions they make as they construct and present their responses, we can begin to determine the fit between the task as intended and as perceived by the participant and assess the magnitude of the threat to validity imposed by a lack of fit. This research could help us to create tasks that are more resistant to multiple interpretations as well as help us to improve scoring criteria to address a variety of interpretations.

Likewise we could ask scorers to think aloud while they scored performance tasks to gain insight into how individual judges interpret standards and assign scores to student work. Through think-alouds, it may be possible to determine the extent to which the underlying conceptualization of reading as represented in the task and scoring rules is guiding judges' decisions as well as the extent to which extraneous factors are influencing scoring.

Dilemma 2: How seriously should we take the inclusion of conative and affective factors in some of these new sets of standards and assessments?

Advocates of performance assessment hold that it is as important to assess habits of mind, dispositions and affect as it is to assess cognitive outcomes to obtain information for improving instruction and influencing accomplishment. These attributes are certainly a part of the rhetoric, if not the reality, of performance assessment. Consider, for example, the original New Standards (New Standards, 1994) ownership dimension for scoring the reading portfolio entries in which initiative, self-confidence, enjoyment and challenge are valued:

- Initiates participation in reading communities outside the classroom.
- Consistently demonstrates self-confidence, independence, and persistence.
- Pursues reading for enjoyment.
- Reads widely and for a variety of purposes.
- Evaluates own reading to set personal goals.
- Analyses personal responses to text.
- Selects challenging texts.

In the USA, matters of motivation and other affective dimensions, as facets of assessment, have become a 'damned if you do and damned if you don't' situation. It is very hard to scale students on these dimensions. Self-report measures are fraught with error, while observations and other surveillance strategies can be personally invasive. On the other hand, motivation is so clearly relevant to most discussions of student achievement that failure to account for it severely limits the validity and utility of the test results. Affective factors occupy a salient, but conflicted position in our assessment logic. Rarely, at least until performance assessments came along, have we included them as a part of formal assessment in our schools, yet we do privilege them in other, often equally important forms of evaluation, such as prospective employer checklists (Is this individual reliable? punctual? cooperative?) and letters of recommendation.

Some designers of assessment systems are attempting to assess both cognitive and affective factors and the relationship among them. The Interstate Teacher Assessment and Standards Cooperative (CCSSO, n.d.) has proposed a set of standards (soon to followed by assessments) for initial licensure. One of its principles illustrates:

Principle 3: The teacher understands how students differ in their approaches to learning and creates instructional opportunities that are adapted to diverse learners.

This principle is unpacked in three interwoven sections: knowledge, dispositions and performances.

Knowledge:
- The teacher understands and can identify differences in approaches to learning and performance, including different learning styles, multiple intelligences and performance modes, and can design instruction that helps use students' strengths as the basis for growth.

Dispositions refer to beliefs and attitudes that teachers would have to hold in order to implement the standard.

Dispositions:
- The teacher believes that all children can learn at high levels and persists in helping all children achieve success.
- The teacher is sensitive to community and cultural norms.

Finally, performances represent the 'evidence' that teachers can meet the standard.

Evidence:
- The teacher identifies and designs instruction appropriate to students' stages of development, learning styles, strengths and needs.
- The teacher brings multiple perspectives to the discussion of subject matter, including attention to students' personal, family, and community experiences and cultural norms.
- The teacher makes appropriate provisions (in terms of time and circumstances for work, tasks assigned, communication and response modes) for individual students who have particular learning differences or needs.

Even though INTASC assessments are still in their formative stages and unavailable for review, it would be hard to imagine performance assessments, at least based upon these standards, that would not include indices of affect, will, and disposition.

Of all the dilemmas discussed in this chapter, this one may prove both the most challenging and most interesting. Both the challenge and the interest come from stepping into a personal world often viewed as the prerogative of the family, or at least of some institution other than the school. By including conative and affective factors in formal assessments, are we in danger of imposing a societally sanctioned view of dispositions? What if a child proves to be a contemptible, anti-social, genius? What if a student shows contempt for reading, shuns goals for improving attitude, does not seek challenges, but performs well? Should we be concerned about affect as long as cognitive performance is solid? The answer is neither clear nor simple, involving an examination of the role of schooling in society and issues of family rights and privacy.

Research possibilities   It is difficult to recommend research on this dilemma. While motivational features are an important part of assessment, they are clearly grounded in academic assessments. We know a great deal about motivation but very little about how professionals use formal evidence of motivational factors in educational decision-making. We seem to want evidence of this sort, but at the same time we are concerned about issues of individual and family privacy and prerogative. What may be needed is a line of inquiry examining the value added to overall decision making when information about motivation, attitudes, and dispositions is available. It seems important to include students and parents as well as teachers in the category of educational decision-makers when we conduct this research.

Dilemma 3: Can we come to terms with the social nature of performance assessments?

In an era in which many extol the virtues of socially grounded views of learning and development (Gavelek and Raphael, 1996; Vygotsky, 1978; Wells and Chang-Wells, 1992, Wertsch, 1985), and regard meaning as an inherently social construction (e.g., Bleich, 1978; Gergen, 1994), it should not be surprising to learn that assessments have developed a social dimension. Indeed, modern assessments not only allow, but sometimes encourage or even *require*, students to work together. Yet, given what we know about the high stakes functions for which assessments are used (e.g. decisions about entry into or exit from special programmes or certification and licensure decisions), what are we to do when we know that the performance of an individual student is influenced by the work, comments and assistance of peers and/or teachers? The essence of this dilemma was captured well in an essay by Gearhart and her colleagues (Gearhart, Herman, Baker and Whittaker, 1993) entitled, 'Whose work is it?'

To illustrate the reality of this dilemma, consider an excerpt from a pilot task in the New Standards Literacy Assessment in which students read and compare two stories by Raymond Carver, the second a variation of the first written some twenty years later. In part of the three-day task, students are asked to conduct a character analysis after reading the first story. They fill in a chart listing the qualities of one of the characters and some words or phrases the author has used to show these qualities. Then they are encouraged to add ideas garnered from the group to their individual responses. The directions to teachers are very specific:

SUGGESTION TO TEACHERS:

When students have completed the chart, ask them to get into small groups. Groups will take turns sharing the ideas on their charts, and collaborate on adding ideas to their charts in the sections marked 'ideas added by my group'.

The social nature of this type of performance assessment clearly creates a dilemma for educators: How to separate out the individual's work from the group's work. Assistance from peers and teachers muddies the waters and makes assessment results less useful in gatekeeping contexts, where only a few candidates can attend, be served, honored, or employed. On the other hand, if assessment is to be grounded in authentic, everyday working contexts, if it is to reward students for the variety of problem-solving behaviours that operate in the workplace and everyday human activity, then it probably should be grounded in a social context. Viewed from the lens of work, collaboration may actually increase the utility of the assessments. If we are to believe the rhetoric of modern industry and total quality management, individuals seldom are required to complete tasks entirely on their own. Their work milieu, like the performance assessment context, may be inherently social, in which case, knowing how they can perform *with the assistance of others* may actually provide a predictive advantage.

This dilemma may not require an either/or solution. Instead it may involve careful *documentation* of the context of an assessment by describing the extent to which assistance was provided and what resources, both human and material, were available. Even better, we might adopt a practice of routinely securing performance judgements about an individual across multiple assessment contexts: alone, in pairs, in groups, in formal contexts, or in relaxed environments. In this way we might learn something about the optimal assessment contexts for different individuals or types of students; for some, social learning environments may enhance performance, while for others prove an impediment.

Research possibilities The central question here is: To what extent is scaffolding in the form of teacher instruction, peer interaction, and/or cooperative learning a legitimate and expected part of the assessment process? If it is, how can it be represented as such? Of course, there are significant research questions here, such as:

- Does the social element actually improve individual performance?
- Does it alter the judgments we make about particular individuals?
- Does it narrow the range of responses to what might be regarded as politically correct for the classroom?
- Is it possible to develop a metric of assisted performance – the degree of scaffolding required for a student to achieve a given level of accomplishment.[1]

If we choose the documentation option, the question may become, what do you do with the documentation once you have it? Do you use it to adjust students' scores? To annotate scores (i.e. with accommodations)?

[1] This, of course, is exactly the logic of dynamic assessment (see Feuerstein *et al.*, 1979).

To produce a 'complementary score' which documents the ability to benefit from assistance? To add narrative elaboration and complexity to an otherwise barren numerical score or a grade? If such support is available, the issue of how access to assistance is determined becomes important. Does everyone have access? Does the student determine what she needs or wants in the way of assistance, or does the teacher control and allocate assistance according to some plan? And, of course, if social support is regarded as one of many forms of assistance, the question of equity and opportunity to perform immediately arises – an issue to which we return when we discuss Dilemma Nine later in this paper.

Theme 2: The usefulness of information from performance assessments

Dilemma 4: Are standards useful reference points for assessing the quality of student performance?

Performance assessments differ from traditional norm-referenced assessments in that performance is referenced to standards rather than norms. In setting standards, a group of experts from a particular domain usually meet to arrive at what they consider to be performance goals or standards for the field. Students' performances are rated according to how well their work reflects the standards. So, it is conceivable that in a highly effective educational setting, the performance of a large number of students would 'meet the standard' by achieving high scores. Similarly, in a less effective educational setting, or in a setting where the standards currently exceed instructional emphasis and/or student performance, the majority of the students could fail to meet the standard.

This method of evaluating student performance differs dramatically from norm-referenced assessment, where an individual's performance is compared to the arithmetic mean of a national or regional sample of age or grade-level peers. Because the scores are interpreted in terms of a normal distribution, only a few students receive top scores, the majority receive average scores, and a few students receive low or below average scores. A problem with norm-referenced scores is that very little diagnostic information is provided about student performance. It is no accident that one of the key arguments provided by the most vocal advocates of performance assessment (e.g., Wiggins 1993) is that the arithmetic mean of a group is a meaningless standard for students to aspire to or by which to evaluate the significance of a particular student's performance.

Whether the public, the educational profession, and even those of us involved in performance assessments can embrace standards without continuing to think in terms of normative comparisons is uncertain. Our answer to this question depends upon the set of data that we examine. In New

Standards, for example, we were able to implement standards-based scoring in several of our task and portfolio experiments. The scoring of students on the 1993 performance tasks indicates that we were not 'curving' our scores. Across all tasks, when the highest score of 4 (on a rubric scaled from 1 to 4) was needed to earn a pass, the passing rate varied from 0 per cent to 17 per cent, with an average rate of 4 per cent. The needs revision group (score of 3) was not much more promising; it varied from 12 per cent to 17 per cent across tasks, with a mean of 15 per cent. Critics might question whether such low scores help students improve their performance or teachers improve their instruction. Whether the low scores are discouraging depends in large part on how high a passing rate we should expect when students have not participated in a curriculum in which standards such as those required for passing were emphasized.

A second experience makes us wonder about 'mean-free' score reporting. In the 1992 and 1994 state by state comparisons of reading performance on the National Assessment of Educational Progress, data were reported in terms of the percentage of students who performed well enough to be placed into the Basic, Proficient and Advanced levels rather than as some mean scale score on the overall assessment (see Salinger and Campbell, this volume). In a special validation study (Pearson and DeStefano, 1993d), we took the verbal descriptors of each of the categories (what it meant to be a below basic, basic, proficient, or advanced reader) and met with classroom teachers whose students had taken the NAEP test. We asked the teachers to use the descriptors – which were supposedly anchored carefully in absolute (not normative) behavioural descriptions of performance at each level – to categorize their students as belonging to one of the four levels. Later, in debriefing interviews, we asked them to describe the bases of their classifications. Overwhelmingly, teachers responded with something like this: 'Well, I sort of thought, high, middle, and low group of readers', or 'who does well on tests and who doesn't' (Pearson and DeStefano, 1993d). Findings such as these make us wonder whether normative comparisons are such an ingrained part of our professional culture of schooling that we cannot escape them even when we are provided with opportunities to examine student performance with entirely different reference points, such as curriculum-based standards of performance.

Research possibilities This dilemma calls for research on how teachers use assessment information. We can imagine some decision-making simulations in which we provide teachers with different sorts of data for individual children (sometimes in the form of evaluated portfolios and performance tasks and sometimes test scores) and ask them to suggest instructional programmes. It would be interesting to see if substantially different instructional suggestions are made as a function of whether the benchmarks to which data are referenced are standards versus norms.

Dilemma 5: Can performance assessments provide teachers with instructionally useful information?

Historically teachers have criticized standardized test reporting on the grounds that it provides little instructionally useful information. As we mentioned previously, standardized test reporting typically is characterized by a single norm-referenced score, usually a percentile or a grade norm score.

Whether scores from performance assessments will improve the type of information gained by teachers for diagnostic and instructional purposes is uncertain. A single, holistic score frequently is what is reported in performance assessments. This single score differs from the type of score reported for standardized tests in that it represents an entire assessment, which may have taken several days (in the case of a complete performance task) or several months (in the case of a portfolio in which artifacts are gathered over time) to have completed. As we pointed out in another paper (García and Pearson, 1991), holistic scores avoid the decomposition fallacy – 'the mistaken idea that by breaking an integrated performance into component processes, each can be evaluated and remediated independently' (380). What we don't know is whether a holistic score will provide teachers with the type of information they need to improve the performance of students who do not meet high standards.

The answers to these questions may depend upon the assumptions made about the role a rubric is supposed to play in the decision-making process. Rubrics are the generic descriptions of performance represented by the levels within a scoring system. For example, consider the differences between score points 6 and 4 in the now defunct California Learning Assessment System (CLAS, 1994, front matter) as illustrated in Figure 2.1.

Clearly both level 6 and level 4 readers are pretty good at what they do, and level 4 readers demonstrate many of the same behaviours and characteristics of level 6 readers, albeit with less confidence, consistency, clarity and ardour. However, when we assign a score to an individual student's performance, we explicitly make the claim that of all the rubric descriptions available, this description provides the best fit to the data in the student's response; we also implicitly ascribe *all*, or most, of the attributes of that level to the individual who generated the performance. Therefore, a performance assessment system would be potentially useful in instructional decision making *if, and only if,* its rubrics provided teachers with guidance for instruction.

Even though the description of performance from a rubric may be richer than that provided by a standard score or percentile rank, teachers need (at least they say they want) much more detailed information in order to plan instruction for individual students. This desire for specificity may explain the popularity of dimensional scoring systems, which provide

Figure 2.1 Excerpts from the CLAS reading rubric

6 Exemplary Reading Performance. *An exemplary reading performance is insightful, discerning, and perceptive as the reader constructs and reflects on meaning in a text.* Readers at this level are sensitive to linguistic, structural, cultural, and psychological nuances and complexities. They fill in gaps in a text, making warranted and responsible assumptions about unstated causes or motivations, or drawing meaning from subtle cues. They differentiate between literal and figurative meanings. They recognize real or seeming contradictions, exploring possibilities for their resolution or tolerating ambiguities. They demonstrate their understanding of the whole work as well as an awareness of how the parts work together to create the whole. *Readers achieving score point six develop connections with and among texts.* They connect their understanding of the text not only to their own ideas, experience, and knowledge, but to their history as participants in a culture or larger community . . . *These readers take risks. Readers performing at level six challenge the text.* They carry on a dialogue with the writer, raising questions, taking exception, agreeing or disagreeing, appreciating or criticizing text features.

4 Thoughtful Reading Performance. *Readers at score point four construct a thoughtful and plausible interpretation of a text.* They fill in some gaps in a text, making assumptions about unstated causes or motivations or drawing meaning from cues in the text. They usually differentiate between literal and figurative meanings. They may recognize real or seeming contradictions, but are sometimes distracted by these contradictions and by ambiguities. They demonstrate a thoughtful understanding of the whole work. *They develop connections with and among texts.* They usually connect their understanding of a text to their own experience and knowledge and sometimes to other texts. *These readers, while confident, rarely take risks. They sometimes challenge or question the text.* They may raise questions and may agree or disagree without explaining their reactions.

separate scores for a number of important dimensions or features of performance. A good example of dimensional scoring is a writing assessment system in which teachers are given information about students' voice, audience awareness, style, organization or content coherence, and mechanics. However, when dimensional scoring is used, there is a natural, if not compelling, tendency for educators to look for the particular weakness – that one valley in a diagnostic profile of peaks and valleys – that will guide them in providing exactly the right instruction for a particular student. This type of approach could have two adverse repercussions: First, teachers might overly emphasize individual dimensions by providing isolated or decontextualized instruction on them. Second, they might ignore or fail to capitalize on the 'peaks' or strong features of performance.

Flexible use of rubrics might be the answer. Holistic rubrics require teachers to apply a 'best fit' approach to scoring. It is unlikely that any response will possess *all* of the characteristics of, say, a level 4 response exactly as described in the rubric. Individual responses are much more likely to mix elements of 'six', 'five', and 'four'. When teachers realize this inevitable blurring among levels and dimensions, one of the important lessons they learn is that there are many routes to a 'four', 'five' or 'six' depending upon the particular mix of features in a given response. The lesson to be learned may be that the lack of statistical independence among dimensions is probably mirrored by their lack of instructional independence – instruction designed to improve performance on one dimension is likely to improve performance on others.

Research possibilities   We know very little about either the perceived or the real utility of different types of evaluative information. What is called for are studies of the ways in which all sorts of assessment information, including norm-referenced, criterion-referenced and standards-referenced (a term we shall use to refer to these newer rubric driven performance assessments), are used by teachers and schools to plan programmes, modify curriculum, or create activities for schools, classes and individuals. All of this debate could turn out to be a moot question if we learn, for example, that curriculum planning, for either individuals or groups, is based more on tradition, textbook adoption, or some other authoritative basis than on information provided by any sort of assessment.

More specifically, we need to understand the ways in which rubrics are actually used to guide instruction. We need to know whether there is any warrant to the claim that teachers apply all, or even most, of the features identified in the rubric. And, if not, what interpretation is being applied to various score points – what exactly do these scores mean in the minds of teachers, students, parents and others who use them?

With the advent of so many forms of performance and portfolio assessments, the time is certainly ripe for careful case studies – a combination of observations and interviews with key constituents – to determine the impact that these assessments have on the lives of teachers and students and to contrast that impact with that of standardized tests. We need to know how everyone involved in these assessments uses the resulting data to construct portraits of individual and collective performance. Put differently, we need to determine the instructional and consequential validity of these assessments. It will be essential, in conducting these studies, to study the effects on students in different tracks and programmes, especially those in compensatory programmes, in order to evaluate whether similar data profiles bear similar consequences across programmes. In other words, if two students have similar profiles, but live and work in different instructional contexts, one in regular education and the other in compensatory education, how do their instructional programmes and opportunities compare?

Dilemma 6: Can we provide teachers with the knowledge and experiences they need to use performance assessments effectively and appropriately?

Successful and appropriate use of performance assessments requires considerable teacher knowledge and expertise, much more than that which is required with standardized tests or commercially developed assessment systems. Interestingly, when standardized tests first were developed, they were heralded as being much more 'objective' and 'efficient' than teacher assessment, which was viewed as being subjective and biased (García and Pearson, 1994). The early concerns about teachers' subjectivity and bias still are valid. They only can be offset if teachers are provided with the appropriate knowledge and experiences needed to become performance experts in learning, instruction and assessment, similar to the experts who score athletic or artistic performance. Either we make an investment in teachers' professional development or we return to tests that require little or no interpretation in order to be used.

Our work in New Standards underscores the importance of teacher knowledge and a shared community of professional judgement. In both the scoring of complex performance tasks and portfolios, the key element in whatever success we experienced was bringing teachers together to examine, to wrestle with, both collaboratively and dialectically, the question of what counts as evidence of quality in student work. This was obvious to the teachers in their evaluations of the conferences, and it was equally as apparent to those of us who organized the events. The same story has been told whenever and wherever groups of teachers assemble to evaluate student work. When asked why such experiences have proven valuable, language arts teachers discover that in the process of judging the quality of student work, they are forced to consider a range of relevant bodies of knowledge – the language arts curriculum (and the opportunities it provides or ignores), the language and cultural perspectives that students bring to their learning, and issues in assessment itself (Pearson, in preparation).

How well teachers use information gained from performance assessments to improve their instruction also turns on the professional development issue. If teachers are involved in developing the rubric, picking the exemplar papers and writing the commentaries, and if they have participated in the rich professional discussions that ensue when teachers get together to evaluate student work, they may be much more likely to view the information from the assessment as instructionally important. By contrast, teachers handed a print-out from an externally imposed and scored assessment, be it performance-based or standardized, may not be inclined to see the utility of the information presented.

36

Research possibilities The research needed to address this dilemma must focus on teacher development. The question is straightforward but hard to answer. We need to know whether advances in teacher knowledge about a range of key domains (subject matter, learning, language, culture and assessment) are associated with more active and effective uses of performance and portfolio assessment. The question is hard to answer for the same reason that all questions of teachers' professional development are hard to answer – we seem not to possess the collective will, in the sense that as a society we are willing to make the necessary investments of resources, to study questions of teacher knowledge thoroughly.

Theme 3: Holding performance assessments to account

Dilemma 7: Will performance assessments stand up to conventional criteria for measurements, such as reliability and generalizability? Or do we need new criteria?

Early efforts to hold performance assessments to traditional psychometric standards, such as reliability, generalizability and validity, have produced mixed results. In New Standards, for example, within-task agreement among scorers approaches acceptable standards. This suggests that teachers can learn how to score open-ended tasks with the help of elaborate rubrics, well-chosen anchor papers and commentaries that explain the logic with which rubrics are applied to the papers to obtain different scores. In the 1993 scoring conference for New Standards, about a third of the English language arts and half of the mathematics teachers had never scored performance assessments before. To qualify as scorers, teachers had to match the benchmark sets on 80 per cent of the papers (8/10 on two consecutive sets). Even with this strict criterion, 90 per cent of the teachers qualified at the national scoring conference. Moreover, these teachers then returned to their states and trained their colleagues on the same tasks and materials; they were able to achieve nearly the same rate of qualification. However, they were not as consistent in matching one another's scores as they were in matching the scores in the benchmark sets. Using a direct match criterion (as opposed to the ± 1 score point criterion used in most states), the between judge agreement ranged from 50 per cent to 85 per cent. The agreement was a little higher in mathematics (69 per cent) as compared to writing (64 per cent), or reading (62 per cent). When agreement was calculated on the cut line between passing and not passing, interjudge agreement ranged from 84 per cent to 96 per cent across tasks.

While the data support the generalizability of scores across raters, there is little evidence to support generalizability across tasks. The data gathered from the first scoring of New Standards tasks (Linn, DeStefano, Burton and Hanson, 1995) indicate considerable covariation between task components and holistic/dimensional scores. However, when we compared the holistic scores across the mathematics tasks of New Standards, the resulting indices of generalizability were quite low, indicating that performance on any one task is *not* a good predictor of scores on other mathematics tasks. Shavelson and his colleagues have encountered the same lack of generalizability with science tasks (Shavelson, Baxter and Pine, 1992), as have other scholars (e.g., Linn, 1993) on highly respected enterprises such as the advanced placement tests sponsored by the College Board. The findings in the College Board analysis are noteworthy for the incredible variability in generalizability found as a function of subject matter; for example, in order to achieve a generalizability coefficient of 0.90, estimates of testing time range from a low of 1.25 hours for Physics to over 13 hours for European History. These findings are consistent with the conceptual problems cited earlier, and they suggest that we need to measure students' performance on a large number of tasks before we can feel confident in having a stable estimate of their accomplishment in a complex area such as reading, writing, or subject matter knowledge. They also suggest that portfolios may provide a way out of the generalizability problem by ensuring that we include multiple entries to document performance on any standard of significance.

In our early work in New Standards, we were very aware of this tension, and we tried to evaluate the efficacy and independence of various approaches to scoring. We examined carefully the statistical relationships (indexed by first order correlation coefficients) between analytic, holistic and dimensional scoring systems (Greer and Pearson, 1993). The data were generated by scoring a large sample of student papers in three ways: (1) *holistically*; (2) *analytically* (question by question by question) using the same rubric for each question, but with the requirement that scorers assign an overall score *after* assigning question by question scores; and (3) *dimensionally* using the dimensions not unlike those implied in the California rubric – thoroughness, interconnectedness, risk and challenge. The bottom line is pretty straightforward (Greer and Pearson, 1993): holistic scores, summed analytic scores and summed dimensional scores tend to correlate with one another at a magnitude in the 0.60 to 0.70 range. There are also consistently positive part-part and part-whole correlations in both the dimensional and analytic scoring systems.

As indicated earlier, our New Standards data are not very compelling on the inter-task generalizability front, although a great deal of research remains to be done before we can legitimately reject even our current crop of tasks and portfolio entries. Even so, we suspect that we will always be hard pressed to argue, as some proponents wish to, that when we include a performance task or a portfolio entry in an assessment system, we are more or less randomly drawing tasks from a large domain that share some common attributes, dimensions, or competencies, and, more importantly, somehow *represent* the domain of competence about which we think we are drawing inferences.

The most provocative criticisms of our current paradigms and criteria for evaluating assessments have been provided by Moss (Moss, 1994; Moss, 1996), who has challenged the very notion of reliability, at least in the way in which we have used it for the better part of this century. She points out that many assessments, particularly those outside school settings, involve a high degree of unreliability, or at least disagreement among those charged with making judgements – scoring performances in athletic or musical contests, deciding which of several candidates deserve to be hired for a job opening, awarding a contract in the face of several competing bids, or reviewing manuscripts for potential publication. She points out that none of us label these assessments as invalid simply because they involve disagreements among judges. Yet this is exactly what we have done in the case of educational assessments; to wit, the allegedly 'scandalous' interjudge reliabilities reported for Vermont (Koretz, Klein, McCaffrey and Stecher, 1992) and Kentucky (Kentucky Department of Education, 1994) in their statewide portfolio assessments.

Moss (1994, 1995) argues for a more 'hermeneutic' approach to studying the validity of assessments. In accepting the hermeneutic ideal and its emphasis on interpreting 'the meaning reflected in any human product', (7), we would not only be admitting that decisions involve interpretation and judgement, we would be doing everything possible to understand and account for the roles played by interpretation and judgement in the assessment process. Instead of scoring performances as 'objectively' and independently as possible, we would seek 'holistic, integrative interpretations of collected performances'. We would privilege deep knowledge of the students on the part of judges rather than regard it as a source of prejudice. We would seek as much and as diverse and as individualized an array of artifacts as would be needed to portray each student's performance fully and fairly. And when differences in process or judgement arose, instead of fidgeting about sources of unreliability, we would try to account for them in our 'interpretation' of performance; we might even opt to document the differences in our account of either individual or group performance. From a hermeneutic perspective, differences can be both interesting and informative, not just 'noise' or error, as they are assumed to be in a psychometric account of interpretation.

In many of our social and professional – indeed our legal – activities, we find other mechanisms for dealing with differences in activity, judgement and interpretation; for example the human practices of consensus, moderation, adjudication and appeals are all discursive mechanisms for dealing with difference. All represent attempts to understand the bases of our disagreements. Additionally they entail, to greater or lesser degrees, attempts to get inside of or underneath our surface disagreements to see if there is common ground (consensus), to see things from the point of view of others (moderation), to submit our claims to independent evaluation (adjudication), and to ensure a fair hearing to all who have a stake in the issue at hand (appeals). These are all mechanisms for promoting trustworthiness in human judgment, and we use them daily in most significant, everyday human activities. Why then do we seem to want to exclude them from the assessment arena?

Research possibilities We are not sure what to recommend for research initiatives on this front. After all, the measurement community has conducted reliability, generalizability and validity studies for decades, and we see little reason to believe that this situation will change. What may change, however, is the set of criteria used to evaluate the efficacy of assessments, particularly performance assessments. While certain criteria, such as authenticity (the assessment activities look like what we think the underlying cognitive process should look) and instructional validity (the assessment prompts teachers to engage children in high quality instruction rather than blind teaching to the test), have been suggested by proponents of alternative assessments, even individuals regarded as champions of more conventional views (e.g., Linn, Baker and Dunbar, 1991) have suggested additional criteria, such as consequences – what happens to students and teachers as a consequence of the scores they achieve (which, by the way, would surely entail our notion of instructional validity), cognitive complexity (does the test engage students in a full, rich and multilayered enactments of the processes), and meaningfulness.

What is probably called for is research that tries to answer questions about the appropriateness, feasibility and credibility of various criteria for evaluating assessment tools. Will audiences and clients accept assessments that employ new and different criteria, especially those that derive from a hermeneutic paradigm? If so, what audiences? For what assessment purposes? Just as traditional criteria have been applied to alternative assessments, so alternative criteria should be applied to traditional assessments. We need to know whether tests created according to psychometric criteria can meet standards of consequences, instructional validity, authenticity, meaningfulness and cognitive complexity.

Theme 4: Political, social and ethical issues in performance assessment

Dilemma 8: Can we achieve and learn to live with a completely open system of assessment?

Perhaps no other spokesperson for performance assessment is more insistent than Grant Wiggins on eradicating the evils that derive from our preoccupation with secrecy and test security. In his book (1993), *Assessing Student Performance*, he argues that no other feature of standardized tests is more inequitable and pernicious than the shrink-wrapping and closeting of tests prior to their administration. Indeed what he argues for is a completely open system of performance tasks so that teachers and students know what a high standard represents. Performance tasks, along with anchor papers and commentaries, would be catalogued in public and/or school libraries and available to teachers, students and parents throughout the political unit in which they are used.

Critics of this approach might contend that students would merely duplicate what they see, invalidating any attempt to evaluate their individual performance. To safeguard against this possibility, Wiggins insists that the public display of performance artifacts be large enough to discourage any sane teacher or student from trying to rehearse or memorize *all* particular tasks and anchor papers. Wiggins' argument is predicated on the assumption that we can specify and exemplify what counts as evidence of quality and accomplishment in any domain of human endeavour. It is important to remember that he often points to art, music, and athletics for examples of domains in which both content and performance standards are completely open and where examples of anchor performances abound (a favourite example being qualifying performances for track and field events).

Another aspect of this issue is self-assessment. Performance assessments frequently include opportunities for students to evaluate their own performances and to set their own goals. If students are to self-evaluate, then the evaluation standards and underlying rubrics need to be made public. Advocates of this approach say that when students are involved in self-assessment, they become more intrinsically motivated, involved and empowered.

Research possibilities   We can learn much about the efficacy, as well as the corruptibility, of open, high stakes performance assessment systems by studying existing examples of successful systems, such as Central Park East (Meier, 1995) and Walden III (Mabry, 1992) high schools. We should also study the international baccalaureate, the advanced placement exams and portfolios used in professional decision making, such as certification examinations in fields like architecture, and, now, with the advent of the National Board for Professional Teaching Standards (NBPTS, 1994), in the teaching profession. We need to know whether students in these open systems are more aware of and better able to articulate and discuss standards and criteria than are students in closed systems, systems in which the standards have to be ferreted out. We also need to research claims, made by advocates of open systems, of better self-evaluation and greater engagement and empowerment. Finally, it would be useful to know whether students in schools that place a premium on performance assessment perform better on genuine high stakes, externally controlled performance assessments, such as freshman writing assessments administered by colleges, grades given in colleges, or success in the workplace (where, if we can believe the rhetoric, these sorts of skills and dispositions will be valued and rewarded).

One last entry remains in the wish list for research initiatives: We should evaluate the 'blinders' effects of both conventional and performance assessments. We already possess convincing evidence, through the low performance achieved on New Standards tasks and portfolios, that students who have been reared in an environment in which they expect multiple-choice tests do not do well on performance assessments. It would be interesting to know if performance assessments are equally as blinding; that is, will students who are reared academically to expect challenging performance assessments do excessively poorly on standardized tests? Anecdotally, we would expect the answer to be, 'Yes'. Any educator who has worked with students of any age for any length of time has accumulated stories about good readers and writers and learners who just do not test well. Even so, it is important to gather evidence to evaluate the validity of such claims.

Dilemma 9: Can we develop new concepts of equity?

Equity is a tricky issue, especially with respect to cultural and linguistic diversity. In discussing issues of equity, it is common for us to use metaphors of equality, such as a level playing field or a common yardstick. This view of equity usually results in students doing the same tasks under the same testing conditions (e.g. level playing field), with their performance evaluated by the same criteria (e.g. common yardstick). Researchers interested in cultural and linguistic diversity are quick to point out that metaphors like 'level playing field' and 'common yardstick' typically reflect a mainstream bias because they are based on a monolithic stance – generally, a White, European-American, middle-class, monolingual, male-oriented view of achievement, which permeates the construction, administration and evaluation of the assessment (García, 1994; García and Pearson, 1994; Geisinger, 1992; Gifford, 1989). Such assessments generally do not take into account varied interpretations of intelligence, achievement or knowledge, nor do they acknowledge the diverse contexts in which students acquire knowledge or the diverse ways in which they might display it. Here, we are reminded of a critical thinking test that evaluated students' responses to a situation where there was litter in a park. The evaluation criteria assumed that the litter was unsightly but not dangerous, reflecting a middle-class suburban view of park litter. The criteria did not take into account how 'street-wise' inner-city students had been taught to respond to a dangerous setting, where park litter could mean drugs or syringes.

If we want to establish an alternative type of equity, an equity in which all students get the opportunity to put their 'best foot forward' or 'show their stuff', then other options may be necessary. For example, students in the process of learning English-as-a-second-language frequently reveal greater comprehension of English text when they are allowed to respond to it – orally and in writing – in their native language (García, 1991). Perhaps, we would want them to respond to the same passage in both languages, so that we could see what they can do in their two languages. Alternatively, we might ask students to choose a familiar and unfamiliar topic or task, and assess their performance on the two.

The best foot forward metaphor for equity would lead us toward *choice* as a primary tool for achieving equity – a choice of tasks (e.g. passages to read, questions to answer, prompts to write to, projects to complete), responses (e.g. ways in which students demonstrate their performance – oral, written, illustrated, constructed, in the language of the assessment or a different language), or even sociolinguistic contexts in which to work (e.g. alone, in collaboration, with expert help, without expert help, at school, at home, at work). In principle, this would not seem to be a problem within a performance assessment milieu. If we take seriously the idea that in performance assessment, students are presenting evidence to demonstrate that they have met a standard, should it matter if students present different bodies of evidence for the same standards?

If we look toward dynamic assessment (Feuerstein, Rand and Hoffman, 1979), we may find guidance on at least one aspect of this dilemma – how to evaluate student performance under different conditions of support. Within the framework of dynamic assessment, instead of holding assessment features and contexts constant and allowing achievement to vary, we end up asking ourselves how much support is needed to help students accomplish a specified goal or level of achievement. In this instance, instead of levelling opportunity, we are levelling achievement and allowing the type and amount of scaffolding provided to vary. Consider the revolution that might occur if choice and scaffolding rather than standardization drove our quest for equity. Conceptually we would have a very different concept of assessment, not to mention a very different concept of curriculum.

Research possibilities   The research questions emanating from this issue are both straightforward and subtle. The straightforward questions have to do with whether we make different judgements about student accomplishment under different criteria and conditions of equity. For example, what does a teacher do when she knows that student A received a great deal more guidance than student B both in putting together a portfolio and in getting pieces ready to go into the portfolio? The issue of assistance was also raised with respect to Dilemma 3 on the social nature of new assessments. As was suggested at that point, perhaps what we need is not so much an answer to the ethical question but a clearer picture of how different individuals perform under different conditions of contextual support. The more subtle questions revolve mainly around the uses of assessment data gathered under such conditions and the potential costs that will accrue to students when users of assessment data – employers and admissions officers and future teachers – realize that the playing fields were levelled in unfamiliar ways. Before travelling too far down this road, we need to know what costs students will incur if users know that they received peer or teacher assistance on a performance task.

Dilemma 10: Can we use performance assessments for wide-scale monitoring and accountability requirements?

Many educators who are quite willing to support portfolios and performance assessments as useful within classroom tools – for teachers and students to use to make decisions about progress within a curriculum-embedded framework – balk at the suggestion that those data might travel beyond the classroom walls (Tierney, in press; Hansen, 1992), either for high stakes decisions for individuals (i.e. the certifying function of the portfolios used by New Standards or Central Park East High School or Walden III High School) or as accountability indices (for comparisons between schools and districts, similar to how standardized tests or state exams are most frequently used). Nonetheless, in the past five years, a few states have jumped headlong into wide-scale use of performance assessments (e.g., California, Maryland, Wisconsin and Indiana) or portfolios (e.g., Kentucky, Vermont and Oregon). These efforts have met with political and technical obstacles. Some of the state efforts (California, Wisconsin and Indiana) have faltered, but others continue to develop and are beginning to be used for monitoring and accountability purposes.

In principle, there is no reason why an assessment built to provide scores or even narrative descriptions of individual students cannot be used for school and district level accountability. In fact, one can argue that precisely such a relationship should hold between individual and aggregate assessment: why would we want to hold schools accountable to standards that differ substantially from those used for individual students? If we can use an assessment to draw valid inferences about individuals within important instructional contexts, why shouldn't we use those same measures for school accountability indices? All we need is a valid, reliable and defensible aggregate index. Who is to say that the percentage of students who score at or above a particular standard – for example the accomplished or proficient level in a rubric used to evaluate individual performance – is not just as useful an indicator of school level programme effectiveness as a mean grade equivalent score, the percentile of the school mean, or a mean scale score on some invented distribution with a mean of 250 and a standard deviation of 50?

If we could aggregate up from the individual and the classroom level, we could meet our school and district accountability (reports to our constituencies) and monitoring (census-like) needs and responsibilities without losing valuable class time getting ready for and administering standardized tests of questionable benefit to students and teachers. As near as we can tell, most standardized tests, and even state tests, serve only this accountability (monitoring programme effectiveness) function in our schools. They convey little instructional information. If accountability functions could be met by aggregating data from assessments that also tell us something about teaching and learning, so much the better.

To suggest that aggregating scores from locally generated assessment tools to provide classroom, school, or district scores might serve accountability purposes is to suggest that we might not need standardized tests. The implications of such a suggestion are politically and economically charged. External assessments, like textbooks, are a key anchor in the economy of education. Of course, knowing what we know about the viability and adaptability of American business, the most likely result is that test publishers, rather than oppose such a movement, will try to become a key part of it. Indeed, the process has already begun with commercially available performance assessments and portfolio evaluation systems.

Research possibilities We need to examine the 'aggregatibility' of performance assessment information from individual to classroom to school to district to state levels. Aggregatibility is dependent not only on the technical adequacy of the scores. It also depends on whether the information collected at the individual level has relevance for accountability and monitoring at the other levels. Such a programme of research could begin by assessing the information needs at various levels within the system, then asking stakeholders at each level to rate the usefulness of different types of information (i.e. average percentile ranks vs. percentage of students at various achievement levels) for the decisions they have to make.

Conclusion

At the outset of this critique, we argued that we were undertaking this critical review of performance assessment in order to improve it not discredit it. We hope that our underlying optimism about the promise of portfolio assessment shines through the barrage of difficulties and dilemmas that we have raised. Perhaps our optimism would have been more apparent had we extended our critique to standardized, multiple-choice assessments. For then readers would have realized that any criticisms we have of performance assessment pale in comparison to the concerns we have about these more conventional tools (García and Pearson, 1994; Pearson and DeStefano, 1993a). For example, for all of their shortcomings, performance assessments stand up much better than their more conventional counterparts to criteria such as meaningfulness, consequential vailidity and authenticity (Linn, Baker and Dunbar, 1991), while they are much less likely to be suscep-tible to phenemona such as test score pollution (Haladayna, Nolan and Haas, 1991) – a rise in a test score without any accompanying increase in the underlying cognitive process being measured – that often results from frantic teaching to the test.

Because so many of these questions and issues are dilemmas rather than problems, attempts at finding solutions are likely to uncover even more problems. So the best we can hope for is to decide which problems we are willing to live with in the process of solving those we believe are intoler-able. Unlike problems, which may, in principle, be solved, the test we can hope for with dilemmas is to 'manage' them (Cuban, 1992).

The issue of privilege brings us to this most central of dilemmas – one that we must all, both the testers and the tested, come to terms with. At every level of analysis, assessment is a political act. Assessments tell people how they should value themselves and others. Assessments open doors for some and close them for others. The very act of giving an assess-ment is a demonstration of power: one individual tells the other what to read, how to respond, how much time to take. One insinuates a sense of greater power because of greater knowledge (i.e. possession of the right answers).

The brightest ray of hope emanating from our recent candidates for assessment reform, the very performance assessments that have been the object of our criticism, is their public disposition. If assessment becomes a completely open process in all of its phases from conception to develop-ment to interpretation, then at least the hidden biases will become more visible and at best everyone will have a clearer sense of what counts in our schools and perhaps even a greater opportunity to become a part of the process.

References

Bleich, D. (1978) *Subjective Criticism*. Baltimore, MD: Johns Hopkins University Press.

California Learning Assessment System. (1994) *Elementary Performance Assessments: Integrated English-language Arts Illustrative Material*. Sacramento, CA: California Department of Education.

Council of Chief State School Officers. (n.d.). 'Model standards for beginning teacher licensing and development: A resource for state dialogue'. Draft from the Interstate New Teacher Assessment and Support Consortium. Washington, DC: Council of Chief State School Officers.

Cuban, L. (1992) 'Managing dilemmas while building professional communities'. *Educational Researcher*, 21(1): 4–11.

Delandshere, G. and Petrosky, A. R. (1994) 'Capturing teachers' knowledge: Performance assessment a) and post-structuralist epistemology b) from a post-structuralist perspective c) and post-structuralism d) none of the above'. *Educational Researcher*, 23(5): 11–18.

Destefano, L., Pearson, P. D. and Afflerbach, P. (1996) 'Content validation of the 1994 NAEP in Reading: Assessing the relationship between the 1994 Assessment and the reading framework'. In R. Linn, R. Glaser and G. Bohrnstedt (eds), *Assessment in Transition: 1994 Trial State Assessment Report on Reading: Background Studies*. Stanford, CA: The National Academy of Education.

Ericsson, K. A. and Simon, H. A. (1984) *Protocol Analysis: Verbal Reports as Data*. Cambridge, MA: MIT Press.

Feuerstein, R. R., Rand, Y. and Hoffman, M. B. (1979) The Dynamic Assessment of Retarded Performance. Baltimore, MD: University Park Press.

García, G. E. (1991) 'Factors influencing the English reading test performance of Spanish-speaking Hispanic students'. *Reading Research Quarterly*, 26, 371–92.

—— (1994) 'Equity challenges in authentically assessing students from diverse backgrounds'. *The Educational Forum*, 59, 64–73.

García, G. E. and Pearson, P. D. (1991) 'The role of assessment in a diverse society'. In E. Hiebert (ed.), *Literacy in a Diverse Society: Perspectives, Practices, and Policies*. New York: Teachers College Press, 253–278.

—— (1994) 'Assessment and diversity'. In L. Darling-Hammond (ed.), *Review of Research in Education* (vol. 20). Washington, DC: American Educational Research Association, 337–391.

Garner, R. (1987). *Metacognition and Reading Comprehension*. Norwood, NJ: Ablex.

Gavelek, J. and Raphael, T. E. (1996) 'Changing talk about text: New roles for teachers and students'. *Language Arts*, 73, 182–92.

Gearhart, M., Herman, J., Baker, E. and Whittaker, A. K. (1993) *Whose Work is It? A question for the validity of large-scale portfolio assessment*. CSE Technical report 363: National Center for Research on Evaluation, Standards, and Student Testing. Los Angeles: University of California at Los Angeles.

Geisinger, K. F.(1992) 'Fairness and psychometric issues'. In K. F. Geisinger (ed.), *Psychological Testing of Hispanics*. Washington, DC: American Psychological Association, 17–42.

Gergen, K. J. (1994) *Realities and Relationships: Soundings in Social Construction*. Carmbridge, MA: Harvard University Press.

Gifford, B. R. (1989) 'The allocation of opportunities and politics of testing: A policy analytic perspective'. In B. Gifford (ed.), *Test Policy and the Politics of Opportunity Allocation: The Workplace and the Law*. Boston: Kluwer Academic Publishers, 3–32.

Greer, E. A. and Pearson, P. D. (1993) 'Some statistical indices of the efficacy of the New Standards performance assessments: A progress report'. Presented at the annual meeting of the American Association of Educational Research, Washington, DC, April.

Haladyna, T. M., Nolan, S. B. and Haas, N. S. (1991) 'Raising standardized achievement test scores and the origins of test score pollution'. *Educational Researcher*, 20, 2–7.

Hansen, J. (1992). 'Evaluation: "My portfolio shows who I am".' *Quarterly of the National Writing Project and the Center for the Study of Writing and Literacy*, 14(1): 5–9.

Kentucky Department of Education. (1994) *Measuring Up: The Kentucky Instructional Results Information System (KIRIS)*. Kentucky.

Koretz, D., Klein, S., McCaffrey, D. and Stecher, B. Interim report: 'The reliability of the Vermont portfolio scores in the 1992–93 school year'.

Linn, R.L. (1993) 'Educational assessment: Expanded expectations and challenges'. *Educational Evaluation and Policy Analysis*, 15, 1–16.

Linn, R. L., Baker, E. L. and Dunbar, S. B. (1991) 'Complex, performance-based assessment: Expectations and validation criteria'. *Educational Researcher*, 20, 15–21.

Linn, R. L., DeStefano, L., Burton, E. and Hanson, M. (1995) 'Generalizability of New Standards Project 1993 Pilot Study Tasks in Mathematics'. *Applied Measurement in Education*, 9(2): 33–45.

Mabry, L. (1992) 'Twenty years of alternative assessment at a Wisconsin high school'. *The School Administrator*, December, 12–13.

Meier, D. (1995) *The Power of Their Ideas*. Boston: Beacon Press.

Moss, P. (1994) 'Can there be validity without reliability?' *Educational Researcher*, 23(2): 5–12.

—— (1996) 'Enlarging the dialogue in educational measurement: Voices from interpretive research traditions'. *Educational Researcher*, 25(1): 20–8.

National Board for Professional Teaching Standards. (1993) *Post-Reading Interpretive Discussion Exercise*. Detroit, MI: NBPTS.

—— (1994) *What Teachers Should Know and Be Able To Do*. Detroit, MI: NBPTS.

New Standards. (1994) *The Elementary Portfolio Rubric*. Indian Wells, CA, July.

—— (1995) *Performance Standards: Draft 5.1, 6/12/95*. Rochester, NY: New Standards.

Pearson, P. D. (in preparation). 'Teacher's evaluation of the New Standards portfolio process'. Unpublished paper. East Lansing, MI: Michigan State University.

Pearson, P. D. and DeStefano, L. (1993a) 'Content validation of the 1992 NAEP in Reading: Classifying items according to the reading framework'. In *The Trial State Assessment: Prospects and Realities*: Background Studies. Stanford CA: The National Academy of Education.

—— (1993b) 'An evaluation of the 1992 NAEP reading achievement levels, report one: A commentary on the process'. In *Setting Performance Standards for Student Achievement*: Background Studies. Stanford CA: The National Academy of Education.

—— (1993c) 'An evaluation of the 1992 NAEP reading achievement levels, report two: An analysis of the achievement level descriptors'. In *Setting Performance Standards for Student Achievement*: Background Studies. Stanford CA: The National Academy of Education.

—— (1993d) 'An evaluation of the 1992 NAEP reading achievement levels, report three: Comparison of the cutpoints for the 1992 NAEP Reading Achievement Levels with those set by alternate means'. In *Setting Performance Standards for Student Achievement*: Background Studies. Stanford CA: The National Academy of Education.

Resnick, L. B. and Resnick, D. P. (1992) 'Assessing the thinking curriculum: New tools for educational reform'. In B. R. Gifford and M. C. O'Connor (eds), *Changing Assessments: Alternative Views of Aptitude, Achievement, and Instruction.* Boston: Kluwer Academic Publishers, 37–75.

Shavelson, R. J., Baxter, G. P. and Pine, J. (1992) 'Performance Assessments: Political Rhetoric and Measurement Reality', *Educational Researcher*, 21(4): 22–7.

Shepard, L. (1989) 'Why we need better tests'. *Educational Leadership*, 46(7): 4–9.

Simmons, W. and Resnick, L. (1993) 'Assessment as the catalyst of school reform'. *Educational Leadership*, 50(5): 11–15.

Sizer, T. (1992). *Horace's School: Redesigning the American High School.* Boston: Houghton-Mifflin.

Smith, M. S., Cianci, J. E. and Levin, J. (1996) 'Perspectives on literacy: A response'. *Journal of Literacy Research*, 28, 602–9.

Smith, M. S. and O'Day, J. (1991) 'Systemic school reform'. In S. H. Fuhrman and B. Malen (eds), *The Politics of Curriculum and Testing.* Briston, PA: Falmer Press, 233–67.

Thorndike, E. L. (1917) 'Reading as reasoning'. *Journal of Educational Psychology*, 8(6): 323–32.

Tierney, R. J. (in press). 'Literacy assessment reform: Shifting beliefs, principled possibilities, and emerging practices'. *The Reading Teacher.*

Valencia, S. and Pearson, P. D. (1987) 'Reading assessment: Time for a change'. *The Reading Teacher*, 40, 726–33.

Valencia, S. W., Pearson, P. D., Peters, C. W. and Wixson, K. K. (1989) 'Theory and practice in statewide reading assessment: Closing the gap'. *Educational Leadership*, 47(7): 57–63.

Vygotsky, L. (1978) *Mind in Society: The Development of Higher Psychological Processes.* Cambridge: Harvard University Press.

Wells, G. and Chang-Wells, L. (1992) *Constructing Meaning Together.* Portsmouth, NH: Heinemann Educational Books

Wertsch, J. V. (1985) *Vygotsky and the Social Formation of Mind.* Cambridge, MA: Harvard University Press.

Wiggins, G. (1993) *Assessing Student Performance. Exploring the Purpose and Limits of Testing.* San Francisco: Jossey-Bass Publishers.

3

FEMINIST POSTSTRUCTURALIST PERSPECTIVES ON THE LANGUAGE OF READING ASSESSMENT

Authenticity and performance

Donna E. Alvermann and Michelle Commeyras

Introduction

The purpose of this chapter is to explore through feminist poststructuralist perspectives some of the humanist assumptions underlying *authenticity*, one of the more common terms currently associated with the new reading assessments. For example, we inquire into the meaning of authentic as 'real life' experiences when used in the context of reading assessment. Similarly, we explore the notion of *performance* and some of its implications for the new reading assessments. But before we begin, a couple of caveats are in order. We have chosen not to distinguish between poststructuralist and postmodernist perspectives in order that our work can be read within the framework discussed in the chapter by Harrison, Bailey and Dewar (this volume). We have also opted to avoid a discussion of what McCoy (in press) calls the performative contradiction in which one's method belies one's message. In avoiding such a discussion, we recognize that critics may point out how our method of writing (nodding as it does to the logico-rationalist form of academic prose) conflicts with our purpose for writing (to question the assumptions that underlie a rationalist or humanist view of reading assessment). Like Spivak (1993), we view this lack of fit between form and function not as a failing but instead as 'the new making-visible of a "success" that does not conceal or bracket problems' (28).

Authentic experiences and reading assessment

Helping 'students become thoughtful, critical, responsible, and effective readers and writers' (Valencia, Hiebert and Afflerbach, 1994: 1) is a central goal among those working to develop the concept of authentic reading assessment. As Valencia *et al.* point out, the past few years have witnessed an explosion in the number of articles and chapters extolling the virtues of this kind of assessment. Although a few writers (e.g., Edelsky, 1990; Myers, 1991; Shannon, 1985) have drawn attention to the ideological assumptions underlying authentic assessment, for the most part the literacy community has seemed disinterested in exploring them. Ambiguities persist and extend, moreover, to what the terms authentic and experience imply.

Defining authentic experiences

The term *experience* has a long history of use. According to Williams (1983), prior to the early eighteenth century, experience meant something closely akin to experimentation, or knowledge arrived at through testing and observation. Although a reliance on observed events remained a part of the definition of experience during the latter part of the eighteenth century, a new dimension was added – a particular kind of consciousness – which in the twentieth century has come to mean what Scott (1992), quoting from Williams, refers to as ' "a full, active awareness" including feeling as well as thought' (27). Speaking of experience in this way, Scott points out, leads to viewing it as the origin of all knowledge – a site of feminist poststructuralist critique.

Authentic, meaning that which is 'genuine or real' (Neufeldt and Guralnik, 1994: 92), is used by assessment experts (e.g., Valencia *et al.* 1994; Wiggins, 1992; Wolf, LeMahieu, and Eresh, 1992) in their description of correspondences linking students' 'real life' experiences to classroom instructional practices and the assessment of those practices. This linkage includes 'using authentic, or "real life", literacy tasks' (Valencia *et al.*, 1994: 8) when applied to reading assessment.

As might be gleaned from these two definitions, the practice of using a student's experience as the basis for authentic reading assessment would seem both appropriate and desirable. However, such a practice, at least as viewed from feminist poststructuralist perspectives, is potentially problematic in that it assumes 'experience is "the great original" ' (Britzman, 1995: 229). Arguing from this point of view, Scott (1992) notes that to appeal to one's experience as the origin of uncontestable evidence is to leave aside the politics of its construction. In other words, treating experience as the origin of one's knowledge (and thus uncontestable) overlooks the ways in which it comes to exist, and more particularly, the historical processes that produce it.

Troubling practice

To trouble a practice is to call the familiar and comfortable into question. Troubling the practice of treating so-called real life experiences as grounds for developing authentic reading assessments entails calling into question the notion of an all-knowing subject, a concept that predates Descartes and is of current interest to feminist poststructuralists (e.g., Butler, 1990; Hekman, 1991; Scott, 1992) who argue for the decentring of the subject as the origin of meaning and truth. For example, Hekman has written:

> Postmoderns reject the notion that meaning derives from a connection between words and the world, positing instead that meaning is a product internal to the mechanisms of language. They argue that meaning derives from the interplay of sign and signified within discursive formations of language. One of the consequences of the postmodern conception of language and meaning is that the subject is decentered as the origin of meaning and truth.
>
> (47)

This movement to decentre the subject is part of a feminist project aimed at exposing the false polarization between the subject as constituting (having agency) and as being constituted by social forces (thereby losing agency). The same feminist philosophers who are working to abandon the modernist concept of the polarized subject (e.g. Hekman, 1991; Scott, 1992) are also working to redefine the notion of experience. We see their work as being important to consider for those involved in developing new approaches to reading assessment (see Hoffman's chapter and Hayward and Spencer's chapter, this volume; also see van Kraayenoord, Moni and Dilena, 1995).

Whereas experience in the classical, Aristotelian sense was viewed as the 'doorway to the apprehension of essence, . . . [in the poststructuralist sense] experience is never as unified, as knowable, as universal, and as stable as we presume it to be' (Fuss, 1989: 114). Therefore, appealing to 'real life' experiences as a basis for developing authentic reading assessments calls for more careful scrutiny and problematizing than has been the case up to now. In particular, it leads us to consider how teachers and students can come to understand how social forces shape, regulate, or even dictate their literacy experiences (Rockhill, 1987).

Whose work is it?

When Gearhart and Herman (1995) in their review of several large-scale portfolio assessment projects raise the question 'Whose work is it?', they are referring to the difficulties that arise when individual student portfolios are constructed in classroom settings that encourage students to share their experiences in a variety of social contexts. Because authorship, like experience, is never as unified or knowable as test developers might like it to be, problems arise. Hampered in their efforts to determine the validity of 'individual' portfolio scores given the social nature of students' shared experiences, developers of large-scale assessment projects find that what is 'real' or authentic often works against their commitment to public accountability.

Teachers, on the other hand, who have agreed to be part of these large-scale assessments often feel a particular commitment to current pedagogical reforms that emphasize engaged communities of learners working on 'real' tasks. Ironically, as Gearhart and Herman point out, 'the more developed the community, the more engaged others will be in the work tagged with an individual student's name' (4). However, teachers who advocate portfolio assessment need not be deterred by this situation if they believe that what counts ultimately is students' engagement in literate communities.

Finding answers to 'Whose work is it?' would seem less important once test developers come to understand that a more basic problem is the detection of biases stemming from their assumptions about whose experiences should count. A case in point is Schafer's (1996) recent content analysis of the items on the *Maryland School Performance Assessment Program*. His analysis demonstrated that test developers had succeeded in making the reading passages 'ethnically neutral' (38) through their misguided effort to create generic passages. According to Schafer, this effort to eliminate possible cultural biases had the unwanted effect of making it more difficult for students to produce inferences, draw analogies, and generally comprehend the passages.

What counts as 'real'?

Not only is it important to determine whose experience counts, but it is also useful to know what counts as 'real' in so-called authentic reading assessments. In an article designed to advance the argument that 'assessment reform is the Trojan horse of real school reform' (Wiggins, 1992: 32), evidence is presented which we believe supports the need to problematize the notion of what counts as 'real' and for whom. In making the argument that 'even our better students are often ill-prepared for real intellectual tasks' (27), Wiggins provides the following item from a freshman final exam in European history:

> Imagine yourself Karl Marx, living half a century later. Write a brief evaluation of the programs of the Fabian socialists and the American reformers such as Teddy Roosevelt to present to the Socialist International.
>
> (27)

To our way of thinking, in this example 'real' is what is valued by the person who wrote the item, and maybe even by Wiggins (1992), who maintains that students will exhibit interest in 'irrelevant but real challenges' (28). This situation reminds us of the phenomenon that Fuss (1989) labels 'inside trading' (115). According to Fuss, when those 'in the know' on the inside (e.g., teachers) agree to do business with others 'in the know' (e.g., test developers), both parties need to rely on their best pedagogical instincts to avoid marginalizing the interests of those outside the circle (in this case, the students).

Performance and reading assessment

Performing 'real life' literacy acts is a central theme of authentic reading assessment. Authentic performance assessments, according to Darling-Hammond and Ancess (in press), 'include oral presentations or performances along with collections of students' written products and their solutions to problems, experiments, debates, constructions and models, videotapes of performance and other learning occasions'. Advocates of such assessments view them as a way to create comprehensive and complete portraits of student achievement (O'Neil, 1992).

The inspiration for new paradigms of reading assessment can be traced in part to practices in the art world, such as the use of portfolios to showcase a repertoire of artistic achievements (Valencia, 1990). Thus, it may come as no surprise to learn that it was in the literature on the arts and artifacts where we found feminist and poststructuralist analyses of *performance*. We explore two ideas from those analyses that seem relevant to the educational project underway to revolutionize assessment within literacy education. First, we consider what Phelan (1988) refers to as the need to reexamine 'the economy between the performer and the spectator in performance' (111). Second, we consider the mimetic assumptions ascribed to performance and their implications for the new reading assessments.

The performer and the spectator

While Valencia and her colleagues (1994) acknowledge that 'procedures and formats for authentic assessment are influenced by the audience for whom information is being gathered' (14), generally speaking there is far less written about the audience's role in performance assessment than there is about what the student, as performer, might be expected to do. When Phelan (1988) writes from a poststructuralist perspective about theatre and performance and when Davis (1995) writes about performance in postmodern museums, there is considerable attention given to the experiences and roles of the audience, the spectator, or the visitor in a performance. The discrepancy that exists in the amount of attention given to the role of audience in the reading assessment world as compared to that in the art world has piqued our interest because of the questions it raises for current practices. To launch our consideration of how the audience/the spectator participates in a performance, we draw upon two examples from our readings.

Performance in postmodern theatre

Phelan (1988) uses Angelika Festa's performance titled 'Untitled Dance with Fish and Others' to reveal certain nuances in the relationship between performer and audience. For twenty-four hours, Festa hung herself from a pole positioned between two supports. She was wrapped to the pole in a white shroud-like arrangement that positioned her face towards the floor. Her eyes were covered with silver tape. Her feet were projected onto a screen so that they appeared as large as the rest of her body. A video monitor in front of Festa played a continuous loop on the embryogeny of a fish. Finally, on a smaller monitor, a video documented the performance by replaying it. In an elaborate analysis of the significance of Festa's performance, which extends beyond this chapter's purpose, Phelan (1988) proposes that the covering of Festa's eyes with tape raises questions regarding the traditional complicity in theatre between watching and doing:

> In the absence of that customary visual exchange, the spectator can only see her own desire to be seen [and for that reason] the spectator has to play both parts of the performative exchange and become the spectator of her own performance in the face of Festa's aversion.
>
> (122)

Thinking about how Festa's performance disrupts the traditional relationship between spectator and performer raises for us new possibilities, particularly in terms of what this might mean to the language of reading assessment. Is it possible that some of the reading performances we ask of students actually require us as teacher-spectators to play both sides of the performance? Are there ways in which students 'blind' themselves or are blinded by us in performing reading tasks that in turn force us, as their audience, to enact the performative exchange? Perhaps when students give us what they think we want from them on an assessment task they, like Festa, can be viewed as engaged in an aversion.

Consider, for example, an assessment activity from the *Maryland School Performance Assessment* (Kapinus, Collier and Kruglanski, 1994) based on Lynne Cherry's (1990) *The Great Kapok Tree*:

> At the end of the story, the man did not cut down the tree. Pretend you are the man. Write a note to your boss explaining why you won't cut down the tree. Use information from the story in your explanation. Because your note will be read by your boss, be sure it is clear and complete. Also, check for correct spelling, grammar, punctuation, and capitalization.
>
> (264)

Students who follow the scripted role of subordinate male subject in this assessment activity may be enacting a performance that tells us more about what we (teachers, policy-makers and test developers) see as literate behavior than what they (students) see as the same. In other words, students' reading performances may only tell us about what we desire to see. When students accept the subject positions we give them, as in the example above, they turn away from considering any number of other valid subject positions, such as an ecofeminist writing a newspaper article about the need to preserve the rain forest or a logging industrialist writing about the benefits to society from using products made from trees.

Performance in postmodern museums

Davis (1995) writes about postmodern museums where 'visitors experience something fundamental to the content and are drawn into performing this themselves, rather than watching others do it' (16). By way of example, she describes *The McMichael Canadian Art Collection* in Kleinburg, Ontario, where the many windows in the galleries offer visitors large and frequent expanses of 'real' landscapes. In their role as spectators, visitors are necessarily engaged in a cross-referencing of the interior European Canadians' and First Nations people's art and the exterior environment that inspired it. In elaborating upon her own role and that of other visitors in this museum she calls postmodern, Davis writes:

> [Because] experience is not restricted to cognitive connections . . . it becomes a performance of artistic insight. We do not just read the captions, listen to the birds, or look at the art, we perform the gestalt affectively, experiencing the creativity, emotion, and ideological attitude of the artists.
>
> (18–19).

Davis (1995) also describes how the museum's designers were able to fuse the bipolar opposition of interior and exterior space in their effort to provoke a gestalt-like understanding that questions 'the hierarchy of authenticity' (19). According to Davis, the results of their effort leave visitors confused as to what is more real – 'the forest landscape unchanged since before the fur trade, the landscape paintings that epitomize what "Canadian" means to dwellers in the modern state, or the material evidence of indigenous people's interpretations' (19).

If we were to imagine an analogous situation involving audience insight as teacher-spectators of reading performances, what might it look like? What kinds of windows would we need to blur the boundaries between the interior (schooling) and the exterior (family and community life)? What conditions would allow us to perform the gestalt as opposed to a narrower cognitive determination of the significance of students' literacy acts? Typically, when we consider the promise of authentic performance assessments for reading, we assume a hierarchy of authenticity by measuring the characteristics of the assessment task against what is 'real' and 'out there' beyond the school and classroom. Thinking about the postmodern museum described by Davis (1995) challenges us to examine our assumptions about the need for such a hierarchy. It also challenges us to think more critically about what is missing in our current conception of audience within the framework of the new reading assessments.

Performance as mimesis (imitation)

Diamond (1989) writes that mimesis 'posits a truthful relation between world and word, model and copy, nature and image or, in semiotic terms, referent and sign, in which potential difference is subsumed by sameness' (58). In relating mimesis to feminist theory and the theatre, Diamond addresses such questions as 'Can feminism do without mimesis?' (59) given that postmodern analyses of language are polemically antimimetic. The temptation in feminist theatre productions to show truthful representations of women's social experience makes it difficult to simultaneously explore a postmodern nonmimetic language in which the speaker can no longer rely on words to mirror or represent experience. Diamond works with this dilemma to explore how women have used mimicry in theatrical performances to represent their exploitation by the dominant discourse without allowing themselves to be simply reduced to it. Using mimesis in this way to deal with the dominant discourse also opens up novel possibilities for multiple nuances in gender identities, which then seem 'real' thanks to the performance (Reinelt, 1989).

The idea that what becomes 'real' follows from the performance leads us to think about the prevailing assumption that reading performance assessments mirror or imitate some notion of what it means to be 'truly' literate. For example, when an assessment activity involves students in reading directions from a manual in order to accomplish some task on a computer, one assumption is that this performance mimics 'real life' literate behaviour in the workplace, at home, or wherever else manuals and computers are found. What happens when we reverse that assumption to consider how reading performances might be conceived that would produce novel or new realities? What happens when students are given opportunities to create what it means to be literate through performance? We are helped to imagine what all of this might mean through an excerpt from Simone de Beauvoir's (1958/1959) *Memoirs of a Dutiful Daughter*. In this excerpt, she writes about her father's passion for stage-acting in a way that illustrates how the audience serves as a mirror, thereby allowing performers to create reality.

Reduced to the role of a mirror, the audience faithfully reflects his image; on the stage he is king and he really exists, he really feels himself to be a king. My father took a special delight in making-up; he could escape from himself by putting on a wig and a false moustache. In this way he could avoid identification; he was neither a nobleman nor a commoner: this indeterminacy lent itself to every kind of impersonation; having fundamentally ceased to be himself, he could become anyone he liked.

(34)

Perhaps as teacher-audiences to students' reading performance assessments we, too, might offer ourselves more as mirrors than as judges, thereby allowing students to impersonate multiple literate personas. And, through that mimetic process, we might provide opportunities for students to create themselves as literate beings. By providing a stage, figuratively or literally, where students could impersonate writers and readers of literature, history, science, and the like, we could become the mirrors. Acting in that capacity, we might be encouraged to communicate to students what we understand from their performances about all the ways in which it is possible to be readers and writers.

Summary

Our efforts to trouble the concepts of authenticity and performance as used in the language of the new reading assessments bring to mind an observation that Lin Goodwin (1993) made at the 14th Annual Meeting of the Ethnography Forum at the University of Pennsylvania. Speaking about her research into the internalized vocabulary of minority students, Goodwin noted: 'In research the answers we get are sometimes not in response to the questions we ask, but rather, to the questions we should have asked.' Reading between the lines of Goodwin's comment, we see a friendly warning: Ask different questions. That is precisely what we have tried to do in this chapter by questioning some of the assumptions underlying authentic reading assessment. Of course, as one of our reviewers reminded us, in advocating that different questions be asked, we may have implied that eventually the right answers would be found. This was not our intention. Perhaps a more appropriate reading of Goodwin (1993) would be that we should explore the answers we get when we question some of the assumptions underlying authenticity and performance.

In gesturing toward experience as an unstable construct, we considered how contesting the notion of an all-knowing subject might inform test developers' concerns about the validity of 'individual' scores in large-scale portfolio assessments. Similarly, in exploring the different roles of performers and spectators in theatrical productions and postmodern museums, we were led to think about the effects of scripted performances on students' creativity and the absent presence of teachers as spectators in performance assessments.

Authors' note

We wish to thank George Hruby, Jennifer Moon, David W. Moore, Richard Robinson and Bettie St. Pierre for helpful comments on an earlier draft of this chapter.

References

Blackburn, S. (1994) *The Oxford Dictionary of Philosophy.* Oxford: Oxford University Press.

Britzman, D. P. (1995) "The question of belief": Writing poststructural ethnography'. *International Journal of Qualitative Studies in Education*, 8, 229–38.

Butler, J. (1990) *Gender Trouble: Feminism and the Subversion of Identity.* New York: Routledge.

Cherry, L. (1990) *The Great Kapok Tree: A Tale of the Amazon Rain Forest.* San Diego, CA: Harcourt Brace Jovanovich.

Darling-Hammond, L. and Ancess, J. (in press) 'Authentic-assessment and school development'. In J. B. Baron and D. P. Wolf (eds.), *NSSE Ninety-Third Yearbook.*

Davis, T. C. (1995) 'Performing and the real thing in the postmodern museum'. *The Drama Review*, 39, 15–40.

de Beauvoir, S. (1958/1959) *Memoirs of a Dutiful Daughter.* (trans. by James Kirkup) New York: Harper Colophon Books.

Diamond, E. (1989) 'Mimesis, mimicry, and the "true-real" '. *Modern Drama*, 32, 58–72.

Edelsky, C. (1990) 'Whose agenda is this anyway? A response to McKenna, Robinson, and Miller'. *Educational Researcher*, 19, 7–11.

Fuss, D. (1989) *Essentially speaking.* New York: Routledge.

Gearhart, M. and Herman, J. L. (1995, Winter) 'Portfolio assessment: Whose work is it?' *Evaluation Comment.* Los Angeles: UCLA Center for the Study of Evaluation and The National Center for Research on Evaluation, Standards, and Student Testing.

Goodwin, L. (1993, February) 'Internalized vocabulary of minorities related to race, class and gender'. Paper presented at the 14th Annual Ethnography Forum. Philadelphia: University of Pennsylvania, Graduate School of Education.

Hekman, S. (1991) 'Reconstituting the subject: Feminism, modernism, and postmodernism'. *Hypatia*, 6(2): 44–63.

Kapinus B. A., Collier, G. V. and Kruglanski, H. (1994) 'The Maryland school performance assessment: A new view of assessment'. In S. W. Valencia, E. H. Hiebert and P. P. Afflerbach (eds), *Authentic Reading Assessment* (255–76). Newark, DE: International Reading Association.

McCoy, K. (in press) 'Killing the father/becoming uncomfortable with the mother tongue: Rethinking the performative contradiction'. *Educational Theory.*

Myers, J. (1991) 'Now that literacy happens in contexts, how do we know if the contexts are authentic?' In J. Zutell and S. McCormick (eds), *Learner Factors, Teacher Factors: Issues in Literacy Research and Instruction* (Fortieth Yearbook of the National Reading Conference) (91–6) Chicago, IL: NRC.

Neufeldt, V. and Guralnik, D. B. (eds) (1994) *Webster's New World Dictionary* (3rd College Edition). New York: Prentice Hall.

O'Neil, J. (1992) 'Putting performance assessment to the test'. *Educational Leadership*, 49(8): 14–19.

Phelan, P. (1988) 'Feminist theory, poststructuralism, and performance'. *The Drama Review*, 32, 107–27.

Reinelt, J. (1989) 'Feminist theory and the problem of performance'. *Modern Drama*, 32, 48–57.

Rockhill, K. (1987) Gender, language and the politics of literacy. *British Journal of Sociology of Education*, 8, 153–67.

Schafer, W. (1996) 'Using performance assessments: Possibilities and pitfalls'. *Reading Today*, 38.

Scott, J. W. (1992) 'Experience'. In J. Butler and J. W. Scott (eds), *Feminists Theorize the Political*. New York: Routledge.

Shannon, P. (1985) 'Reading instruction and social class'. *Language Arts*, 62, 604–13.

Spivak, G. (1993) *Outside in the Teaching Machine*. New York: Routledge.

Valencia, S. (1990) 'A portfolio approach to classroom reading assessment: The whys, whats, and hows'. *The Reading Teacher*, 43, 338–40.

Valencia, S. W., Hiebert, E. H. and Afflerbach, P. P. (eds) (1994) *Authentic Reading Assessment*. Newark, DE: International Reading Association.

van Kraayenoord, C. E., Moni, K. B. and Dilena, M. (1995, December) 'Authentic assessment approaches and the use of a national reporting framework: An Australian perspective'. Paper presented at the annual meeting of the National Reading Conference, New Orleans, LA.

Wiggins, G. (1992) 'Creating tests worth taking'. *Educational Leadership*, 49(8): 26–33.

Williams, R. (1983) *Keywords*. New York: Oxford University Press.

Wolf, D. P., LeMahieu, P. G. and Eresh, J. (1992) 'Good measure: Assessment as a tool for educational reform'. *Educational Leadership*, 49(8), 8–13.

Part II

WHAT ARE THE NEW APPROACHES, AND WHAT ARE THEY ATTEMPTING TO ACHIEVE?

4

AUSTRALIAN PERSPECTIVES ON THE ASSESSMENT OF READING

Can a national approach to literacy assessment be daring and progressive?

Paul Brock

Introduction

In 1991 Australia adopted a national language and literacy policy expressed in a White Paper endorsed by the Cabinet of the Federal Government. The many Commonwealth Government programmes generated by *Australia's Language: The Australian Language and Literacy Policy* (Dawkins, 1991) and the funding of research projects in the teaching of literacy and English as a Second Language within the school and adult education contexts, have had a major impact upon the quality and diversity of literacy teaching throughout Australia.

Significant contributions to the national curriculum framework for English K-12 and the professional development for school teachers of English across all interdependent modes of reading and viewing, writing and speaking have been made by four of the five Australian language and literacy professional bodies under the umbrella of the Australian Literacy Federation (ALF): the Primary English Teachers Association; the Australian Association for the Teaching of English; the Australian Literacy Educators Association; and the Australian Council of Teachers of English as Second Language. Australian programmes such as the Early Literacy Inservice Course (ELIC) which had been undertaken by some 20,000 teachers by the end of 1986, the School, Home and Reading Enjoyment (SHARE) programme, First Steps, The Talk to a Literacy Learner (TALL), and Frameworks programme have enjoyed widespread support and success in Australia. Some have been exported to a number of countries.

In the adult literacy field Australian research and development has also been substantial. For example, the National Framework of Adult English Language, Literacy and Numeracy Competence and the National Reporting

System for adult literacy provision broke new ground within the whole field. The Australian Council for Adult Literacy, the fifth association sitting under the ALF umbrella, has played a key role in curriculum debate and professional development.

The Australian history of the assessment of reading and viewing, writing, listening and speaking is more akin to the British than the American tradition (see Brock, 1996; Brock and Smaniotto, 1997). For example, Pearson, DeStefano and García's accurate assertion that conventional, multiple-choice assessment is still the dominant force in (the American) society (see chapter 2 in this volume) could not have been made about Australia. In recent years there has been greater use of standardized testing as a diagnostic, systems-wide tool and, occasionally, as a small component of a far broader canvas of assessment and reporting. But standardized testing has never experienced in Australia the supreme power and ubiquity as the dominant mode of assessing and reporting student performance which it has enjoyed in the USA. In Australia, the assessment of students' performance in English (or Language Arts) has traditionally drawn upon holistic and relatively comprehensive indicators which acknowledge the interrelationships between speaking and listening, reading and viewing, and writing. While there is considerable reliance on external modes of assessment, the judgement of classroom teachers plays a crucial, and substantial, role in the formal assessment of students at the end of secondary education in Australia.

Australia's national collaborative curriculum

In Australia's system of federated government it is not easy to establish national goals upon which the Commonwealth and all State and Territory governments might agree. Tensions usually can be found to exist between government bodies at the local, regional, State and Commonwealth (i.e. the federal) levels. Striving for creative and productive outcomes involves resisting the twin tyrannies of unfettered partisan localism and conformist centralism, and harnessing the strengths of both these local and central educational forces. The Hobart Declaration on Schooling issued by the Australian Education Council (AEC) of Ministers in 1989 marked the start of extremely significant national co-operation between Commonwealth, State and Territory governments in school education and formed the basis of the national collaboration on curriculum frameworks. It commences with five broad goals:

The agreed national goals for schooling in Australia

Goal 1 To provide an excellent education for all young people, being one which develops their talents and capacities to full potential, and is relevant to the social, cultural and economic needs of the nation.

Goal 2 To enable all students to achieve high standards of learning and to develop self-confidence, optimism, high self-esteem, respect for others, and achievement of personal excellence.

Goal 3 To promote equality of educational opportunities, and to provide for groups with special learning requirements.

Goal 4 To respond to the current and emerging economic and social needs of the nation, and to provide those skills which will allow students maximum flexibility and adaptability in their future employment and other aspects of life.

Goal 5 To provide a foundation for further education and training, in terms of knowledge and skills, respect for learning and positive attitudes for life-long education (Curriculum Corporation, 1994, 46).

Goal 6 focuses upon specifics:

Goal 6 To develop in students: the skills of English literacy, including skills in listening, speaking, reading and writing; skills of numeracy, and other mathematical skills; skills of analysis and problem solving; skills of information processing and computing; an understanding of the role of science and technology in society, together with scientific and technological skills; a knowledge and appreciation of Australia's historical and geographic context; a knowledge of languages other than English; an appreciation and understanding of, and confidence to participate in, the creative arts; an understanding of, and concern for, balanced development and the global environment; and a capacity to exercise judgement in matters of morality, ethics and social justice (Curriculum Corporation, 1994, 46).

In July 1996 all Australian Ministers of Education agreed to add an extra goal: that 'every child leaving primary school should be able to read, write, spell and communicate at an appropriate level'. It must be said, however that those of us who have researched the history of education in Australia would hardly describe this as a startlingly new addition to the goals of primary education in the States and Territories: 'appropriate' is the most flexible and forgiving of words. In 1989 all Ministers for Education had agreed that there would be eight Key Learning Areas: English; Mathematics; Science; The Arts; Health and Physical Education; Languages Other Than English; Studies of Society and the Environment; and Technology. In some cases these Key Learning Areas (KLAs) were the direct equivalents of traditional school subjects; in others they represent amalgams – e.g. The Arts and, especially, Studies of Society and the Environment which includes at least history, geography, consumer education, legal studies, environmental education and religious studies. Languages Other Than English (LOTE) covers many different languages.

Interpenetrating all of these Key Learning Areas, schools have to incorporate the non-subject-specific but generic Key Competencies expected to be demonstrated by all students prior to entering the workplace: communicating ideas and information; collecting, analysing and organizing information; planning and organizing; working with others and in teams; solving problems; using mathematical ideas and techniques; and using technology.

In its processes, as well as in its products, the Australian national curriculum experience has been rather different from what has happened in the United Kingdom. Collaboration among all governments and other national teaching, parent, and research bodies had been central to the Australian process, although it must be acknowledged that such collaboration has been better in some areas than others.

The Australian Education Council of Ministers established a comprehensive committee known as the Curriculum and Assessment Committee (CURASS) to construct the eight curriculum frameworks and profile frameworks to be deployed in assessment and reporting. The Commonwealth was only one of a number of bodies with a vote on CURASS. Membership also included representatives of each State and Territory curriculum authority and public education system; the National Catholic Education Commission; the Australian Teachers' Union; the Independent Teachers' Association of Australia; the Australian Parents' Council; the Australian Council of State School Organizations; the Australian Council of Educational Research and the Australian Curriculum Corporation. The New Zealand Government was also represented on the committee.

Dr Ken Boston, Director General of The Department of School Education in New South Wales and Chair of the CURASS committee has succinctly highlighted the principal differences between the Australian and the British experiences as follows:

> Our so-called national curriculum has not – as in the United Kingdom – been developed by a National Curriculum Council appointed by the Secretary of State and charged with the responsibility of preparing fully detailed curriculum material to be tabled in Parliament. Nor, as in the UK, has it been driven by a particular political agenda. The Statements and Profiles are the result of a voluntary and fragile alliance which has held together only because each of the States and systems judges it to be of benefit to them and the nation. (Boston, 1994, 44).

Dr Boston has also sketched the processes of consultation involved across the whole national project.

The work took eighteen months. Some hundreds of people – selected competitively from across the nation and on the basis of their expertise – were involved in writing the briefs, the statements and the profiles for the (eight) key learning areas. More than 250 national organisations were consulted along with their State and Territory chapters. No fewer than 70,000 students, 2,400 teachers and 480 schools were involved in trialing the profiles. The validation process carried out for us by the Australian Council for Educational research, involved a further 1,600 teachers and 20,000 students (Boston, 1994, 44).

But any implication that the quality of construction, consultation and trialing was of consistent quality within and across all of the eight key learning areas would be false. English was arguably the best as far as both the process and the product are concerned. The late Garth Boomer, who was the initial Chair of the Curriculum and Assessment Committee before what proved to be, tragically, his fatal illness led to his resignation and replacement by Dr Boston, also chaired the sub-committee which took responsibility for the English curriculum project (the author was a member of both bodies, representing the Commonwealth Government, in 1990–1). Boomer enjoyed an eminent international reputation in the field of English curriculum. The Australian National Statements were not formal classroom curricula. Rather, they were nationally agreed curriculum frameworks endorsed by all Australian Ministers for Education which each State and Territory is free to use and adapt – or even not use at all – in establishing their own specific curricula.

The national Statement and Profile in English

The basic goals, within which *A Statement on English for Australian Schools* is framed, are as follows:

GOALS OF THE ENGLISH CURRICULUM

English is that area of the curriculum where students study and use English language and literature (including literature translated into English).

The English curriculum encompasses studies which, in Australia, are called by a number of names, among them Language Arts, English and English language. It also includes a significant part of English as a second language (ESL) programs.

The English curriculum aims to develop the following:

1   The ability to speak, listen, read, view and write with purpose, effect and confidence in a wide range of contexts.

2   A knowledge of the ways in which language varies according to context, purpose audience and content, and the ability to apply this knowledge.

3   A sound grasp of the linguistic structures and features of standard Australian English ... and the capacity to apply these, especially in writing.

4   A broad knowledge of a range of literature, including Australian literature, and a capacity to relate this literature to aspects of contemporary society and personal experience.

5   The capacity to discuss and analyse texts and language critically and with appreciation.

6   A knowledge of the ways in which textual interpretation and understanding may vary according to cultural, social and personal differences, and the capacity to develop reasoned arguments about interpretation and meaning.

Students come from diverse socio-cultural and language backgrounds. The school curriculum must recognise this diversity and the important part language plays in students' educational achievements.

(Curriculum Corporation, 1994b, 3)

The English Statement insists that literacy is more than a set of static, decontextualized skills. It makes a strong endorsement of the view that at school, as in the early formative years, language is best learnt in use, with the aid of well-chosen teacher demonstrations, explanations, correction, advice and encouragement.

Effective teaching is based on what children already know and can do. The teaching of English will achieve most where the considerable informal language knowledge and competence of students, whatever their cultural or language backgrounds, is acknowledged, used and extended.

(Curriculum Corporation, 1994b, 5)

Within the Statement there are four Bands: A – roughly School Years 1–4; B – roughly School Years 4–7; C – roughly School Years 7–10; and D – roughly School Years 11–12. There are two content Strands within the national Statement: Texts and Language.

The 'Text Strand' in the National Statement on English

The 'Text Strand' in the National Statement on English definition of texts for reading and viewing is inclusive. But the framework mandates no specific texts. There is, for example, no prescription that all 14-year-olds must study a Shakespearian text. 'Texts' include three categories: literature, media and everyday communication.

The definition of texts for reading and viewing is as follows:

> The Texts strand defines texts broadly as any communication, written, spoken or visual, involving language. It may thus include novels, newspaper articles or personal letters, conversations, speeches or performances of plays, feature films, television programs or advertisements. To ensure that the range of texts is balanced, the statement proposes that teachers draw texts for study from three categories: literature, everyday texts and mass media. In the literature category, the statement suggests that teachers select from classic texts, contemporary texts and popular texts. The everyday category includes texts such as letters, forms, summaries, essays, reports, labels, diaries, notices and telephone conversations. Mass media texts include print, film and electronic forms directed to a mass audience. The categories overlap considerably.
>
> Balance of content, complexity and intended audience is an issue within all these categories. The selection should include both Australian and non-Australian texts, which may be translated as well as written originally in English. It should reflect the interests and values of both women and men. It should reflect the diversity of Australia's population, and draw from the past as well as the present. It should represent a range of forms and styles, and include the student's own work. Selecting a text depends as much on how it is used as on its nature or complexity. The same text may be used at different levels of schooling for different purposes. The range of texts used should in general increase in conceptual, linguistic and cognitive complexity as the student moves through the bands of schooling.
>
> (Curriculum Corporation, 1994b, 6)

In passing, one notes that in a era when there is increasing debate on the place of 'literature' within studies of English, (or Language Arts), the emphasis in the Australian Statement's treatment of literature is upon pluralism and diversity without abandoning a commitment to quality education:

> Literature is fundamental to the English curriculum, although opinions differ on what distinguishes literature from other texts. Typically, literature involves the use of language and the imagination to represent, recreate, shape and explore human experience. Literature can be based on actuality or fantasy and includes written,

spoken and visual texts. Examples include picture books, traditional stories (written and oral), novels, feature films, short stories, plays, poetry, newspaper journalism, translated works, students' own speaking and writing and non-fiction such as biographies and filmed documentaries. Literature texts provide readers, viewers and listeners with rich meanings and significant imaginative experiences.

(Curriculum Corporation, 1994b, 6)

The educational goals for the teaching and learning of literature are stated as follows:

- Literature's potential to provide a source of enjoyment.
- Literature's potential to inform and educate through its imaginative representation of human experience.
- The opportunity literature presents to discover a diverse range of socio-cultural values, attitudes and beliefs.
- The opportunities literature provides to reflect on the ways writers use language, including its linguistic structures and features.
- The ways in which literature can shape the reader or listener's perceptions, and the ways these can be discussed and challenged. The different ways people can respond to texts, depending on their context.
  Because it is important that a balanced range of literature is taught, literature texts have been loosely categorised. The categories that follow are neither conclusive nor rigid and immutable; for example, classic texts would all once have been contemporary or popular. It is important that teachers attend to each category to ensure a balanced study of literature.

(Curriculum Corporation, 1994b, 7)

The 'Language Strand' in the National Statement on English

In addition to the Texts Strand there is the Language Strand, which emphasizes three modes: speaking and listening; reading and viewing; and writing. The National Statement neither shies away from the controversial issue of whether students need to have an understanding of the linguistic structures of our language, nor does it advocate any one particular theoretical or ideological approach to grammar. But it does repudiate any mere learning of sets of skills in isolation from linguistic contexts. The language strand fills up what in recent years has become too much of a vacuum in the English curriculum area by setting out what students should know about the structure and features of written, spoken, and visual language and the ways in which the use of English varies according to situation and social or cultural context. It also sets out the strategies students need to learn in order to understand and use language. The document proceeds to articulate a number of sociocultural contexts, situational contexts, and linguistic structures and features. But it also proposes some specific strategies within the various modes. The following is an example:

STRATEGIES FOR READING AND VIEWING

Students need to develop strategies for (examples in parentheses): selecting texts (referring to the recommendations of others and to bibliographies; browsing; skimming and scanning; reading cover information).

Reading or viewing for specific purposes (browsing, skimming and scanning; identifying key words and phrases; using organisational features such as titles, headings, tables of contents and indexes; making notes, adjusting reading pace and level of concentration; viewing key segments).

Monitoring understanding (relating ideas and information to personal knowledge and experience; asking questions while reading or viewing; discussing ideas with others; making notes, using journals and logs) interpreting meaning (predicting, checking, confirming and self-correcting using knowledge of the topic, patterns of language and text structure and letter-sound relationships or other visual cues; considering relationships between visual and non-visual parts of the text; identifying the socio-cultural orientation of the text; detecting bias and prejudice; recognizing that literature will not always offer complete closure and provide neat answers to issues) coping with difficult texts (finger pointing and voice pointing; maintaining attention; re-reading and re-viewing; highlighting; adjusting reading pace; note-making; drawing diagrams; using cues provided by illustrations, tables, sound effects) recording and organising information (constructing summaries of texts; organising notes chronologically, by author/text, thematically; noting bibliographic information about sources used; using a personal abbreviation system).

(Curriculum Corporation, 1994b, 14–15)

The English Profile

In some ways the national English Profile is a more strategically important document, since it sets out the principles upon which assessment of student achievement in English language and literacy should be based, as well as providing work samples and 'pointers' or indicators of levels of student attainment. It also incorporates an English as a Second Language (ESL) component. The Profile has been used in, and adapted to, the specific curricular contexts developed by most States and Territories as an assessment and reporting framework to enable teachers to make judgements about students' ability to use their English knowledge and skills to speak, listen, read, view and write with purpose and effect and are to be used as part and parcel of classroom teaching and learning strategies.

The national Profile refers to reporting on students outcomes only from Year 1 (called Kindergarten or Reception, Preparatory, depending on the system) to Year 10 which is the last year of compulsory secondary education. But more than 70 per cent of all Australian school students proceed to Year 12. University matriculation is contingent upon credentials awarded at the end of Year 12 – but, increasingly, such credentials have assumed a comprehensive status well beyond their use for matriculation purposes.

It is my view that, at least in some systems, insufficient attention may have been placed on situating the assessment and reporting guidelines of the Profiles within the broader educational contexts of the curriculum frameworks established in the eight Key Learning Areas' Statements (KLA's). Unfortunately, as with all eight key learning areas, the English Profile was published separately from its curriculum framework Statement. I would wish to argue that the further that assessment instruments are removed from their relevant curriculum statement, the greater the risk that relatively content-free assessment and testing processes will drive the school curriculum.

As is often the case in such global assessment and reporting frameworks, a number of the so-called levels of achievement run the risk of being exercises in semantics rather than descriptors of real development that classroom teachers observe in their students as they develop across the years. Some of the examples of progress from one 'level' to the next are problematic. There is always a danger that in constructing reporting and assessment templates like the Australian English Profile, those relatively remote from classrooms can make assumptions about student progression which fail to take account of some of those outside-of-school pressures with which those of us who have spent years in the classroom are very familiar. These include, for example, socio-economic and cultural inhibitors including the effects of poverty, as well as the regression inevitably brought on by discontinuities as a student moves from being 'on top of the pile' in one schooling environment before hitting the 'bottom of the heap' in the next as they proceed from pre-school through to tertiary and other forms of post-school education.

The English Profile booklet provides teachers with:

- Strands (Speaking and Listening, Reading and Viewing), and Strands Organizers: Texts; Contextual Understanding; Linguistic Structures and Features; and Strategies;
- Levels (eight from K-10) which indicate progression in students' learning, and Level Statements which are general descriptions of student performance at each of the eight levels within the Profile;

- Outcomes which describe in progressive order the essential skills and knowledge in English which students typically acquire as they become more proficient;
- Pointers which are indicators or signals of the achievement of an outcome; and
- Annotated Work Samples which show student work which demonstrates the achievement of one or more outcomes at a level. The samples are annotated to show reasons for the judgements made.

By way of illustrating the kind of information given about reading and viewing in the national English Profile, Figure 4.1 reproduces about half of what appears in the document by way of texts, contextual understanding, linguistic structures and features, and classroom strategies for level 4 (i.e. halfway across eight levels from Year 1 to Year 10).

Implementation of the National Statements and Profiles in the eight Australian States and Territories

Most State and Territory systems acknowledged the need for progressive implementation and review over two or three years, and are using the Statements and Profiles as the basis for curriculum development, while incorporating variations that reflect local policies and/or priorities. A survey of the eight State and Territory systems conducted by Australia's Curriculum Corporation indicated the perceived strengths of the documents and included the assurance they offer of comprehensive curriculum provision, the benefit of a shared language for planning courses and for describing and reporting student achievement, and the usefulness of the outcomes for making expected student achievement explicit. Dissatisfaction was expressed about the perceived complexity and volume of the documents, some imprecision and inconsistency in articulating outcomes, and the amount of time demanded of teachers in recording student performance. Most respondents indicated their intention to use Profiles (modified if necessary to reflect local situations) as the basis for reporting to parents. The widest range of responses concerned the question as to whether profile levels should be linked directly to specific years of schooling (i.e. Years 1 to 10). Some were emphatically opposed to such a linkage; others have already quite explicitly made such a linkage within their policies.

One State, New South Wales, has chosen no longer to mandate the national Profiles and their levels in all NSW syllabuses, but nevertheless to deploy an outcomes-based approach as driven by the objectives of each subject syllabus in that State's school curriculum, and as specified across the five stages of compulsory schooling (K–2; 3–4; 5–6; 7–8; 9–10). The Minister for Education in NSW has affirmed the prime role of syllabuses in defining curriculum content – knowledge, skills and understanding – in

Figure 4.1 Level 4 Reading and Viewing

Texts	Contextual understanding	Linguistic structures and features	Strategies
At level 4, a student; **4.5 Justifies own interpretation of ideas, information and events in texts containing some unfamiliar concepts and topics and which introduce relatively complex linguistic structures and features.** *Evident when students, for example:* • Read for their own pleasure and interest novels and books of a series such as C.S. Lewis's Narnia stories and construct considered responses to them, justifying opinions with references to the text. • Find information on an unfamiliar topic in reference sources such as encyclopaedias and reference books, recognizing the breadth of information in complex texts. • Explore and discuss humour in stories, novels, film and television, showing an awareness of how humour is constructed (bizarre or unusual situations, events, people, dialogue as in Randolph Stow's *Midnite* or Lewis Carroll's *Jabberwocky*). • With teacher guidance, identify another level of meaning in a text (allegory in a picture book such as Mem Fox's *Feathers and*	At level 4, a student: **4.6 Explains possible reasons for people's varying interpretations of a text.** *Evident when students, for example:* • Recognize that interpretations of some texts are more readily agreed upon than others (compare agreement on the meaning of a full stop with agreement on the motivation of a character from a novel such as Libby Hathorn's *Thunderwith*). • Consider how their different interpretations of or reactions to a text can be explained (by differing purpose or circumstances when reading or viewing). • Report on different interpretations of a text after a group discussion or interviewing people (what different people considered to be the reasons for a character's actions; whether they thought the resolution to a story was appropriate) • Discuss and justify their own preferences for a particular interpretation of a text, referring to text details and their own knowledge and experience.	At level 4, a student: **4.7 With teacher guidance, identifies and discusses how linguistic structures and features work to shape readers' and viewers' understanding of texts.** *Evident when students, for example:* • Justify inferences about information and ideas implicit in texts by referring to text features such as vocabulary and text structure. • Discuss the effect of language forms such as figurative language, jargon and technical words in texts and the possible impact of these on different readers (ambiguity or conflicting messages). • Recognize and discuss the purpose of important organizational elements of different types of text (main elements of story in narratives; main argument, supporting points and conclusion in persuasive texts; general statement and descriptive details in reports; acts and scenes in plays). • Identify text features which may help readers to distinguish fact from opinion (use of 'I think . . .';	At level 4, a student: **4.8a Selects, uses and reflects on strategies appropriate for different texts and reading or viewing purposes.** *Evident when students, for example:* • Use a range of automatic monitoring and self-correcting methods when reading (rereading, reading on, slowing down, sub-vocalizing). • Use word identification strategies (apply knowledge of words and their parts such as root words, morphographs, prefixes). • Select information important to the purpose for reading (scan a novel for sections that support a particular interpretation of text). • Attempt several strategies when reading more difficult texts such as Tolkien's *The Hobbit* or Kenneth Grahame's *Wind in the Willows* (talking to others about the ideas and information; keeping a reading log to reflect on interpretation; rereading or reviewing parts of the text; making notes about key features; consulting the index, contents page, diagrams; searching for links with personal experience). • Make predictions about plot in film and television based on setting (underground car parks are often the scene of violent action).

74

Table 4.1 Continued

Texts	Contextual understanding	Linguistic structures and features	Strategies
Fools or a story such as Lilith Norman's *Dream of Seas*). • Consider events in texts from characters' points of view (roleplay or write in the role of a character, being consistent with the original character). • Discuss the treatment of information in articles from a magazine or tabloid newspaper and television news broadcasts on a local issue or newsworthy event (a large fire, a visit by a pop star). • View a documentary film made for a general audience and extract information from the text using a set of key questions provided by the teacher (a documentary film on the life cycle of a crocodile). • Justify interpretation of rock video view clips, plays or print advertisements that use some abstract or symbolic images.	• Recognize that an interpretation of a text will be more readily accepted by others if evidence from the text supporting that interpretation is cited. • Consider how changes to aspects of a text can alter people's interpretation of meaning such as reversing the roles of males and females in a novel, poem or play (consider the effects of making Judy a boy in Ethel Turner's *Seven Little Australians* or change the point of view from which Alfred Noyes's poem 'The Highwayman' is narrated).	'It has been reported that . . .,' citing of sources). • Consider how logical relationships (time, cause and effect, comparison and addition) are signalled by linking words in texts (because, then, soon, first of all, after that, however, like, different from, otherwise, on the other hand). • Identify the viewer position in visual texts and how this affects meaning (an over-the-shoulder shot from the point of view of one character looking at another). • Recognize a variety of film and television genres from features of the setting and characters' dress (westerns, outback dramas). • Discuss some techniques used to establish mood in films (sombre lighting to imply mystery or fear, music and sound effects to convey a variety of emotions).	**4.8b With peers, identifies information needs and finds resources and information for specific purposes** *Evident when students, for example:* • Discuss with peers key characters and events in texts read and viewed to select information and ideas needed for particular tasks (writing a description of a character, describing conflict and its resolution) • Work with peers to identify and narrow a research topic (brainstorm and cluster ideas, develop focus questions). • Predict possible resources, considering a wide range of possibilities, and devise a search plan. • Identify and locate resources by using a range of strategies (subject/key word/author/title searches; consulting encyclopaedias, atlases, yearbooks, data bases (PressCom and Nexus), CD-ROMs in the reference section of resource centres; considering and sometimes using information sources such as government departments, local people, and organizations, magazines, pamphlets and newspapers). • Make notes on focus questions and record details of research sources.

Source: Curriculum Corporation (1994b)

each subject area as recommended in the Report of the Review of Outcomes and Profiles in New South Wales Schooling. The committee was chaired by Professor Eltis of the University of Sydney. But NSW has agreed to develop support documents containing units of work and work samples showing how these relate to the corresponding levels within the national Profiles.

The National School English Literacy Survey

The most significant national project on the assessment of literacy (incorporating reading, viewing, writing, speaking, and listening) in Australia in 1996 was the National School English Literacy Survey.

In Australia, as in most if not all developed and developing countries, one hears cries from employers that school leavers do not have adequate literacy skills to meet the demands of the contemporary workforce. The claims are, of course, not new: they have been made repeatedly throughout this century (and earlier, stretching at least back to Ancient Greece). In a major policy decision in its Working Nation White Paper of May, 1994, the former Labour Commonwealth Government of Australia allocated nearly $A3 million (£1.5 million) for a national survey of the English literacy of school students – based upon the English Profile, in order to obtain a clear view, based upon properly researched data and its analysis of English literacy levels of attainment among Australian school students. Three stages of schooling were eventually chosen; Year 3, 5 and 10. The Commonwealth Government also set out to identify those student characteristics associated with different levels of literacy; to clarify any misconceptions that employers and the community may hold about the adequacy of the English literacy skills of Australian students; to enable governments to assess literacy needs so that resources can be targeted more effectively; and to establish national benchmarks against which teachers, schools and systems could assess the effectiveness of current programmes and can adjust their goals and programmes to improve literacy attainment.

A national steering committee was set up by the Australian Ministers of Education (the author was a member). This committee was resolute in rejecting any simplistic, reductionist approach to assessment. Procedures deployed have classroom teachers' judgements as central. It set out to model good practice. The whole process provided professional development programmes of undoubted quality.

In mid April 1996 the Federal Minister for Schools, Vocational Education and Training in the newly elected Liberal-National Party Commonwealth Government announced that the School English Literacy Survey would proceed in August and September 1996, as planned by the former Labor Commonwealth Government. The National Survey has been fully funded by the Federal Government.

The Survey Trial conducted in October 1995

In agreeing to undertake a Trial Survey for October 1995, the National Steering Committee agreed on a number of underpinning principles:

- teacher judgement was to be central to methodologies trialled;
- the finally approved methodology must model exemplary classroom practice in assessing English literacy and not be confined to such restrictive practices as 'ticking boxes';
- professional development must be central to the whole venture: external assessors (mostly classroom teachers) must undergo quality professional development; participating classroom teachers must undergo appropriate training; and the whole enterprise must enhance the professional skills of participating teachers;
- student performance in relation to the outcomes described in the national English Profile was a good practical indicator of English literacy and provided a valid framework; and
- the trial survey had to address all three modes: reading/viewing; speaking/listening; and writing.

Methodologies used in the 1995 Trial

The Steering Committee decided to trial two methodologies prior to making a final decision as to what methodology it ought to deploy in the 1996 Survey proper. The two procedures used in the 1995 have been summarized as follows:

PROCEDURE 1

In Procedure 1, teachers were given a set of outcomes from the English Profile for Australian Schools and asked to judge how often five individuals displayed each outcome (hardly ever, occasionally, or almost always). These 'outcome judgements' were the data for Procedure 1. Anticipating that teachers' outcome judgements might not be directly comparable for teacher to teacher, and that it might be necessary to statistically 'moderate' teachers' outcome judgements, a set of English literacy tasks was also administered to each participating student. Literacy measures based on teachers' outcomes judgements were then compared with students' performances on the provided literacy tasks ('common tasks').

PROCEDURE 2

In Procedure 2, teachers worked with external assessors to assess five students' work against provided assessment criteria. The assessed student work was of two kinds: students' performances on a set of provided Reading, Viewing, Speaking, Listening, and Writing tasks ('common tasks'), and classroom work assembled into portfolios. The assessments made by teachers/external assessors were the data for Procedure 2.

(Masters and Forster, 1996, 3)

Analysis of the Procedure 1 data showed significant differences between teachers' outcome judgements and the performances of the same students on the common Reading, Viewing, Speaking, Listening, and Writing tasks. Some teachers' assessments placed all students above their performances on the common tasks. Individual students also demonstrated more varied task performances across the literacy strands than was evident in teachers' assessments. An attempt to statistically 'moderate' each teacher's assessments by bringing them into line with students' average performances on the common tasks was only partially successful. For large numbers of students, teachers' moderated assessments remained significantly different from their performances on the common literacy tasks.

Procedure 2 built on earlier studies which had demonstrated very high levels of inter-marker agreement in the assessment of students' performances on the Reading, Viewing, and Listening common tasks. (Performances on these tasks are marked using provided marking keys). The 1995 Survey revealed relatively high levels of agreement between teachers' assessments of student writing and independent reassessments of this writing by ACER project staff. High levels of agreement were obtained for writing completed under timed conditions (the 'common tasks') and also for classroom writing collected into portfolios. The highest levels of inter-marker agreement for writing occurred between ACER markers working independently. Since Procedure 2 proved to be the more reliable, it is worth making a few observations about the portfolio process. As is central to the Australian tradition of assessing 'literacy', all modes were included: reading/viewing; speaking/listening; and writing. Specific criteria for portfolio inclusion and assessment were stipulated. For example the reading/viewing criteria for portfolio inclusion in Year 5 were expressed as follows:

WRITTEN RESPONSE TO READ OR VIEWED TEXT

Each student's portfolio should include a written response to read or viewed text. Responses could include, for example:

- a book or film review (details of the book – author, title, publisher should be provided)
- reflective comments on a book or film

Each student's portfolio should include a list, annotated if possible, of the student's recent reading and viewing. The list could include, everyday, mass media and literature texts, for example:

- regularly watched television programs
- videos seen in class
- a range of text types (short stories, autobiographies, novels, non-fiction).

(Masters and Forster, 1996, 14)

There have been increasing pressures from the Council of Australian Governments, known by the acronym COAG (made up of the Prime Minister, the Premiers of States, and the Chief Ministers of Territories), for education systems to establish national benchmarks of student attainment in literacy and numeracy which would enable governments to deliver education outcomes more 'efficiently' as well as to assist governments to make comparisons between State and Territory using national benchmarks of student performance. Realizing that this pursuit had at least the potential for the COAG to support measures of literacy attainment using a 'standardized' skills testing instrument rather than the more sophisticated approach deployed in the National School English Literacy Survey, the State of NSW recently proposed a way of ensuring that the benefits of the Survey's methodology could be applied to the COAG exercise. Subsequently, all Australian Ministers for Education agreed to facilitate a process whereby benchmarking in literacy for Australian school students might be determined not by narrower forms of standardized testing but rather by the more eclectic and validated approach to literacy assessment established by the Survey's methodology.

The 1996 National School Literacy Survey

A number of decisions were made following the 1995 Trial Survey and its review. First, because of methodological unreliability revealed in the Trial, as well as structural and other difficulties for schools, the Year 10 candidacy was omitted in the 1996 Survey. Second, the 1995 Trial demonstrated that Procedure 2, based on portfolios of students' best work, was the preferred methodology for the Survey in 1996. The original three interrelated categories of Reading and Viewing, Speaking and Listening, and Writing were treated as five interrelated modes: Reading, Viewing, Writing, Speaking and Listening.

The 1996 Survey was conducted over a six week period between August and September. There were two separate cohorts samples; 4,500 students in Year 3 and 4,500 students in Year 5. The categories were over-sampled to compensate for the fact that individual students and/or their parents as well as teachers were given the right not to participate. Schools were randomly selected. Indigenous students make up around 3 per cent of the primary school population. But because the literacy attainments of these Aboriginal and Torres Strait Islander children are of particular concern to all Australian governments, this group was also over-sampled (500 in each Year 3 and Year 5 sample) so as to arrive at statistically reliable data.

It has been the consistent policy of the national steering committee that the Survey should not be used to establish 'league tables' involving comparisons between States/Territories and between the government and non-government school sectors. Hence, the nature and size of the samples has made it impossible to make any such valid comparisons. One hundred teachers participated from all States and Territories. Each teacher assessed ten students in their class. The methodology deployed was that described in Procedure 2 (above). Teachers used five sets of specially designed assessment tasks covering Reading, Viewing, Writing, Speaking, and Listening to assess students' best classwork as collated in the portfolios. The assessment processes were integrated within the normal teaching programme over the six weeks. All data on individual students remained confidential to the classroom teacher and the students' parents.

Reliability

There were three principal sources of reliability built into the methodology to provide consistency in teachers' assessments:

- Common tasks: the use of common assessment tasks developed and previously trialed by the ACER.
- Common training: consistency in professional development both for the External Assessors and the participating classroom teachers.
- Reliability checks: all students' data was collected by the ACER so that reliability checks on the methodology could be conducted by a team of the most experienced External Assessors. Where the checking process revealed an unacceptable level of reliability of teacher assessments, the student work was reassessed by the team.

Classroom teachers were assisted by ninety External Assessors (one for every ten teachers). Mostly classroom teachers themselves, drawn from all State and Territory systems in both the government and non-government sectors, the External Assessors participated in a three-day live-in intensive professional development programme in Geelong, Victoria. This proved to be a most successful exercise in equipping them to assist the teachers assigned to them. Each External Assessor then provided two days of intensive professional development for their team of ten teachers. While the principal role of the External Assessors was to act as moderators of teacher judgement to assure methodological reliability, they played a key role as working partners for the classroom teacher. The External Assessors visited each of their ten teachers and liaised constantly with them during the Survey itself to assist the teachers in making accurate assessments. This careful and intensive focus on professional development was central to ensuring a high level of reliability for the data collected by the Survey.

In a time of ever-dwindling financial resources, the Australian Government invested heavily in this Survey. The previous government had set aside nearly $A3 million. Its successor agreed to continue and enhance this funding. With the support of the State/Territory governments the Australian Government has eschewed the cheaper, 'pencil and paper', options of traditional standardized testing. For the cost of around $A15 per student the Australian Government could have opted for the 'basic skills' test approach that can be found in many places. But the National School English Literacy Survey with its alternative and complex strategies for assuring statistically reliable data is both a much more educationally comprehensive and much more expensive exercise: it cost around $A200 per student. In an era of economic rationalism and 'quick fix' solutions to assisting literacy achievements and the pursuit of outcomes-based benchmarks, the National School English Literacy Survey is perhaps unique.

In addition to the Survey itself, participating classroom teachers, students and school principals were asked to provide data to investigate school and personal factors that may influence literacy attainment. Data collected included: the background characteristics of the school; information on classroom practices linked to student development in literacy; details of the student's personal characteristics, learning and home background; and information about the student's attitudes to and experiences of reading, writing, viewing, speaking and listening at school and at home. The results of this questionnaire are expected to add further to the overall validity of the Survey.

Outcomes of the National School English Literacy Survey – 1997 and beyond

The outcomes of the Survey will provide a very rich picture of literacy performance across Australia. However the data will not be directly comparable by State or Territory or by government and non-government school sectors.

The July 1996 meeting of Commonwealth, State and Territory and Education Ministers agreed:

- to a new national goal; that every child at primary school-going level should be able to read, write, spell and communicate at an appropriate level;

- to the development of common literacy benchmarks at year 3 and year 5;
- to invite States and Territories and non-government schools authorities to participate in the process of developing these benchmarks and report to the first meeting of the Council of Ministers in 1997;
- that the Curriculum Corporation and Boards of Studies or their equivalents (in the States and Territories) should also be involved in developing these benchmarks;
- that if the Survey were to be repeated the sample size should be large enough to enable State and Territory comparisons.

In benchmark-setting exercises of this type there is a risk of setting benchmarks at a relatively low level because of a desire by standard setters to set realistic standards that can be achieved by most students. An alternative to this approach could be more flexible yet realistic, by asking the standard setters to set, for example, realistic but challenging standards to be achieved by 90 per cent of students, with higher standards to be achieved by at least 50 per cent of students and very high standards to be achieved by the top 10 per cent of students. In the longer term, it would be possible for individual teachers using the materials developed by ACER for the National School English Literacy Survey to assess all their students in Year 3 and Year 5 against these benchmarks and against the norms from the Survey.

Conclusion

It is necessary to acknowledge that there will always be gaps between what research and scholarship demonstrate about reading competence and assessment, and what 'public opinion' (especially as massaged by the media) believes; and between what politicians – especially within advisory systems of governments – assert, and what those in bureaucracy (who are charged with assuring that 'tax payers'' funds are dispersed effectively) deliver.

This chapter has focused on processes and issues that are still developing and evolving in response to a variety of influences impacting on Australian education. Heraclitus' observation that you cannot put your foot into the same stream twice is an apt motif to represent the ever-changing nature and scope of educational assessment, reporting and accountability. As this manuscript was being written, for example, the author was organizing a national forum convened by New South Wales and funded by the Australian Government on the impact of national frameworks upon teaching and learning, reporting educational outcomes and educational accountability.

There is a tradition of healthy scepticism within Australian education towards claims made for global instruments of assessment that are neatly efficient, simple to administer and overly ambitious in aspiration. I believe that the view shared by most Australians with expertise and experience in the field would be that we are still on the journey towards achieving reliable instruments of assessment of reading, rather than having arrived at the destination. And as we continue both to refine and amplify what is meant by the terms 'reading' and 'literacy', as well as developing assessment instruments that achieve greater reliability in assessing these evolving constructs, we will need to fortify our scepticism towards the simplistic claims made by those who promote one-fix 'solutions' that too often are heralded as a panacea. But, as much of recent Australian experience suggests, that scepticism need not degenerate into cynicism. Good things can be found swimming in Heraclitus' stream!

References

Australian Committee for Training Curriculum (ACTRAC) (1994) *National Framework of Adult English Language, Literacy and Numeracy Competence.* Frankstone.

Boston, K. (1994) 'A perspective on the so-called National Curriculum'. *Curriculum Perspectives,* 14(1): 43–5.

Brock, P. (1995) on behalf of the Australian Language and Literacy Council of the National Board of Employment, Education and Training, *Teacher Education in English Language and Literacy.* Canberra: AGPS.

Brock, P. (1996) 'Telling the story of the NSW secondary English curriculum: 1950–1965. In B. Green and C. Beavis (eds) *Teaching the English Subjects: Essays on English Curriculum and History and Australian Schooling.* Geelong: Deakin University Press, 40–70

Brock, P. and Smaniotto, I. (1997) (eds) *Forum on National Statements and Profiles in Australian Schools: Teaching and Learning; Reporting Outcomes; Educational Accountability.* Sydney: Department of Training and Education Co-ordination.

Cairney, T. and Munsic, L. (1990) *Talk To A Literacy Learner.* Penrith: University of Western Sydney, Nepean.

Coates, S. *et al.* (1995) *National Reporting System: a mechanism for reporting adult English language, literacy and numeracy indicators of competence.* Melbourne: Ministry of Education.

Curriculum Corporation (1994a) *English – A Curriculum Profile for Australian Schools.* Melbourne: Curriculum Corporation.

Curriculum Corporation (1994b) *A Statement on English for Australian Schools.* Melbourne: Curriculum Corporation.

Dawkins, J. The Hon. (1991) *Australia's Language: The Australian Language and Literacy Policy.* Canberra: AGPS.

Keating, P. The Hon. (1994) *Working Nation: The White Paper on Employment and Growth.* Canberra: AGPS.

Masters, G. and Forster, M. (1996) *Assessing English Literacy Skills: Report of the National School English Literacy Survey Trial.* Melbourne: Australian Council of Educational Research.

5

ASSESSING READING IN THE ENGLISH NATIONAL CURRICULUM

Sue Horner

Introduction

The year 1989 was the first time that, in England and Wales, curriculum provision in schools was the subject of legislation. This legislation included a statutory Order for English, which includes requirements for reading within an integrated programme of speaking, listening, reading and writing. During 1994–5 the original National Curriculum was revised to slim down the content of what is to be taught and to refine arrangements for the assessment of pupils' achievement. In 1996 teachers in England began to teach a revised National Curriculum, consisting of eleven subjects in all, of which English, mathematics and science are core subjects and are compulsory for all pupils between the ages of five and sixteen.

The National Curriculum in England and Wales is unique, when compared to that in other countries, in that it has not only provision for what should be taught but also has a mandatory system for assessing what pupils have learnt related to that curriculum, at specific intervals in their progress through school, at ages seven, eleven and fourteen. There has been a period of rapid changes in the curriculum and assessment systems in the last eight years, and the arrangements are just beginning to stabilize. The government has promised that there will be no more changes to legislation for five years, so this will give opportunities to build familiarity and confidence in what has been put in place.

This paper first outlines the structure of the curriculum and its assessment arrangements and then goes on to show how reading fits within this structure. The final section makes some comparisons between the experience of such curriculum innovation in England and that in other English speaking countries.

The structure of the English National Curriculum

The curriculum for each subject is structured in a similar way. What is to be taught is outlined in Programmes of Study related to key stages of schooling. The programmes of study for English include the framework of what is to be taught in relation to Speaking and Listening, Reading, and Writing for Key Stage 1 (5–7-year-olds), Key Stage 2 (7–11-year-olds), Key Stage 3 (11–14-year-olds) and Key Stage 4 (14–16-year-olds). These programmes of study are organized in terms of the Range of activities and material to be covered, the Key Skills which pupils need to learn, and the aspects of Standard English and Language Study which are relevant at each key stage. They do not seek to prescribe classroom activities or teaching methods, but rather to define the range of experiences which must be provided, the skills which must be developed and the knowledge pupils need about language and how it works.

Alongside these provisions for the curriculum are the Attainment Targets, which outline progression in achievement in each of the aspects of English. In each of the three Attainment Targets – Speaking and Listening, Reading, and Writing – progression is described in eight levels to characterise achievement in relation to the curriculum for ages five to fourteen. Each level is described in a prose statement of characteristics of pupils achieving at that level, and these statements are called Level Descriptions.

The Level Descriptions are designed to be used on a 'best fit' principle. The model is not one of mastery, determining that pupils move from one distinct goal to another, and so up through the levels. Rather, it is expected that through the teaching of the contents of the programmes of study in a range of contexts, pupils will progress and then, at specific points, namely at ages seven, eleven and fourteen, pupils' achievement will be assessed and compared to the Level Descriptions. The work of a pupil is judged to be at a particular level because that description is the closest match and best fit. It is not necessary to show achievement of every aspect of the description to gain that level. Although this does, in one sense, free the assessment from the straitjacket of identifying specific hurdles, in another way it puts a greater onus on the assessment instruments to deliver judgements which do not undermine the complex nature of speaking and listening, reading and writing.

The Level Descriptions cannot, of course, attempt to cover all the ground that is in the programmes of study, and it is assumed that, if the programmes of study are taught, pupils will give evidence of their abilities which may then be assessed. How the curriculum is taught is not subject to statute, that is up to teachers and schools. In particular, the provision for identification of progress within a key stage, that is, formative assessment, is for teachers to decide as part of their ongoing, day-to-day teaching.

The assessment arrangements

The arrangements by which judgements are made about pupils' levels are also statutory. At the ends of the Key Stages pupils are assessed in two ways: on their performance in the National Curriculum tests, and on their work over time through Teacher Assessment. Both these assessments are anchored to the standards described in the Level Descriptions. The essential distinction between them is that they are based on different evidence, and the assessments are therefore complementary.

The National Curriculum tests are designed to target the skills outlined in the Level Descriptions, in relation to a sample of the range of activities and texts in the programmes of study. They are designed, and extensively pre-tested, to ensure continuity of standards from year to year. The same tasks are given to all pupils in a cohort and, at ages eleven and fourteen, they are undertaken in limited time and independent of teacher help. These tests give a snapshot of what pupils can do, and, since they are the same for all pupils at a particular age, they enable comparisons to be made on the basis of similar evidence.

Teacher Assessment, which is akin to coursework or portfolio assessment, is based on teachers' knowledge of pupils' work over a range of situations and takes account of pupils' strengths and weaknesses in aiming at the 'best fit' judgement. Since teachers decide on how to teach the curriculum, according to their pupils' needs, the work in one class on which Teacher Assessment is based is unlikely to be the same as that for other classes or pupils. This allows pupils' particular achievements to be recognized and their future needs to be identified. Teachers' records and observations are vital to this process. In order for this to be a credible national system it is very important for teachers to agree the standards that are being applied in a school and that these reflect national standards.

The interrelationship of these different parts of the system is shown in diagrammatic form in Figure 5.1.

What we are in the process of setting up, as the figure shows, is a system of assessment which works on parallel, complementary tracks. Both the tests and the Teacher Assessment are referenced to the same Level Descriptions and hence, the same standards. They are predicated on different sets of evidence to serve different purposes. The two levels resulting from the two assessments are to be reported in parallel to parents, and there is no expectation that the two levels will necessarily be the same.

Reading in the English National Curriculum

In the revised English statutory Order the overall aims of English are to 'develop pupils' abilities to communicate effectively in speech and writing and to listen with understanding'. It should also enable them to

Figure 5.1 English National Curriculum: assessment arrangements

PROGRAMMES OF STUDY

- Speaking and Listening, Reading, Writing
- Range, Key Skills, Standard English and Language Study
- Skills, content, processes to be taught

LEVEL DESCRIPTIONS

- Summative, end of key stage
- Based on a range of evidence
- Holistic, 'best-fit' judgement
- Single scale for ages 5–14

TEACHER ASSESSMENT

- Includes Speaking and Listening, Reading, Writing
- Based on pupils' work over a period of time and teachers' knowledge
- Standardized within school
- Strong on curriculum validity

TESTS

- Include Reading and Writing
- Based on a range of skills in limited conditions
- Pretested to ensure standards
- The same for all pupils

Two sets of evidence
Two different purposes
– reported to parents in parallel

be 'enthusiastic, responsive and knowledgeable readers' (HMSO 1995). Within these, the requirements for reading, in particular, specify that to develop as effective readers, pupils should be taught to:

- read accurately, fluently and with understanding;
- understand and respond to the texts they read;
- read, analyse and evaluate a wide range of texts, including literature;
- this literature to come from the English literary heritage and from other cultures and traditions.

The details of what should be taught are in the programmes of study for reading. The Level Descriptions relate to major aspects of that curriculum, so that those for reading describe features of attainment related to fluency and accuracy, to understanding and response, and to critical evaluation of texts. The intention of these Level Descriptions is to show that progress relates to increasing sophistication in reading and response. This progress is largely a qualitative development of the necessary skills rather than gradual coverage of specific, discrete hurdles. This is illustrated by the following level descriptors:

> Level 2, the average level for seven year olds, describes achievement in Reading in these terms:
> 'Pupils' reading of simple texts shows understanding and is generally accurate. They express opinions about major events or ideas in stories, poems, and non-fiction. They use more than one strategy, such as phonic, graphic, syntactic and contextual, in reading unfamiliar words and establishing meaning.'

> Level 4, the most common level for eleven year olds, says:
> 'In responding to a range of texts, pupils show understanding of significant ideas, themes, events and characters, beginning to use inference and deduction. They refer to the text when explaining their views. They locate and use ideas and information'.

> A fourteen year old who is just above average may be expected to be best described by Level 6:
> 'In reading and discussing a range of texts, pupils identify different layers of meaning and comment on their significance and effect. They give personal responses to literary texts, referring to aspects of language, structure and themes in justifying their views. They summarise a range of information from different sources.'
> (HMSO, 1995)

The model of reading

Reading is a complex activity and accomplished readers operate at a number of levels simultaneously. They are decoding and establishing meaning at the same time as they are responding to what they read, selecting particular aspects for consideration and evaluating effects. At the lower levels emphasis is placed on accurate and fluent reading and on reading with understanding. Response to texts is included at all levels but becomes more prominent later, as do strategies for information retrieval. It is the sense of a text as an artefact and critical evaluation of it which distinguishes pupils' responses at the upper levels. Throughout the levels, there is reference to all the following aspects, with different emphases:

- reading accurately and fluently, using different strategies;
- establishing meaning and showing understanding;
- using inference and deduction;
- locating key aspects, ideas, information and using them as appropriate;
- identifying and commenting on character, language, theme, structure;
- responding to what has been read, expressing preferences and making critical evaluations;
- referring to texts as appropriate to explain and support views.

Challenges posed by the model

A range of problems has always beset assessors of reading, including fundamental issues such as whether to try to get directly at the reading act or whether to rely on evidence derived from speaking or writing. The systems being set up in England provide several challenges, both to test developers and to teachers applying the Level Descriptions:

- how to 'weight' the different elements of reading and so of the level descriptions;
- whether such 'weightings' should vary at the different key stages;
- whether a description can or should be interpreted differently depending on the age of the pupils;
- whether and/or how to separate decoding, understanding, responding and evaluating for assessment purposes;
- how to judge the degree of difficulty of a test passage or a book, and how that influences pupils' performance, since affective engagement is recognized as important in the level descriptions;
- what significance to attribute to the mode of response (written or oral), since the level descriptions are not prescriptive about this.

The ways these issues are tackled is likely to vary at different ages and between tests and Teacher Assessment. Both modes of assessments are related to the same Level Descriptions and the same model of reading, but are based on different evidence. What is important is their complementarity, since both have strengths and drawbacks.

The tests

How does this format of assessment bring together the model of reading and the Level Descriptions? The ways the tests are set up for the different age groups does vary, but there are commonalities. The Levels 1 and 2 are awarded through very similar procedures at each key stage. The teacher and the pupils select a text for a reading interview. After initial discussion of the choice, the pupil reads the text, (or an extract) aloud. The teacher notes successes and failures in the reading, using a running record. There is then some further discussion of the text, looking for the pupil's views, understanding and preferences. The questions the teacher asks about the reading are related to the features in the level descriptions, so, in the light of a pupil's reading and responses, the teacher can decide which level best describes the pupil's achievement. This procedure is followed to award Levels 1 and 2 in all key stages and also Level 3 for 14-year-olds. The evidence in this test is obviously oral not written.

For 7- and 11-year-olds, written papers are required for Levels 3 to 6, and for Levels 4 to 8 for 14-year-olds. At each age, pupils are expected to read more than one type of text, literary and non fiction; that range is important, even in timed, written tests, because it allows students to demonstrate different strengths. At the earlier ages the tests are mainly focused on comprehension, that is, location, inference and deduction, and retrieval of information, although some comment on aspects such as character and plot is invited. At Key Stage 2 some questions invite comment on how language is used and on pupils' likes and interest. In the main, the tests for 7- and 11-year-olds contain questions which expect short, correct answers, so the opportunity for recognizing multiple readings of texts is not extensive.

In the tests for 14-year-olds, the nature of the questioning is slightly different. There are two tests in the package at this level: Paper 1 includes two passages to read which are previously unseen by the pupils, and Paper 2 is a test of prior reading, on scenes from plays by Shakespeare which have been taught. In both these papers the model of questioning differs from that at the earlier key stages. The questions all follow a similar pattern, which is to invite comment about a lead idea central to the text, and help with structuring the answer is provided by a number of bullet points or prompts. It is assumed that all readers, regardless of ability, on first reading of such a piece, find it natural to engage with the central impact of the text. For example, one of the texts in the 1995 tests was a letter from the Red Cross appealing for donations, and pupils were asked to comment on how the letter seeks to persuade readers to send money and how successful pupils thought the letter was in accomplishing its goal. The questions expect that pupils will retrieve specific information, comment on what they find, and state their reactions to it, doing so in a way which integrates the various aspects of their reading. In this model, the Level Descriptions are a helpful mechanism, since they allow credit to be given wherever it is possible, whilst recognizing that better answers contain more to value than weaker ones. Indeed, the performance criteria in the mark schemes resemble the Level Descriptions, customized to the particular tasks in the tests.

Teacher assessment

The other assessment system which is currently being developed for the National Curriculum is Teacher Assessment. To help these assessments, materials have been sent to all schools; these include collections of pupils' work in different key stages. The evidence for reading which is shown in the pupils' work is particularly interesting, because it indicates the great variety of students' work. These exemplification materials show different pupils at work at different key stages:

> Navi is seven years old. Navi's collection contains her teacher's records of reading conferences when Navi read aloud and talked about her reading, as well as her attempts to engage with a computer game, a retelling of a story she has heard, and a voluntary piece of writing about a book. This collection is related to the level descriptions and a judgement made about which level best describes Navi's achievement.
>
> A similar approach is taken with Bethan, an eleven year old, whose work includes a record of the range of her reading and a review of one story from that range, a letter in role as a character in a novel and a diary by the same character.
>
> Adam's work, from Key Stage 3, includes a different range. Not only is there work based explicitly on his reading, such as works by Shakespeare and Dickens; there is also literary comment on his own poetry and a story which owes much to his liking for science fiction. The other work included in Adam's collection, a letter and a retelling of a traditional story, shows his familiarity with different genres, which could also be taken as evidence of his reading.
>
> (HMSO, 1995)

The purpose of these collections is to help teachers by establishing the standards in the Level Descriptions, and by modelling the process by which the judgements are made. Nor does the evidence stop here – in the written mode. Video material has also been published which focuses on pupils in each key stage, and shows them in different activities. Although this video has been made principally to establish standards in speaking and listening, there is also plenty of evidence of pupils' reading ability in the different activities. In these materials, it is explicitly stated that the work included can only be a part of what teachers know about their pupils, and that they might take a great range of evidence into account when making a judgement at the end of the key stage.

The international context

The developments in England and Wales, which have put in place both curriculum and assessment arrangements, have their parallels in several other English-speaking countries. New Zealand and Australia have been involved in similar initiatives. In the UK, Scotland and Northern Ireland have their own documents and provision. In the USA, a move to develop national standards has been taking place, accompanied by much debate. There are also moves to formalize and standardize curriculum and assessment arrangements in at least some parts of Canada.

There are interesting differences in the terminology used, the way the debate is enacted, the format of the documents and the reaction of the teaching profession in each of these countries. These differences are, of course, partly dependent on the educational culture in which the work takes place. For example, in a system where norm-referenced tests are regularly used and school performance is partly measured through the results, then to develop other means of assessing pupils' performance and give more scope for teacher judgement may be welcomed. Alternatively, if assessment has traditionally been teacher based and related to individual pupils rather than to the overall effectiveness of a school, then to develop tests for all pupils at various stages of schooling and to publish the results is potentially a much more threatening process to teachers. Similarly, the strength of minority or local control over what is taught will have considerable influence on the acceptability of proposals for a national curriculum. In Australia, for example, the development of the curriculum statements and profiles was cooperative between states but, at the point of implementation, this agreement broke down and the states now have taken up the initiative to different degrees and in different forms. Campagna-Wildash (1995) outlined some of the controversies that accompanied these developments. Pearson (1993) presaged the issues in the USA in his article outlining a taxonomy of 'standards' and the arguments, in the American context, for and against national standards. Salinger and Campbell (this volume) describe the National Assessment of Educational Progress that is used in the USA to survey students' achievement in various disciplines; it is completely independent of any effort to establish national standards or national curricula and serves only as a monitoring device.

That so many of these countries should have similar initiatives leads to speculation as to what they have in common which has led to this work. One notable aspect is that the initiatives have resulted from increased political interest in what the education services should and do provide for the country, given the level of investment in them. The development of public interest and the political will to define what should be taught and assessed in schools seems to have two main sources. First, in diverse societies with a range of educational provision and increasingly insistent demands from different minority groups, there has been a perceived need to determine the basic educational entitlement for all pupils. Second, there have been public anxieties about the levels of achievement of pupils leaving school, and how their supposed lack of skills affects the competitiveness of the nation. These twin concerns have led to attempts to define what should be taught and what pupils should achieve, to ensure fair and equitable provision for all and to provide benchmarks of achievement against which pupils may be measured.

There are interesting differences in the models of the curriculum adopted. In England and Wales, since the recent revisions, the curriculum documents lay down, in succinct form, the content, skills and processes that must be taught. Linked to these are the level descriptions which define a scale of achievement against which pupils must be measured at different points of schooling. In other words, although there are expectations about which levels are 'average' for an age group the measurement is defined separately from the curriculum entitlement. There are similar models operating in Scotland and Northern Ireland. In contrast, the models from Australia, New Zealand and the USA define the expected outcomes and then what must be done so that pupils achieve them. This model is much more likely to be seen as a mechanism for defining minimum competences, whereas the UK model could be seen to fail to make the vital link between what is taught and what is learnt, since differentiation is made evident at the end rather than during the process of teaching the curriculum.

What counts as reading varies between these models. The main differences centre round the treatment of media and IT texts, the area of visual literacy. In New Zealand that term, visual literacy, has currency, whereas in Australia one of the profiles is called Reading and Viewing. At one point in the development of the American IRA/NCTE Standards the term 'mediacy' had been coined, but it was widely criticized as jargon and subsequently not used. In England, media texts are a part of the Reading requirements, though this does not amount to anything like a structured programme of television and film studies. There is clearly no single way to link these areas to the more long-standing facets of English and literacy which feature in all the documents. Although the treatment of the English literary canon has attracted much attention in England, it has been less contentious in other countries, where recognition of a literary canon, as part of the reading diet, has been relatively uncontested.

Further differences between countries can be seen in the level of detail in the documents and the closeness of the reference to what teachers actually do in the classroom. The first national curriculum in England (1989) was considered too detailed and cumbersome. The revisions in England aimed to retain the specifics of what should be taught without going into what it should look like in the classroom. The Australian curriculum profile leads with numerous statements about what pupils should be able to do, supported by examples of the classroom experiences which will enable them to show this achievement and work samples of what it looks like. This is likely to be more instantly recognizable by teachers since the classroom activities and the work samples show, in practical terms, what the requirements mean. It does, however, lead to lengthy and complex documentation. What takes thirty-one pages in England needs 157 in the Australian equivalent. (The English exemplification of standards of achievement through work samples was published separately.) The recently published examples of Standards documents from the USA (International Reading Association, 1996) has tended to follow the Australian model and to be outcomes-led, offering illustrative 'vignettes' of classroom experiences and including work samples instead of stating specific levels of attainment.

A national companion to the defining of entitlement is a demand for accountability, both to ensure the entitlement is available for all and to look at the adequacy of levels of achievement. In many of these countries there is frequently concern expressed about levels of literacy and numeracy in the workforce and public debate about what education can and should be achieving. Methods of achieving accountability vary greatly. It seems likely that the systems now in place in England are amongst the most rigorous, since there are requirements to report to parents both test and Teacher Assessment levels at ages seven, eleven and fourteen, as well as public examinations for 16-year-olds and beyond. In addition to this there is a system of inspections where teams of members of the Office for Standards in Education go into schools to assess the effectiveness of the school in teaching the national curriculum and in managing pupils' learning. This completes the cycle – the curriculum is defined, the assessment of pupils through tests and Teacher Assessment is mandated, schools are required to report these results and schools are inspected to see if they are fulfilling their duties effectively.

The speed of change, as well as how radical it is, affects the acceptability of what is proposed. Scotland and Northern Ireland have also been developing their own curriculum documents, at a slower pace than England, and these have met with greater professional approval. The other major contrast within the UK has been the compulsory implementation of assessment, particularly tests. In those countries where the tests are optional or the timing is at the teacher's discretion, there has been more acceptance of them, but since they are not completed by all pupils under standardized conditions, the effects of the tests on schools' accountability are less obvious. The degree of teacher control over assessment also affects professional reaction. Where the assessment is closer to the English system of Teacher Assessment, there has been more consensus from teachers, who are clearly in control of the assessment when compared with centrally set tests.

In those countries where the accountability issues have been most evident there has been greater professional concern over the innovations. These professional concerns have often centred round what Afflerbach *et al.* (1996) describe as the need for a 'systematic approach that provides the resources to support change of classroom practice, helpful communication between those people involved in the curriculum, instruction, and assessment change processes, and ongoing refinement of the assessment programme and the performance assessment materials'. Even where systems are in place there is continuing need for such development and support. The challenge of raising expectations and achievement is a real and continuing one to which both teachers and policy-makers are committed. The next few years will prove interesting in considering the impact of all these new developments and whether they do indeed achieve all that is hoped for.

References

Afflerbach, P., Almasi, J. and Guthrie, J. (1996) 'Barriers to the implementation of a Statewide Performance Program: School Personnel Perspectives. National Reading Research Center, Universities of Georgia and Maryland.

Campagna-Wildash, H. (1995) 'For the record – An anonymous hack comes out'. *Australian Journal of Language and Literacy*, 18(2): 91–104.

Curriculum Corporation (1994) *A Statement on English for Australian Schools*. Carlton: Curriculum Corporation.

HMSO (1995) *English in the National Curriculum*. London: HMSO.

——— (1989) *English in the National Curriculum*. London: HMSO.

International Reading Association/National Council of Teachers of English (1996) *Standards for English Language Arts*. Newark, DE: International Reading Association.

Learning Research and Development Centre (1996) *New Standard Performance Standards*. Pittsburgh, PA: University of Pittsburgh.

Ministry of Education, Wellington, New Zealand (1994) *English in the New Zealand Curriculum*. Wellington: Ministry of Education.

Northern Ireland Curriculum Council (1989) *Proposals for the English Curriculum*. Belfast: Northern Ireland Curriculum Council.

Pearson, P. D. (1993) 'Standards for the English Language Arts: a Policy Perspective'. *Journal of Reading Behaviour*, 25(4): 457–75.

SCAA (1995) *Exemplification of Standards: English*. London: School Curriculum and Assessment Authority.

6

THE NATIONAL ASSESSMENT OF READING IN THE USA

Terry Salinger and Jay Campbell

Introduction

Since 1969, the National Assessment of Educational Progress (NAEP) has been a part of the American educational scene, offering reports on students' achievement in numerous content areas, contrasting achievement according to various demographic categories, and reporting upward and downward trends in achievement across the years of its history. Administration of assessments that will enable state-by-state comparisons of reading and maths achievement have recently been added to the NAEP list of purposes. After first providing some background information, this chapter discusses the ways in which NAEP has monitored students' reading achievement throughout its many administrations. A brief but enlightening history of NAEP, with specific attention to the procedural changes that have occurred over its nearly thirty years, can be found in Jones (1996).

Background

Planning for the National Assessment began in late 1963 as representatives from the US Office of Education, the Carnegie Foundation and the Center for Advanced Study in the Behavior Sciences met to devise a way to provide data on the 'condition and progress of American education' in accordance with the original congressional mandate that established the Office (Jones, 1996). The original intent was to develop an assessment system that would differ substantially from the norm-reference cognitive testing that predominated then and on into the present. According to the original plan, one or more of the following subject areas would be included in each bi-yearly assessment: reading, writing, mathematics, science, literature, social studies, art, music, citizenship and career/occupational development. In its original plan, the assessments would contain primarily open-ended, constructed response items. All but the last two subjects continue to be cycled through the NAEP administrations, with reading and mathematics tested most frequently; until very recently, however, most of the items were of machine-scorable, multiple-choice format.

Designers of the original NAEP model made two important assumptions as they developed what was intended to be a national assessment. They assumed, first, that commonality exists in what was taught in the target subject areas in schools nationwide, and, second, that panels of experts could reach consensus on test frameworks and item content for the necessary instruments. Consensus would be essential if NAEP were to be valid, for even though the assessment has always been intended to reflect what is taught nationwide, there has never been a United States national curriculum on which to base the content area tests.

It is important to stress this point: the National Assessment of Educational Progress differs from assessments such as the Key Stage exams in England and Wales and other examinations based on a national curriculum. Educational decision-making is a state and local concern in the USA, a 'states' rights' issue that is passionately guarded in many quarters and fiercely questioned in others. Thus, the USA has no national curriculum and no nationally administered high stakes examinations with which to monitor students' achievement (American Federation of Teachers, 1995). Although administered nationally, for students NAEP is a low-stakes test. This is especially true for twelfth grade students, who sit for the exam in the spring of their last year in high school. Further, there is no linked system of state-level exams that measure what students nationwide know and can do at any given age. Admittedly, tests administered to rank students for entry into colleges do report average scores, can provide breakouts of scores by states and by districts, and do provide trend data; but their share of the student populace is not fully representative of the nation as a whole. As discussed in chapters by Salinger and by Hoffman (this volume), decisions about accountability testing are sometimes made at the state level and sometimes left to individual districts. Thus, there is only the National Assessment of Educational Progress, with its own purposes, strengths and limitations, to provide a 'report card' on America's students. Figure 6.1 presents information about the National Assessment in the same categories used by Brooks (this volume) to contrast assessments in England and Wales and in Northern Ireland.

The National Assessment of Educational Progress can be thought of as an academic survey of a nationally representative sample of students enrolled at three points along the continuum from elementary to secondary schools (Grades 4, 8, and 12 or at ages nine, thirteen, and seventeen). Every two years, students are tested on several of the 'school subjects' previously named; they take 'blocks' of items developed from a framework or test 'blueprint' that has been determined by a discipline-specific consensus panel and subjected to extensive public and governmental review. Large item banks are periodically developed for each subject area, and multiple blocks of

Figure 6.1 Aspects of the NAEP Reading Assessment (see chapter 7)

Ages/grades tested	9, 13, 17 4th, 8th, 12th
Genres of text	Literary, expository, documentary Long, intact passages 'Authentic' texts
Degrees of central control	High National Assessment Governing Board is federally-appointed oversight board; National Center for Educational Statistics within the Department of Education subcontracts on competitive bid with test development and data analysis firms; large field reviews are conducted, including federal review by Office of Management and the Budget
Coverage	Light sampling of students Matrix sampling for test assembly
Intended data	By group, by region, by background variables Also reporting by state for comparative purposes
Political purpose	Monitoring; preparing 'Nation's Report Card' Documenting trends in academic achievement Leveraging change through state comparisons
Backwash	Incidental to schools; extensive media coverage
Cash value to students	None
Learning benefit to students	None
Cost to students	Little
Stakes	Low
Fitness for purpose	Medium to high
Value to society	Unrealized

items are developed to sample each domain to be tested. Matrix sampling governs test administrations, so each examinee responds to only about 10 per cent of the entire pool available in each assessment cycle. Results are issued in terms of the percentage of students whose performance falls within the bands of distinct descriptive scales. This information provides quantitative and qualitative data, but as discussed in the chapter by Pearson *et al.* (this volume), this kind of reporting may not communicate as completely as intended. Figure 6.2 presents the five points on the current NAEP reading scale. The reports published after each assessment cycle discuss students' achievement in terms of the relevant content area framework and along numerous demographic and educational variables such as size of community, number of hours of television watching reported by test takes, or parents' educational accomplishment.

The National Assessment of Educational Progress seeks to accomplish two goals: to provide information about trends in student achievement across time, and to report students' achievement of current educational objectives. In order to meet these two sometimes conflicting goals, what has emerged over the history of NAEP is an assessment programme consisting of two distinct instruments. The first instrument contains items developed during the early years of NAEP that have been administered periodically since 1969 to comparable age-cohort samples using identical administration procedures. By replicating procedures and content in each administration, NAEP has been able to assess long-term progress of the nation's students in reading, writing, mathematics and science.

The second instrument recognizes that while documenting trends in achievement requires that the instrument remain unchanged across assessment years, educational priorities and pedagogical practices within the various fields within education have hardly remained static, in terms of educational priorities and pedagogical practices. Thus, in response to evolving theories and practices, NAEP has developed new instruments for different subject areas that have been administered at different times; these are revised as needed to reflect more current objectives. For example, in both 1988 and 1992 the NAEP reading assessment underwent substantial revisions in response to changing perspectives on reading and reading instruction. New frameworks were written and new instruments were developed that incorporated the changes taking place in the field of reading.

At present, the National Assessment administers both instruments concurrently on a biannual basis: the instrument to gather trend data and the instrument that is periodically revised. However, because of differences in the content of the two instruments and because the long-term trend assessment samples students by age and the more current instruments sample students by grade, the results of the two assessments are not directly comparable. This situation sometimes causes confusion in the media and among users of NAEP data: two different reports are often released in the same year, one describing the progress or lack thereof in students' achievement since the first assessment year, and the other reporting student's performance relative to currently held educational priorities. For example, in 1992 both the long-term trend assessment in reading and the newly developed

Figure 6.2 NAEP Proficiency Levels for Reading

Rudimentary (150)

Readers who have acquired rudimentary reading skills and strategies can follow brief written directions. They can also select words, phrases, or sentences to describe a simple picture and can interpret simple written clues to identify a common object. *Performance at this level suggests the ability to carry out simple, discrete reading tasks.*

Basic (200)

Readers who have learned basic comprehension skills and strategies can locate and identify facts from simple informational paragraphs, stories and news articles. In addition, they can combine ideas and make inferences based on short, uncomplicated passages. *Performance at this level suggests the ability to understand specific or sequentially related information.*

Intermediate (250)

Readers with the ability to use intermediate skills and strategies can search for, locate, and organize the information they find in relatively lengthy passages and can recognize paraphrases of what they have read. They can also make inferences and reach generalizations about main ideas and author's purpose from passages dealing with literature, science and social studies. *Performance at this level suggests the ability to search for specific information, interrelate ideas and make generalizations.*

Adept (300)

Readers with adept reading comprehension skills and strategies can understand complicated literary and informational passages, including material about topics they study at school They can also analyse and integrate less familiar material and provide reactions to and explanations of the text as a whole. *Performance at this level suggests the ability to find, understand, summarize and explain relatively complicated information.*

Advanced (350)

Readers who use advanced reading skills and strategies can extend and restructure the ideas presented in specialized and complex texts. Examples include scientific materials, literary essays, historical documents and materials similar to those found in professional and technical working environments. They are also able to understand the links between ideas even when those links are not explicitly stated and to make appropriate generalizations even when the texts lack clear introductions or explanations. *Performance at this level suggests the ability to synthesize and learn from specialized reading materials.*

Source: National Center for Education Statistics (1992)

reading assessment were administered. Results of the two instruments were reported in separate publications, but the two could still be confused by those not familiar with NAEP's dual purposes.

In addition to reporting trend data and assessing students periodically, the National Assessment of Educational Progress has several other important purposes. One is to collect background data on students, teachers and schools. In addition to collecting routine demographic information, background questionnaires are routinely administered to teachers and students; these have yielded valuable information about factors such as the number of hours of television-watching children engage in, the extent of home and school support for students' academic achievement, the 'climate' within schools, teachers' curricular approaches, the resources available to teachers and students and the extent to which innovations such as 'process writing' have been incorporated into routine instruction. Students' achievement can be reported in terms of these variables, so that we know, for example, that as of 1986, 'more than 45 per cent of the students at grades 7 and 11 [had] never [had] the opportunity to exchange ideas in group discussion' (Applebee, Langer and Mullis, 1988, 15).

Another valuable NAEP purpose has been to provide opportunities for small special studies. These have allowed researchers to look closely at student behaviour, experiment with innovative item types, or gather data in ways that are not feasible in the large-scale assessment. Several of these studies will be discussed below.

What NAEP reports

The end products of NAEP administrations have always been quite varied. Statistics about students' achievement are reported in the media, with accompanying hand-wringing or congratulations as appropriate. The focal point of the media releases is whether scores have gone up or down, usually with little attention to the nature of the examination on which students scored better or worse than their predecessors.

Students' achievement can also be reported in terms of the background, demographic, or curricular variables described above. Thus, we know that as of 1994, 36 per cent of eighth graders and 61 per cent of twelfth graders were asked by their teachers to discuss various interpretations of what they had read at least once or twice a week. Furthermore, the data indicated that these students demonstrated higher average reading achievement than students who were asked to do so less than weekly (Campbell, Donahue, Reese and Phillips, 1996, 72).

Data are published in both technical and summary reports; these provide glimpses of item types, report statistical analyses of students' achievement, discuss background information to some extent; yet they routinely avoid making direct statements about instructional approaches to teaching the content areas that have been assessed. Compilations of data are also routinely produced for researchers who wish to perform secondary analyses. As more and more 'constructed response', that is, non-multiple choice items, are used, actual student answers have been reproduced in the reports, providing valuable benchmarks of the kinds of work students at different achievement levels can actually perform. This practice represents a small-scale attempt to achieve the 'criteria- and exemplar-guided norm referencing' advocated by Brooks (this volume).

State assessments

At its inception, the National Assessment was mandated by law to report results only for the nation. However, in 1988 Congress changed the legislation to include state-by-state assessments of selected subjects on a voluntary basis. Individual states could choose to participate at their own expense, and in return, receive individual reports on the achievement of students within their jurisdiction as well as be provided with comparative information in relation to students from other states and the nation. In 1990, the first state assessments were conducted along with the National Assessment in mathematics, followed by state assessments in 1992 in both mathematics and reading. State-level assessments in reading were again conducted in 1994. In each case, more than two-thirds of the states participated in these assessments.

Proponents of the state assessment programme claim that more valuable information is gained from these costly but 'low stakes' tests than is provided by 'high stakes' state-developed or commercial tests that may not be comparable from state to state (Phillips, 1991). Critics cite the cost and point out that the state comparisons merely reinforce what is already known: students from certain states, mostly in the northeast and northern tier of the country, out-perform students from other states, notably southern states and those with large immigrant populations (Koretz, 1991, 1992).

Additional proposed changes

Many changes are proposed for the NAEP for the years ahead, mostly to increase efficiency and cut costs. The National Assessment Governing Board, the Congressionally mandated and appointed oversight body, has suggested that fewer small-scale experimental studies be undertaken and that the usual rich vein of background information still be collected during administrations but that it not be left unmined during the initial, federally funded statistical analysis of test results. Special investigations and fine-grained analyses of background data may still be conducted, but by those who have secured their own funding to cover costs. An additional change will be to decrease the time between test administration and publication of the results in booklet form. Obviously, these three changes are related, in that data may be available sooner but it will not be as deeply contextualized within the lives and school experiences of the test-takers. What will remain constant about the National Assessment is that it will be a low-stakes test, only tangentially related to curricula nationwide, and taken by a small number of students.

Reading in the National Assessment of Educational Progress

Reading is the most frequently assessed of all the NAEP subject areas, and as one might expect from a project based on broad-based consensus, changes in the assessment of reading in NAEP have reflected the history of the field over the past thirty years. Consider, for example, the 'blueprint' from which items are developed and which guides data reporting; see Figure 6.3 (National Assessment of Educational Progress, 1970). The definition of reading one can derive from this outline is congruent with the kinds of reading programmes commonly used at the time (e.g., Wisconsin Design).

Contrasting the 1970–1 objectives with those developed for the 1978–80 and 1992 assessments provides a vivid picture of a changing field (see Figures 6.4 and 6.5). Over these twenty years or so, reading researchers offered new ways of thinking about reading, about how it is learned, how it should be taught, and how it can best be assessed (Ruddell, Ruddell and Singer, 1994). Thus, by 1992, NAEP reading had been officially redesigned (Langer, *et al.*, 1995), to include lengthy authentic texts and innovative instrumentation. No longer was the assessment driven by objectives; it now emerged from a framework dependent upon a definition of reading for meaning as 'a dynamic, complex interaction among three elements: the reader, the text, and the context [of the reading act]' (Council of Chief State School Officers, 1992, 10). In discussing the assessment, the framework developers talked about 'reading literacy', stating that the term 'is not intended to imply only basic or functional literacy. Rather the term connotes a broader sense of reading, including knowing when to read, how to read, and how to reflect on what has been read' (6).

The summary of the 1992 NAEP objectives presented in Figure 6.5 only begins to suggest the extent of change from the objective-driven assessments of earlier years. Even more subtle changes concern assessment itself. The impact of important research findings from the twenty intervening years was being felt by assessment experts, who were being asked to reformulate the assumptions that undergirded assessment development, scoring and reporting. The reformation included recognition that readers bring different stores of background knowledge to their reading and that reading is in no way a simple, unidimensional skill that can be measured validly by items with one best answer. As a result, the assessment featured longer passages of both literary and informational texts, reproduced in their entirety, and authentic 'documents' such as bus schedules that required analysis and interpretation of print and non-print texts. There were more

Figure 6.3 Reading Objectives 1970–1 Assessment

1 **Comprehend what is read**:
   (a)   read individual words
   (b)   read phrases, clauses and sentences
   (c)   read paragraphs, passages and longer works
2 **Analyse what is read**:
   (a)   be able to trace sequences
   (b)   perceive the structure and organization of the work
   (c)   see the techniques by which the author has created his effects
3 **Use what is read**:
   (a)   remember significant parts of what is read
   (b)   follow written directions
   (c)   obtain information efficiently
4 **Reason logically from what is read**:
   (a)   draw appropriate inferences from the material that is read and 'read between the lines' where necessary
   (b)   arrive at a general principle after examining a series of details
   (c)   reason from a general principle to specific instances
5 **Make judgements concerning what is read**:
   (a)   relate what is read to things other than the specific material being read
   (b)   find and use appropriate criteria in making judgements about what is read
   (c)   make judgements about a work on the basis of what is found in the work itself
6 **Have attitudes about and an interest in reading**

Source: National Assessment of Educational Progress (1970)

short and long 'constructed response' items requiring analytical scoring by teams of trained scorers. Subsequent assessments in 1994 and 1996 have maintained changes introduced in 1992.

How NAEP reached its current point

The intervening assessments, from 1970 to 1996, are in their own way as interesting as the changes in the 1992 assessment. Although rarely departing radically from the original format and design and employing primarily multiple-choice items, these intervening assessments often differed strikingly from the routine commercial, norm-referenced instruments that dominated high-stakes accountability testing. For example, a discrete assessment of literature study was administered in 1970, but during the next ten years, literature and reading were consolidated conceptually for NAEP assessment purposes. This merger is a precursor to the kinds of curricular changes that the whole language movement would bring about

Figure 6.4 Reading and Literature Objectives 1979–80 Assessment

---

1 Values reading and literature:
  (a) Values the benefits of reading for the individual
     i Recognizes that reading can be a source of enjoyment; demonstrates a commitment to reading for enjoyment
     ii Recognizes that written materials can contribute to a personal growth; demonstrates a commitment to reading as one means of developing self-understanding
     iii Recognizes that reading can be a means of acquiring knowledge and solving problems; demonstrates a commitment to reading as a means of acquiring knowledge and solving problems
  (b) Appreciates the cultural role of written discourse as a way of transmitting, sustaining and changing the values of a society

2 Comprehends written works:
  (a) Comprehends words and lexical relationships
  (b) Comprehends propositional relationships
  (c) Comprehends textual relationships

3 Responds to written works in interpretive and evaluative ways:
  (a) Extends understanding of written works through interpretation
     i Demonstrates awareness of emotional impact of written works
     ii Applies personal experience to written works
     iii Applies knowledge of other works or other fields of study
     iv Analyses written works
  (b) Evaluates written works

4 Applies study skills in reading:
  (a) Obtains information from non-prose reading facilitators
  (b) Uses the various parts of a book
  (c) Obtains information from materials commonly found in libraries or resource centres
  (d) Uses various study techniques

Source: National Assessment of Education Progress (1981)

---

nationwide. The result was the 1979–80 assessment of reading and literature which included fairly long selections to read and numerous constructed response items (see Figure 6.3 for objectives). The resulting report was *Reading, Thinking, and Writing* (National Assessment of Educational Progress, 1981). The introduction to the resulting report seems quite contemporary: 'This report on students' academic performance looks beyond the boundaries traditionally ascribed to subject areas. It rests upon the assumption that in order to understand how well people read, we must look at their ability to read a range of materials and to express and explain their interpretations of what they have read' (National Assessment of Educational Progress, 1981, ix).

Figure 6.5 1992 Reading Objectives

Forming an Initial Understanding
Write a paragraph telling what the story/poem is about.
1   Which of the following is the best statement of the theme of this story?
2   Write a paragraph telling what this article generally tells you.
3   What is this supposed to help you do?
4   What would you tell someone about the main character?

Developing an Interpretation
5   How did the plot begin to develop?
6   What caused the character to do this? Use examples from the story to support your answer.
7   What caused this event?
8   What type of person is this character? Use information from the text to support your answer.
9   In what ways are these ideas important to the topic or theme?
10   What will be the result of this step in the directions?
11   What does this character think about _____?

Personal Reflection and Response
12   How did this character change your ideas of _____?
13   Do you think that _____ (a grandmother and a 5-year-old) would interpret this passage the same way? Explain.
14   How is this story like or different from your own personal experience? Explain.
15   What current event does this remind you of? Explain.
16   Does this description fit what you know about _____? Why?
17   What does this passage/story say to you?
18   Why do you think _____ (bullfrogs eat dragonflies?) Is there anything else you think they might eat? What parts of the passage, information from other books, or your own knowledge helped you answer this?

Demonstrating a Critical Stance
19   Compare this article/story to that one.
20   How useful would this be for _____? Why?
21   Do you agree with the author's opinion of this event?
22   Does the author use (irony, personification, humour) effectively? Explain.
23   What could be added to improve the author's argument? Why?
24   Is this information needed?
25   What other information would you need to find out that you don't know now?

Source: Council of Chief State School Officers (1992)

The reading/literature assessment and its report were important milestones in the NAEP history. The innovative nature of the assessment, the model of comprehension upon which it was developed, and the strength of its recommendations are often forgotten in the debates over the value of NAEP and other nationally administered tests. For example, the report called for more writing and more discussion in classrooms at all levels, more institutional support and inservice training for teachers, and more instruction in problem-solving strategies; it stated that 'essay questions that require students to explain their points of view should be a regular part of any testing program' (4); and it bade teachers to analyse the text books they are using to see if 'students can stop after stating an initial opinion . . . or do [students] have to find and organize evidence in support of what they have said or written?' (4).

The special studies

The reading/literature assessment was the regular assessment, not a 'special study'. Small, special studies have been incorporated into more recent assessments. In planning the 1992 assessment, the National Assessment Governing Board approved supplemental studies to be conducted with nationally representative sub-samples of students. In one study, the Integrated Reading Performance Record, over 1300 fourth graders were interviewed individually, and an array of literacy indicators were collected ranging from students' oral reading fluency to samples of classroom work completed during reading instruction. As a part of the interview, students were asked to describe their reading preferences and habits, their school experiences related to reading and their impressions about their classroom work.

The study was designed to incorporate some of the more innovative reading assessment practices being implemented in classrooms and to provide more in-depth information about the literacy development of fourth graders than could be collected in the main assessment. Two published reports detailed the results of this special study: *Listening to Children Read Aloud* (Pinnell, et al., 1995) and *Interviewing Children about their Literacy Experiences* (Campbell, Kapinus and Beatty, 1995). One of the findings from this study was that oral reading fluency, but not necessarily accuracy, had a direct relationship with reading comprehension. Also, it was apparent that students who had been exposed to more diverse types of reading materials had higher reading achievement than students who had more limited exposure to different types of texts.

Another special study, referred to as The NAEP Reader, was conducted in both 1992 and 1994 and involved eighth- and twelfth-grade students in a self-selection literary reading task. Concern about the role of interest and motivation in the reading process led to the design of this study in which students were given the opportunity to select one of seven short stories to read for the assessment. A compendium of stories written by various, and in some cases, well-known authors was given to each student in the special study sample. A different compendium comprising a range of topics, genre and cultural contexts was used at each grade. The compendiums contained a table of contents and brief story summaries that students could use in making their story selections. To assess their comprehension of the stories they selected, students were given twelve constructed-response questions worded generically so as to be applicable to each of the stories in the compendium. The 1994 study included a comparison sample of students, each of whom was asked to read a story without the opportunity for making a selection. The results from the 1994 special study (scheduled for release in 1997) may provide important insight into the effect of offering students choice in reading assessment.

These special studies were important additions to the 1992 and 1994 reading assessments, but it does not diminish their worth to remember the reading/literature assessment conducted more than a decade earlier. Surveying the history of NAEP reading assessments makes it evident that the National Assessment can be an invaluable resource for experimentation and implementation of assessment innovations, without impinging on local curricular decision-making. By doing so, it can remain a vital contributor to the ongoing debates about assessment practices and instructional approaches. Clearly, if the National Assessment is to maintain its relevance and usefulness, it must continue to be responsive to the changing needs and priorities of the education community and to push educational practices forward by gathering, analysing, and disseminating information on innovative approaches to assessment.

Readers who are interested in data and interpretations of data are referred to the bibliography at the end of the chapter, for the intent here has not been to summarize all that NAEP has found over its years. Instead, the intent has been to provide information about a 'national' assessment system that is very different from the systems against which Europeans may rail but which they more or less take as part of their educational landscape.

Postscript

At the time this chapter was written, the National Assessment of Education Progress was the only test administered nationwide. Its sampling design allows for reporting on students' abilities according to numerous groupings (by states, region, grade levels, gender, ethnic group) but not by individual test takers. As this book is going to press, voluntary national tests of reading in fourth grade and mathematics in eighth grade are in early stages of development, with spring 1998 as the first date of the tests' annual administration. States and districts would be invited, but not required, to participate in the testing program, and no aggregate data would be reported by the federal government. The tests would be constructed from specifications similar to the NAEP frameworks, and reports would be issues in terms of the NAEP proficiency levels.

References

American Federation of Teachers (1995) *What Secondary Students Abroad are Expected to Know.* Washington: Author.

Applebee, A. N., Langer, J. A. and Mullis, I. V. S. (1988) *Who Reads Best? Factors Relating to Reading Achievement in Grades 3, 7, and 11.* Princeton, NJ: Educational Testing Service.

Campbell, J. R., Donahue, P. L., Reese, C. M. and Phillips, G. (1996) *NAEP 1994 Reading Report for the Nation and the States: Findings from the National Assessment of Educational Progress and Trial State Assessment.* Washington, DC: National Center for Educational Statistics.

Campbell, J. R., Kapinus, B. and Beatty, A. S. (1995) *Interviewing Children about their Literacy Experiences.* Washington, DC: National Center for Educational Statistics.

Council of Chief State School Officers (1992). *1992 NAEP Reading Objectives.* Washington, DC: Author.

Jones, L. J. (1996) 'A history of the National Assessment of Educational Progress and some questions about the future'. *Educational Researcher,* 25(7): 15–22.

Koretz, D. (1991) 'State comparisons using NAEP: Large costs, disappointing results'. *Educational Researcher,* 20(3): 19–21.

—— (1992) 'What happened to test scores, and why?' *Educational Measurement: Issues and Practice,* 11(4): 7–11.

Langer, J. A., Applebee, A. N., Mullis, I. V. S. and Foertsch, M. A. (1990) *Learning to Read in Our Nation's Schools.* Princeton, NJ: Educational Testing Service.

Langer, J. A., Campbell, J. R., Neuman, S. B., Mullis, I. V. S., Persley, H. R. and Donahue, P. L. (1995) *Reading Assessment Redesigned.* Princeton, NJ: Educational Testing Service.

Mullis, I. V. S. and Jenkins, L. B. (1990) *The Reading Report Card: 1971–88: Trends from the Nation's Report Card.* Princeton, NJ: Educational Testing Service.

National Assessment of Educational Progress (1970) *Reading Objectives.* Ann Arbor, MI: Author.

—— (1974) *Recipes, Wrappers, Reasoning, and Rate: A Digest of the First Reading Assessment.* Denver: Educational Commission of the States.

—— (1981) *The Reading Report Card: Progress Toward Excellence in Our Schools.* Princeton, NJ: Educational Testing Service.

——(1987) *Reading Objectives: 1986 and 1988 Assessments.* Princeton, NJ: Educational Testing Service.

—— (1989) *Reading Objectives: 1990 Assessments.*

Phillips, G. (1991) 'Benefits of state-by-state comparisons'. *Educational Researcher,* 20(3): 17–19.

Pinnell, G. S., Pikulski, J. J., Wixson, K. K., Campbell, J. R., Gough, P. B. and Beatty, A. S. (1995). *Listening to Children Read Aloud.* Washington, DC: National Center for Educational Statistics.

Ruddell, R., Ruddell, M. R. and Singer, H. (1994) *Theoretical Models and Processes in Reading,* 4th edn. Newark, DE: International Reading Association.

7

NEW EMPHASIS ON
OLD PRINCIPLES

The need for clarity of purpose and of
assessment method in national testing
and for national monitoring

Greg Brooks

Old principles

It seems to me unarguable that any system of assessment which purports
to be fair to those assessed should meet at least the following standards:

- There should be clarity over the purpose which the assessment is meant
  to serve.
- The instruments used should be valid in relation to the intended
  domain.
- The instruments used should be as unbiased as possible.
- The system of assessment should be clear, and only as complicated as
  the purpose served requires.
- The outcome measures should be reliable.
- The experience of taking the assessment should be useful to those
  assessed, and the outcome measures should be useful both to those
  assessed and to the wider society.

This list is, of course, a counsel of perfection; no assessment system can
achieve all these desiderata both fully and simultaneously. The requirements of validity, reliability and utility are notoriously impossible to
reconcile. However, any assessment system which fails on several of these
criteria at once must be in urgent need of revision. This must be particularly the case with nationally important systems.

These principles remain entirely theoretical, of course, unless tested in
practice; the purpose of this chapter is to use them in an analysis of two
recent British projects, and then to draw more general conclusions. In

particular, I shall argue that the requirements of strict criterion-referencing and of national monitoring are inherently incompatible.

Two British assessment projects

In 1993 the National Foundation for Educational Research (NFER) carried out two projects on the assessment of English for different branches of the British government:

- a national evaluation of the tests of English at Key Stage 3 (age fourteen) in England and Wales; this was done for the (then) School Examinations and Assessment Council (SEAC), now merged in the School Curriculum and Assessment Authority (SCAA)
- a survey of reading standards of pupils aged eight, eleven, fourteen and sixteen in Northern Ireland; this was carried out for the Department for Education in Northern Ireland.

The 1993 Key Stage 3 English tests in England and Wales

A full description of these tests is given in Ruddock *et al.* (1995), but since that report may be difficult to obtain, the following summary is given. These tests were meant to occur in June 1993, to be taken by all Year 9 pupils (age fourteen) in state secondary schools in England and Wales, to assess pupils' achievement against parts, specified by SEAC, of the National Curriculum in English for England and Wales (1990 version), and to deliver assessments of every pupil in reading and writing in the form of levels on the (then) ten-level National Assessment scale. The tests were specially designed. There were three papers, each of which was set at three tiers of difficulty:

- Paper 1 (1.5 hours) was a test of factual reading and directed writing
- Paper 2 (1.5 hours) was a test of prior reading, based on an anthology of extracts from English literature and on either a Shakespeare play or a text from a set list
- Paper 3 (1 hour) was a test of extended writing.

Though the tests were devised, rather little of the testing actually happened. Because of teacher opposition, arising from doubts about both the workload involved and the quality of the tests, only about 2 per cent of the 5000 secondary schools in England and Wales both administered the tests and reported the results.

The boycott of the tests reduced the intended scope of the NFER evaluation, so that it actually consisted (for present purposes) of a detailed desk review of the tests (covering mainly judgements of validity and reliability), plus an analysis of the marking and aggregation systems, and a small quantity of test data from about 100 schools which reported results. However, even this incomplete set of data raised acute issues about the validity and reliability of these tests in particular, and about the practicality of criterion-referencing in general. The evaluation reached the following conclusions:

- Some of the test arrangements were unduly complex.
- There was satisfactory coverage of what SEAC required, but, since there were substantial discrepancies between SEAC's specification and the National Curriculum, coverage of the National Curriculum was unsatisfactory. In particular,
  - the section of Paper 1 consisting of vocabulary and grammar items seemed to have no relevance whatever to the National Curriculum;
  - most of the reading tasks were judged to be invalid;
  - a heavy emphasis was placed on narrative (60 per cent of the marks in writing, 71 per cent in reading) in relation to other genres.
- The test items, considered individually, gave little concern over possible bias. However, the division of the anthology of literary extracts into compulsory and optional texts made it possible to select for study and assessment texts which entirely excluded the female and non-white authors represented, but not vice versa.
- The marking system as a whole was too complex. In particular, the marking system for writing was liable to distortion by the large weightings to be applied to some raw marks.
- The mark schemes for writing, spelling and handwriting, and most of those for reading, were considered satisfactory.
- A number of the mark schemes for reading, however, were insufficiently clear to ensure adequate reliability, and one section of the marking system appeared to award no marks to positive evidence of (admittedly low) attainment.
- Where the number of texts was large, it was thought unlikely that options were of similar difficulty.
- Progression in difficulty across test tiers in writing was largely satisfactory, except that it was achieved in part by setting more demanding question types rather than more demanding questions. However, in reading, progression in difficulty across tiers was judged to be inadequate; this was largely because too few items assessed understanding beyond the literal. This in turn meant that parts of the tests seemed to be too easy for the levels awarded. Both the test data available to the evaluation (Ruddock *et al.*, 1995, section 7.2) and a small-scale study in which pupils in one school took the papers for two adjacent tiers (Harding, 1993) supported this view.
- The assessment system, though operating within a framework designed to be criterion-referenced, was a compromise between criterion-referencing and norm-referencing.

In terms of the principles enumerated at the beginning of this chapter, this implies that there were problems with the validity and reliability of the tests, and possibly also with bias; that the assessment systems were unclear and unduly complex; and therefore that their value both to those assessed and to the wider society was likely to be low.

At the time, the official line was that these assessments were to serve various purposes simultaneously: they were to be formative, summative and diagnostic, and provide a basis for monitoring trends over time. The NFER researchers took the view that the assessments should be evaluated as though their purpose was principally summative; given the severe doubts about their validity and reliability, it was concluded that their summative value was low. Furthermore, since an absolute precondition for a reliable system of monitoring progress over time is that the assessments at any one point must be reliable, these tests clearly could not serve this purpose either.

At the time, the official line was also that these assessments were to be criterion-referenced. In practice, only small parts of the tests were criterion-referenced in any full sense, and the remainder were assessed by various blends of criterion-referencing and norm-referencing. This issue, and that of clarity of purpose, will be analysed in more detail below.

The 1993 Northern Ireland reading surveys

These surveys are reported in Brooks *et al.* (1995). They took place in June and September 1993, involved light samples of pupils aged eight, eleven, fourteen and sixteen in the various types of primary and post-primary school in Northern Ireland, used existing tests (most of which had been used in previous surveys in the province); assessed pupils' achievement against the model of reading embodied in the tests and on a norm-referenced basis; and used straightforward systems for administration, marking and aggregation. For individual pupils, the tests took between ninety and 200 minutes; none of the tests required prior reading. The surveys were intended to serve a single purpose, namely monitoring; that is, they were to estimate the current level of achievement of groups of pupils of the relevant ages (rather than of individuals), relate that level to previous surveys where possible, and provide a basis for possible future work.

The surveys yielded sufficient data to achieve this objective, and were judged by the Northern Irish teachers who marked the tests to have been largely appropriate for the purpose and the pupils involved. Again, in terms of the principles enumerated at the beginning of this chapter, this implies that these tests were largely valid, reliable and free from bias; that the assessment systems were clear and of an appropriate complexity; and that their value to the wider society was satisfactory. Their value to those assessed, however, might still be low, since they had little intrinsic learning value and led to no certificates; the only compensatory factor for this was that they were short and took little time away from other teaching and learning.

Figure 7.1 attempts to summarize the similarities and differences between the tests in these two projects. (For further details, and comparisons with experience in Romania, see Mihail, 1995, 171, Table 1; see also Salinger and Campbell, this volume, for a summary of the US National Assessment which charts similar comparisons.

It seems to me that most of the differences noted in Figure 7.1 do not co-occur coincidentally; they were inherently linked. That is, it was precisely because the English tests were trying to achieve an incompatible variety of

Figure 7.1 Comparisons between 1993 tests in England and Wales, and Northern Ireland

	England and Wales	Northern Ireland
Ages tested	14	8, 11, 14, 16
Genres of text	literary and factual	literary and factual
Assessment system	in theory criterion-referenced; in practice a mix of criterion- and norm-referencing	norm-referenced
Degree of central control	high	arm's-length
Coverage	blanket	light sampling
Intended data	individual, school, area, etc.	group
Political purpose	raising standards	investigating standards
Educational purpose(s)	formative, summative, diagnostic, monitoring	monitoring
Backwash	intended to affect and police curriculum	incidental, but should not be harmful
Cash value to pupils	none	none
Learning benefit to pupils	a little	a little
Cost to pupils	teaching to tests took time away from other teaching	very little – tests were short and could not be taught to
Stakes	high	low
Fitness for purpose	low	high
Value to society	low	high

purposes, carried high-stakes politically and attracted a high degree of central control that they did not achieve what they were intended to (and would not have done so, even if there had been no boycott).

Correspondingly, in my judgement the Northern Irish tests were successful precisely because the authorities there had a single, clear purpose in mind, kept the political stakes low, and allowed the researchers responsibility for all the professional aspects of the task. The moral would seem to be that a professional job is more likely to be achieved with loose political control, partly because this makes clarity of purpose more likely. The criterion- versus norm-referencing issue is not necessarily implicated here, however, and will be discussed separately below.

Changes since 1993

The Northern Ireland surveys of 1993 were repeated in 1996 and were again successful, but there are currently no plans to repeat them again. The 1993 tests in England and Wales, however, were intended to be the first in a permanent annual series. Many changes and improvements have been made to the system in the intervening four years (see Horner, this volume). A new National Curriculum in English for England and Wales was devised, and came into effect in September 1995. The vocabulary and grammar items, and the anthology of literary extracts, were not continued. The testing and marking systems were greatly simplified. The tests were made more valid, and reliability improved. The move away from strict criterion-referencing continued. Above all, one month after the date at which the 1993 assessments were (intended to be) carried out, the range of purposes of such national tests was officially narrowed to become summative and, by implication, a monitoring system:

> National tests have . . . a summative purpose. They are undertaken in order to contribute to an objective view of pupils' achievements . . . at the end of key stages 1, 2 and 3 [ages seven, eleven and fourteen]. The information they supply can then be reported to parents and can be used to help form judgements about the progress being made by the class, the school and the education system as a whole.
>
> (Dearing, 1993, para. 5.9)

This long-delayed but welcome clarity of purpose offered the possibility that the tests, if they continue, will achieve satisfactory validity, freedom from bias, and clarity and economy of means. Certainly, the changes brought about a return to peace in the classroom; about two-thirds of secondary schools implemented the age fourteen tests in 1994, and over 90 per cent in 1995.

However, there are three important, linked issues which remain to be settled. The first is whether a nation-wide test system can achieve sufficient reliability, in the technical sense of inter-marker consistency and test/re-test or split-half agreement, to provide reliable information that can be trusted by those who use it. The second is whether even a fully reliable annual system of blanket summative testing can also serve the purpose of monitoring 'the progress being made by the class, the school and the education system as a whole', as Dearing suggested should be the case. The third is the balance within the system of criterion- and norm-referencing. The links between these issues are that the second and third logically depend on the first; however, I would argue that the second and third are in inherent contradiction with each other.

National reliability

If national assessment results are to be trusted, then those using them must be sure that particular results mean, within narrow limits, the same thing across the whole country. This has traditionally meant, in public examinations for instance, that assessors need to be supported with adequate training, exemplars, the socialization into the 'interpretive community' of markers through calibration exercises and meetings and years of experience, and moderation of their assessments through cross-marking and the monitoring of their consistency, both with themselves and with each other. Moreover, even after all this effort chief examiners have had the responsibility of carrying the 'standard', particularly the 'pass mark' (if there is one), forward in their heads from year to year, and judging, with statistical aids including re-marking exercises, whether the 'standard' is being kept consistent over time. Good assessment practice requires all this in order to make the system as reliable as is humanly achievable, and does not come cheap.

The national tests in England and Wales have only parts of this set-up. There is a little training, there are some exemplars, and there is a system (called 'audit') for checking that the mechanics of the marking have been carried out accurately. But there is little opportunity for teachers to meet or otherwise test their consistency with each other, and the 'interpretive community' that is needed may therefore never come into existence. Above all, the level boundaries are pre-determined during test development and trialling; there is no chance at all for the boundaries to be adjusted after the event, even if the test developers should conclude that the 'standard' has not been kept consistent (for instance, if part of the test should prove unexpectedly easy or difficult). In my judgement this means that the system is unable to achieve the degree of reliability that is needed if the results are to be genuinely useful either to those assessed or to the wider society.

National monitoring

The basic reason for national monitoring was stated with definitive clarity over twenty years ago:

There will always be keen interest in the movement of standards, and it is perfectly natural that there should be. Where there is no information there will be speculation, and the absence of facts makes room for prejudice . . . Information of the right quality will be of value to teachers and researchers and will be a reference point for policy decisions at the level of central and local government.
(Department of Education and Science, 1975, 36).

In order to monitor the trend of achievement, surveys need to be carried out at regular intervals; annual or even biennial surveys seem too frequent, but any frequency greater than five-yearly runs the risk of irrelevance and of tests beginning to go out of date. It is also highly desirable to use the same instruments on at least two occasions, so that as far as possible like is being compared with like; but on the second occasion also to introduce new tests which can then replace the old ones on the next occasion before the first set become too dated. This is not unlike the collection of 'trend data' described by Salinger and Campbell (this volume).

Blanket surveys designed to provide individual information on all pupils (such as the national tests in England and Wales) are unnecessarily large for monitoring the performance of the system as a whole; light sampling is sufficient, provided that great care is taken to draw equivalent samples on all occasions. Moreover, blanket surveys seem incapable in principle of serving monitoring purposes, for two main reasons. First, nationwide tests inevitably become high-stakes, so there will always be teaching to the test, because teachers know that their pupils cannot give of their best if they are inadequately prepared. Second, again because such tests inevitably become high-stakes, it is impossible to keep them secure. This entails the use of new instruments every time, thus destroying one aspect of comparability between occasions of testing, and introducing into the results uncontrollable variation that is not due to the pupils' performance.

A way out of both this problem and that of nation-wide reliability was meant to be offered by criterion-referencing; but can it work?

Criterion- and norm-referencing

The implied theory seems to have been as follows. Even though blanket testing means that the assessment instruments cannot be kept secure, and have to be changed for every round of testing, and the 'standard' has to be pre-set, this is irrelevant. Provided that sufficiently explicit, clear and detailed criteria can be set out, performance on any appropriate instrument can be assessed against them; in this way the standard can be maintained irrespective of the particular instrument used. Assessment against the criteria then becomes the guarantee not only of the reliability of the results in any one year, but also of the direct comparability of the results obtained in different years. Thus national tests in English (and other subjects) in England and Wales could serve both summative and monitoring purposes.

This theory seems to me to have been proved hopelessly optimistic in practice, and to such an extent that the theory in turn has had to be materially altered. In order to demonstrate this, I should first attempt to define what I mean by criterion-referencing, since definitions of this term seem fluid, especially in the context of National Curriculum assessment. My definition (and much of the following critique) is based on the work of Wolf (1993). She provides this description:

> The crucial idea underpinning criterion-referenced assessment is that one should look at the substance of what someone can do; in effect, compare a candidate's performance with some independent, free-standing definition of what should be achieved, and report on the performance in relation to this 'criterion'.
>
> (Wolf, 1993, 5)

All forms of criterion-referencing thus require specifications of the domain to be assessed and for constructing items to assess it, items designed to meet the specification, and rules governing not only the scoring of separate items but also aggregation of item scores to levels or grades for the complete domain. In strict forms of criterion-referencing not only are all item-scoring rules dichotomously Right/Wrong, but even aggregation rules are 'all or nothing' – either candidates have demonstrated complete mastery of the domain (by achieving every criterion) and pass, or they haven't and fail. Less strict forms have less absolute rules – a high percentage, say, or every criterion but one.

What Wolf goes on to show is that this ideal picture of criterion-referencing goes wrong at several points in practice:

- Domain and item specifications become too narrow: 'The attempt to map out free-standing content and standards leads, again and again, to a never-ending spiral of specification' (Wolf, 1993, 6).
- Item writing becomes much more problematic than anyone expects: 'Test questions which authors may think are approximately equal in difficulty, or test the same domain, have the universal habit of proving very different indeed' (11).
- Above all, no matter how tightly the specifications, items and assessment rules are written, the assessors are always called upon to make judgements: 'While assessment systems may vary in the *degree* to which . . . judgements come into play, such judgements are universal to all assessments' (17, Wolf's emphasis). And this is just as true of 'objective' item types as of more 'subjective' ones, since judgements on 'objective' item details and responses still have to be made, but largely during the construction stage and *before* the candidates attempt them.

Wolf gives key examples of all these tendencies, and supporting evidence is abundant from the story of the national tests in English for pupils aged fourteen in England and Wales. The development of these tests began in 1990. Small-scale pilot tests were carried out in 1990 and 1991, and a larger pilot in 1992. Nationwide testing was planned for each year from 1993, though as already stated the amount implemented was about 2 per cent in 1993, 66 per cent in 1994 and 95 per cent in 1995. In each of these years, the domain specifications, the criteria to which performances were to be referenced, were (officially) the Statements of Attainment contained in the National Curriculum. In practice, each year the test developers (of whom there have been four different teams over the six years so far) grappled with the Statements of Attainment, found them impossible to apply directly as criteria, and produced 'operationalized' adaptations of them.

Furthermore, by 1993 the attempt to operate with even the operationalized adaptations of the Statements of Attainment as though they were strict criteria had already been largely abandoned:

- Only for spelling, handwriting, and the two lowest levels of attainment in reading and writing did teachers award national curriculum levels directly from the number of Statements of Attainment achieved. This was a purely criterion-referenced system, but it applied to only a very small part of the tests.
- For all other parts of the tests, the systems used were criteria-related, in the sense that they were derived from the Statements of Attainment; but they were mark-based or at least mark-mediated.

Most of the systems were therefore an attempt to combine certain features of impressionistic and criterion-referenced assessment. Having mark scales at all within what had been intended to be a criterion-referenced system was a recognition that, even amongst candidates who have all met the criterion for achieving a particular level for part of the domain called 'English', there will still be gradations of achievement, and that those gradations may well need to be gathered together as 'partial credit' towards the award of an overall score. And in fact the final award of National Curriculum levels within most of the 1993 age fourteen English tests was an entirely arithmetical process based on score ranges within totals of marks on a 0–100 scale; these score ranges were pre-set and could not be adjusted in the light of the actual results.

Both the presence of mark-related sections within this system and the gathering together within it of partial credit reflect what Wolf has to say about the role of assessors' judgement:

What assessors do, when deciding whether an observed piece of evidence 'fits' a defined criterion, is operate with a 'compensating' model. This takes account of both the context of the performance and of its own characteristics . . . For example, assessors will 'make allowances' for whether a question or task was particularly difficult . . . The more complex the behaviour, the more this type of process comes into play.

(Wolf, 1993, 17)

This implies that assessors try to relate judgements of performance not only to the criteria but also to what it is reasonable to expect of candidates on the task set. But that is precisely the central process within norm-referencing, and there seems to be no logically possible escape from the conundrum that criterion-referencing has this impressionistic, norm-referenced element at its very heart.

(Re)new(ed) emphases

The conclusions I draw from this analysis are five:

First, criterion-referencing, precisely because of the judgemental element at its heart, is in principle incapable of delivering results at the level of precision required of it in national testing.

Second, the national tests in England and Wales have tested criterion-referencing to destruction, and it should be abandoned.

Third, the attempt to base a national monitoring system on criterion-referenced national tests cannot succeed. This is because the need to use strict criterion-referencing to sidestep the need for new instruments on every occasion falls foul of the fact that criterion-referencing in practice is operated by assessors as though it must take account of the difficulty of the task, which in turn can only be judged in relation to the candidates taking it. This is equivalent to reinterpreting the criteria for application to each new task, instead of applying the criteria unaltered no matter what the task.

Fourth, the designers of assessment systems need to build the human factor into those systems. All assessment is built on assessors' judgements; it is therefore essential to recognize the limits of reliability of those judgements. This means, for instance, restricting the precision of assessment scales to what is humanly possible, and not purporting to deliver a degree of precision which, given the human element, can only be spurious. It also means (and see again Wolf, 1993, 29) that assessors need to be supported not only with domain specifications, item requirements and scoring rules, but also (as hinted above) with training, exemplars, socialization into the 'interpretive community' and moderation.

Fifthly and finally, the debate over norm- versus criterion-referencing has been sterile. Pure norm-referencing is inadequate for any form of national assessment because it leaves too much to chance variation between markers. But strict criterion-referencing is no better off. We all need to recognize that there is a middle way, which also happens to be the most that is humanly achievable in this sphere, namely criteria- and exemplar-guided norm-referencing.

References

Brooks, G., Fernandes, C., Gorman, T. P. and Wells, I. (1995) *Reading Standards in Northern Ireland Revisited.* Slough: NFER.

Dearing, R. (1993) *Interim Report on the National Curriculum.* London: Department of Education and Science.

Department of Education and Science (1975) *A Language for Life* (The Bullock Report). London: HMSO.

Harding, P. (1993) 'Reduced to tiers'. *Times Educational Supplement.* 25 June, 20.

Mihail, R. (1995) 'Assessing reading in secondary schools: a Romanian perspective'. In: B. Raban-Bisby, G. Brooks and S. Wolfendale (eds) *Developing Language and Literacy* (Proceedings of the 1994 UK Reading Association conference). Stoke-onTrent, UK: Trentham Books for UKRA, 161–76.

Ruddock, G., Brooks, G., Harris, D., Salt, S., Putman, K. and Schagen, I. (1995) 'Evaluation of National Curriculum Assessment in English and Technology at Key Stage 3: 1993'. Final report from the NFER and Brunel University Evaluation of Key Stage National Curriculum Assessment in English and Technology 1993. Slough: NFER.

Wolf, A. (1993) *Assessment Issues and Problems in a Criterion-based System.* London: Further Education Unit.

8

CURRICULUM-BASED ASSESSMENT OF READING IN ENGLAND AND WALES

A national pilot study

Denis Vincent and Colin Harrison

Introduction

This chapter offers an account of a pilot study of a curriculum-based approach to the assessment of reading which was undertaken in England and Wales in the early 1990s. The assessment was government-commissioned, and was intended to measure children's performance related to the National Curriculum for English (the subject broadly comparable to that implied by the term 'Language Arts' in the USA), which was introduced in England and Wales in 1988.

During the period 1988–96, there was a good deal of turmoil in education in England and Wales: three different statutory National Curriculum documents, each defining in a different way how English should be taught, were put in place, and no fewer than seven different approaches to the National Assessment of English were piloted. British readers of this chapter will hardly need an account of these; however, an account of what happened during this period of hitherto unprecedented political intervention into curriculum and assessment permeates all the chapters in this book written by British authors, and for non-British readers, Harrison's (1995) paper in the *English Journal* offers further contextualization.

Prior to 1988, and the introduction of the first National Curriculum in England and Wales, there had never been nationally mandated testing of reading in the UK, except that based on stratified samples of the population. In the late 1980s, ministers in the Conservative government, whose stated intention was to enable parents to have access to full information on how every child was progressing within the school system, and subsequently to produce 'league tables' of schools' performance, introduced legislation to mandate nationwide tests, most of which would be administered by teachers, at ages seven, eleven, fourteen and sixteen. Assessment at age sixteen, the earliest point at which students may leave school in England, had been in place for many years, and was based on examinations in traditional school subjects such as mathematics, English, French, science and so on. But national assessment for every child at ages seven, eleven and fourteen was wholly new, and, understandably, the establishing of totally new procedures opened up heated debate within the educational community about what assessment approaches should be used, and what the overall objectives of those assessment procedures should be. The government's intention was to provide valid and reliable summative data on the standards achieved by school students; naturally, there were strong movements within teachers' organizations arguing for the place of formative assessment within the new arrangements. This tension was never fully resolved, essentially because close attention was never given to the question of whether the goals of simultaneously collecting formative and summative data on students are mutually exclusive.

Other tensions were also present at this time: many teachers in secondary schools who prepared students for the examinations at age sixteen were already familiar with and confident in using assessment procedures which made use of portfolio data collected under reasonably authentic classwork and homework conditions over a period of eighteen months. These teachers were keen to see similar status given to teacher-assessed data collected within what to them seemed much more authentic assessment conditions than those of a formal reading test or timed examination. Interestingly, as we shall see, although the government used the word 'tests' to describe the new assessment procedures, there did not seem to be a strong determination on the part of the government to develop new standardized group tests of reading of the type traditionally used for large-scale measurement exercises in the past.

These, then, were some of the contextual factors which frame the pilot study reported in this chapter.

The background to the pilot assessments

Pencil-and-paper group objective tests of reading have often been the preferred choice of administrators seeking to introduce large-scale assessment programmes. In the period up to 1988, some use of tests such as these was to be found in the UK, but their use was restricted to the monitoring of national or local standards longitudinally or for screening certain age groups of children in order to identify failing readers (Gipps et al., 1983; Gipps et al., 1995).

Although objective testing in the UK has never approached the degree of intensity noted by Pearson, DeStefano and García, and Hoffman in their chapters in this volume, the practice has been fairly well-established in many primary schools and, on a more limited scale, in some secondary schools in the UK. Administrators have been able to justify the use of objective group tests on the grounds that they minimize demands upon time or teacher skill to administer and mark. When the intended role of testing is extended to functions such as individual diagnosis or assessment of reading specified as a curriculum subject, such merits have to be weighed against the quality of the information that such a test can provide (Vincent, 1996). Hayward and Spencer, in their chapter in this volume, present an account of an alternative to the traditional psychometric approach to reading diagnosis.

When a National Curriculum was proposed for England and Wales the government placed considerable emphasis on the requirement that it should be assessed. The objective pencil-and-paper test retains an appeal to some administrators and politicians for this purpose, and such an approach was no doubt in the minds of some of those responsible for the political legislation: the public perception is that the results of such tests do not depend upon the expertise or knowledge of the test marker and that the system is fair and impartial. Against this must be set concerns that the assessment does justice to the content of what has been taught and that assessment methods enhance rather than distort teaching methods.

Such concerns were uppermost in the minds of the East London and Macmillan Assessment Group (ELMAG) team which won the contract to develop and pilot the National Curriculum assessments in English at Key Stage 3 (age fourteen) which are reported in this chapter. For the assessment of English (of which reading was an important part) the model initially developed by this team contrasted with conventional notions of testing by:

a) requiring assessments to be made in the course of a sustained programme of work;
b) placing reliance on the teacher's capacity to observe and interpret student performance as it occurred naturally in response to the curriculum activities.

Basis for assessment

The goal of the national assessments in all National Curriculum subjects was to place children on a ten-point scale which was assumed to represent progression through nine successive years of compulsory schooling (TGAT, 1988). The assessments were to be carried out at the ages of seven, eleven and fourteen. An advisory group of assessment experts set up to advise the government recommended that the assessments at these ages should be through a combination of teacher assessment and so-called 'standard assessment tasks'. These would use varied presentation and response modes (not only written) and would be broader and more flexible than conventional tests. They were to be, in the words of the advisory group, 'externally provided tasks and procedures designed to produce performance data on a national scale'.

Panels of subject experts were commissioned to specify the content of each national curriculum subject. English (DES, 1989) was divided into Speaking and Listening, Reading, Writing (essentially compositional skills) and Presentation (essentially spelling and handwriting). For each of the four sub-divisions the subject panel was also required to describe the attainments which corresponded to successive levels on the ten-point scale.

The specification for Reading was notable for the emphasis it placed on assessing through oral rather than written responses to texts. In general, the descriptions of the attainment were couched in terms which would have been very difficult to measure using conventional group objective testing. The Statements of Attainment, each notionally identifying criteria which were intended to represent achievement at one of the ten levels, were similar to many of the Standards documents produced by individual states in the USA: they tended to be general, were often complex, and multidimensional, and extremely difficult to apply, as this example demonstrates:

STATEMENT OF ATTAINMENT, READING, LEVEL 3:

[Students should be able to] Demonstrate, in talking about stories and poems, that they are beginning to use inference, deduction and previous reading experience to find and appreciate meanings beyond the literal.

(DES, 1989)

Statements of Attainment such as this one might be extraordinarily difficult to link reliably to student achievement, but they did reflect a set of values that many teachers of English found acceptable. The complexity within the statement, which makes it very difficult to use from a formal assessment point of view, was what made it attractive to many teachers, who liked the multidimensionality because it coincided with their preference for wholistic assessment.

The materials

The materials which the ELMAG group developed consisted of classroom activities for completion over successive English lessons, over a period of either three or five weeks. These activities were linked by theme or purpose and designed to allow students to demonstrate the highest level (on the ten-level scale) of which they were capable. They were intended to reflect good practice in National Curriculum English, for example by integrating reading with other written and oral activities for assessment purposes. The student activities included group work, discussion and oral presentations as well as individual reading and writing assignments. The texts to be read included fiction and non-fiction in a range of genres and some audio and video stimulus materials. The intention behind the choice of materials was to create 'opportunities' for assessment in a naturalistic context. This was consistent with the way reading was specified in the national curriculum and would, the team hoped, reflect good classroom practice rather than lead to its distortion.

Assessment was, unequivocally, to be curriculum-based and reflect practitioners' definitions of how English should be assessed. Practising teachers were closely involved in the work, either as full-time members of the development group or in working parties recruited to work on particular themes or topics. The materials were flexible. Teachers were free to amend, select, substitute or add to them as local classroom conditions dictated.

It should be made clear that the materials did not in themselves constitute items or tasks which 'tested' specific behaviours. The activities were however 'flagged' to indicate where opportunities for particular assessments were likely to arise. This certainly disappointed some teachers who were expecting tests against which students could 'pit their wits'.

The assessment model

The Assessment Guide prepared by the team to accompany the curriculum materials encouraged teachers to see themselves as important agents within the process of assessment. Implicit in this was the view that teachers would need to exercise pragmatism to make sense of the Statements of Attainment, although it was recognized from the outset that this was likely to be a difficult matter, since the statements themselves were difficult to relate reliably to student performance. To structure this a three-column 'Assessment Chart' was developed for each language skill (Speaking and Listening/ Reading/ Writing). This document was an attempt to build a link between the raw phenomenon of student behaviour and the way the skills were described in the official documentation.

The first column grouped the ten-level scale into three major developmental stages. The second identified National Curriculum levels at which important sub-skills or attributes were first mentioned in the statements. The third column presented summary 'snapshots' of each level.

For trial purposes teachers were asked to endorse or qualify each of the assessments which they recorded in relation to whether they felt 'tentative', 'reasonably confident' or 'very confident' in making the judgement. The team suspected this would be helpful for teachers, given that the National Curriculum was still in the process of being introduced into schools, and teachers might reasonably feel uneasy at making unqualified judgements at that stage. Moreover, it seemed a desirable feature for an assessment system that is based on individual judgements rather than objective measures.

A complication of the arrangements for National Curriculum assessment in England and Wales was the ambiguous status of teacher assessment. In general, politicians were willing to have teachers administer and record test scores, but they were less willing to have teachers' judgements of progress, as judged independently of this extended (but government-commissioned) assessment, included in the final decision about what level the student had achieved. The combination of this global assessment with judgements made on the basis of the specially-prepared assessment materials to derive an overall assessment remained contentious. For trialling purposes, teachers were asked to record assessments in all three English National Curriculum areas (Speaking and Listening/ Reading/ Writing), and then the final assessment was to be a balanced overall judgement given the evidence from teacher assessment and the ELMAG materials.

The need for evaluation

The proposed model was a considerable departure from conventional pencil-and-paper testing. To a great extent it reflected the views of the teacher educators and leading practitioners who worked on the project as to how, ideally, assessment should be done. It remained to be seen how far it was practicable as the mandatory way in which all teachers of English to 14-year-olds should assess their students. Some of the most important questions that needed to be answered about practicability and acceptability and some of the relevant evidence we obtained are presented in the following section.

Evaluation trials: some findings

The materials underwent evaluation in two large-scale pilot trials in 1990 and 1991. In 1991 three sets of assessment materials were trialed. Two of these were randomly distributed so schools took one of them. Schools were also randomly allocated to complete the work in either a three-week or five-week period. The findings reported here are from the 1991 pilot. The evaluation was wide-ranging using a variety of criteria, including questionnaires, interviews and classroom observation.

Could teachers carry out the teaching programme? By the various indicators used for the evaluation most schools found the operational demands of the exercise manageable; those allowed three weeks somewhat less so than those with five weeks. On average the three-week group reported spending an estimated total of thirteen hours on the work while the five-week group's mean estimate was 9.3 hours. Those who had taken part in previous trials reported somewhat less difficulty in managing the activities compared to other teachers and said they found it easier the second time round. Most felt their previous experience in portfolio-based assessment, and in assessment of 16-year-olds' oral performance, had been valuable. Manageability and convenience are not the same, however: most participants reported that they had spent more time than usual in preparing for the trial and that the workload during it was greater than normal. Case study evidence and supplementary school visits suggested that in at least some schools the exercise proved 'just about' manageable.

Eight schools failed to return data in time for statistical analyses but there were no non-returns because schools had found the exercise fundamentally unworkable.

Could teachers make the assessments? Teachers did manage to complete assessments for most students – this was not something that the ELMAG team had assumed would necessarily be the case. Assessment record sheets for a total of 9,092 students were returned from eighty-one schools. For reading, non-assessments were slightly higher (at 3.0 per cent) than for the other skills.

Were the assessments credible to the teachers making them? The above relative difficulty in assessing reading is reflected in other data. In questionnaire responses fewer than 35 per cent of teachers thought the assessment materials we had developed gave 'adequate opportunities to assess student performance against the statements of attainment' for reading although approaching 80 per cent felt that the materials were adequate for each of the other three language skills. The weaker position of reading was reflected, but much less strongly, in the 'confidence ratings' teachers recorded alongside their assessments on the ten-point scale. Although, on average, reading assessments were rated as 'reasonably confident', they attracted slightly more 'tentative' endorsements and fewer 'very confident' endorsements.

Further comparisons showed that teachers who took part in the previous trial endorsed fewer assessments as 'tentative' and made more 'reasonably confident' assessments of reading.

Overall, as a model for the way 14-year-olds should be formally assessed for National Curriculum purposes, most teachers (over 65 per cent) rated it 'fairly manageable' although less than 10 per cent rated it 'very manageable'. Somewhat over 25 per cent found it 'fairly' or 'very' unmanageable.

Were the teachers assessing reading? The statistical evidence suggested that teachers had some difficulty in conceptualizing reading as a construct process separate from other aspects of English. Intercorrelations between assessments made of each language skill under teacher assessment and on the assessment materials we had provided indicated some 'convergent' validity for each skill, 0.91 in the case of reading. For example, correlations between the assessments for reading on the pilot material and all other assessments ranged from 0.72 to 0.85.

These results must be evaluated in the light of the newness both of the curriculum and the method of assessment. Teachers were aware of this. Questionnaire data included the following comments:

I need to get used to the statements of attainment and levels.

[I am] . . . still trying to absorb the levels et cetera and it's helping me to understand the national curriculum better than I did before.

There's a lot more to Reading than I thought. A lot of 'tentatives' in that column.

The materials themselves came in for criticism. Questionnaire comments included:

Opportunities to assess reading (even if one can be very sure about what 'reading' means in the N.C. context) are really insufficient.

I was particularly disappointed in the opportunities offered for assessing Reading . . . the materials did not allow sustained discussion to occur . . .

(ELMAG, 1991)

Was the written guidance useful? The Assessment Guide was rated as easy to follow and helpful in preparing for and administering the prepared assessment materials. Over 80 per cent reported it as helpful in the crucial task of completing the assessments. The 'Assessment Charts' were rated favourably by well over 75 per cent of the questionnaire respondents and there were favourable comments volunteered during interviews. In line with other findings, the chart for Reading was rated least favourably of the four, attracting a larger percentage of 'unhelpful' ratings.

Interview comments also referred to the charts as helpful and useful (in one case 'a lifeline'). Teachers were also observed in schools to refer to the charts both during lessons and at the point of completing the assessment sheets. However, not all teachers found this attempt to bridge the void between classroom performance on the curriculum activities and the formally stated assessment criteria adequate. One interviewee praised the quality and educational value of the curriculum materials but said of the assessment process: 'I feel angry having to spend the time making it work. I had difficulty translating what I saw into National Curriculum levels.' Another teacher said: 'There was no step between the work and the assessment . . . just a big gap.'

How did they make the assessments? A protocol which requires the assessment of a largely private process going on in the head of one individual (the reader) using a second equally private process in the head of another person (the assessor) might be expected to attract such criticisms. We were of course able to gather plenty of evidence that teachers made as serious and considered assessments as they could. For example, teachers were observed to make running notes during or at the end of lessons. Their self-reports were also compelling: 'The process of keeping a running assessment is not easy – exhausting! – you have to be aware of so much. . . . I have spent a great deal of time reading the statements of attainment and trying to decide where these pupils fit.'

Twelve teachers kept 'audio logs', using cassette recorders to think aloud into as they made their assessments. Transcripts of these confirmed that teachers were attempting thoughtful, honest and detached assessments, also showing the need to take account of existing knowledge of students:

> Reading: an eight – just let me refer again to the booklet. Now level eight says 'compare literary texts'; she didn't do any of that [during the assessed programme] at all but she's quite able to give a considered opinion of features of non-literary texts. In her work in researching the history of . . . she talked very convincingly about what she was reading and she read critically . . . she can do the re-combining of information located and retrieved from these texts, too, because it's not simply a matter of copying out with her – she actually uses the material in a creative way herself.
>
> He was given a two for his reading initially: he can read aloud using context and phonic cues, he does listen and respond to stories – and poems – not that he has done so in this particular project. He can read silently and can find some information from books and certainly can devise questions to be answered from reference books – so far as the reference aspects are concerned he does and has achieved level three although he would not achieve these, I don't think, as far as the literary side of things, because he finds it difficult to move beyond literal meaning when talking about stories.

It is worth pausing to ask why such accounts should be considered a less acceptable form of evidence for a student's attainment than the result of a standardized test.

Did the teachers find the curriculum-based model credible? Many teachers received the materials and assessment model with some relief. They had feared an approach less attuned to their current practices. Yet, not all teachers were satisfied. In particular, there were reservations about the degree of flexibility and scope for teacher discretion in the way the programmes of work were to be managed and assessed. Some trial teachers were certainly concerned that the assessment would not be 'standard' for all 14-year-olds but would depend upon highly local factors, unlike a set test/examination which would be the same for all testees: 'I can't see where "standard" applies to work with such flexibility.' Such concerns about the reliability of the assessments are understandable. The pilot did not include the various moderation procedures and other checks to calibrate teachers' assessments which would be a necessary part of the final assessment system.

Circumstantial evidence in favour of the 'standardness' of the approach was provided by the distribution of assessments made over the ten-level scale on the two sets of prepared assessment materials which were randomly allocated to schools. They were remarkably similar: the difference in proportion of assessments at any one level never exceeded 1.4 per cent.

Ninety-two teachers were interviewed near or at the end of the pilot. They were asked whether they would have preferred 'a short written examination' to the model trialled. Only eleven teachers answered with a clear 'yes'. The remaining eighty-one answers could be loosely categorized as either clear rejection ('no – it wouldn't have done my children justice'), rejection 'on balance' ('On practical grounds it would be easier. Educationally I won't support that'), or abstentions ('Depends on what the exam is. I like the idea of continuing assessment but I have not learned much about our pupils that I didn't know before').

Although the question was not asked in the questionnaire, a small number of teachers did take the opportunity to express disappointment at the format of the assessment and to voice a preference for a formal test or examination. Against such views must be set those of the panel of subject experts who were asked to evaluate the proposed model who, while expressing reservations about workload and manageability, were generally supportive of the overall assessment model.

'Elaborate Nonsense'

Just as the second pilot year was about to commence the senior government minister responsible for Education dismissed the assessment materials that were about to be trialled as 'elaborate nonsense'. The development contracts were terminated and a new specification for tests for English was drawn up. This stressed that the tests were not to be 'extended curriculum materials' but 'straightforward' objective tests prepared at a series of 'tiers' corresponding with restricted ranges of levels on the ten-point scale. At the higher tiers a Shakespeare play was specified as a set comprehension text for Reading.

An innovative classroom-based approach to national assessment was curtailed before it could be fully put in place; the Prague Spring was over.

Reflections

The model of assessment practice developed by the ELMAG team had aimed to accord with secondary English curriculum experts' ideals of best practice. This was a preference for assessment as a longitudinal process in which the reflective teacher accumulates evidence to reach a view, often tentative, on a student's progress and attainments. This proved a politically fragile model which was rejected even before the (extensive) evaluation report was completed.

This chapter began by noting that most administrator-initiated assessment schemes appeal because they minimalize disruption to teaching, additional workload and costs and that they favour instruments which are not overly dependent upon teacher skill or judgement. By contrast, the approach reported here went to the other extreme in making significant demands upon teachers and placing considerable trust in their judgement. Although there were problems, it is remarkable that such an ambitious model worked so well at such an early stage.

Not all teachers welcomed the burden that accompanied a model that so fully respected their professional competence. However, the subsequent history of National Curriculum assessment in England and Wales suggests it might have been better to persevere on this basis. In 1993 (the first year for mandatory assessments for 14-year-olds) all but a few schools boycotted the tests in all subjects. This boycott was led by English teachers, opposing the tests as educationally unsound (see also the account of Brooks, this volume). The majority of schools did so again in 1994, although in 1995 and 1996 opposition became more muted.

Lessons for the future: psychometrics and psychology of teacher assessment

Assessment in which professional judgement is central, but which is to have a national or at least public standing, has many obstacles to overcome. Firstly, more needs to be known about the dynamics of teacher judgement. Our findings suggest this would be a fruitful quest. If the teacher is to be the 'instrument' of assessment then the psychometric properties of this instrument need to be laid out. There are some grounds for optimism. For example, it is a commonplace finding in standardized reading test development that teachers' class rankings correspond substantially with rank order of test scores. However, as our 1991 trial results showed, there remains some question as to how well secondary teachers were able to differentiate the construct of reading from other language modes.

This points to a second area where more needs to be known: the psychology of reading assessment. Assessment is, after all, as much a behaviour as reading itself but it has been little studied. Ironically this particular behaviour shares with reading itself the property of being private and internal to the individual assessor. The audio logs kept by teachers taking part in the 1991 trial suggest one way forward; these sought to record the assessment process in action rather than retrospectively. There is a parallel with the use of 'think aloud' protocols for assessing reading itself.

The teachers we studied clearly varied in their definitions and their expectations of the assessment process. Gipps *et al.* (1995) present evidence for a typology in the way teachers of 7-year-olds carried out National Curriculum Assessment: intuitives (sub-grouped as 'children's needs ideologists' or 'tried and tested practitioners'); evidence gatherers; systematic planners (sub-grouped as ' systematic assessors' or 'systematic integrators'). The differences between these models of assessment could have implications for the way in which the assessment process itself is designed and disseminated. In retrospect, it seems likely that (had time and resources allowed) a comparable exercise would have been useful with the sample of teachers of English at fourteen years.

The need for a coherent theory of fluent reading

The quality of teachers' assessments will be constrained by what they know (and indeed believe) about reading and by the models of reading available as the basis for assessment. There are well-developed psychological models of early reading and the initial development of reading skill. However, psychology has less to offer the teacher of reading at secondary school level, particularly with regard to helping readers respond to full-length literary texts. There have been some provocative insights. For example, schema theory has provided us with evidence about the way readers process new texts in the light of their existing knowledge and expectations but this is far short of a comprehensive model which might inform the planning and design of a reading curriculum.

In practice this has relied upon expert opinion to define its content. The problem is to determine the extent to which reading can be defined by committee. A committee is no doubt satisfactory for advising on matters of value: should there be a canon of set books? Should such a canon include Shakespeare? Is it desirable to include non-print media? Is a film a 'text'? Such expert committees are on weaker ground when defining the constituents of the reading process. There are dangers in quasi-psychologizing, but we will continue to rely upon this until more scientific methods manage to overtake or falsify it. Better use must be made of introspection and subjectivity in the meantime. The first task would be to specify ways in which it might be done effectively.

As a starting suggestion, it might be argued that the process will have to be iterative, that is to say that whatever analysis of reading is posited, it would only be a starting point. As teachers began to apply it to real-life situations a redefinition would emerge on the basis of increased understanding of what good readers really do with texts.

The future for curriculum-based reading assessment

At the time of writing it seems unlikely that the assessment model described here will be reinstated for National Curriculum Assessment in England and Wales. It might seem to some that such a fate was inevitable. Yet, it is interesting that similar approaches have managed to flourish and enjoy greater administrator acceptance in the USA, where standardized objective testing is also far more deeply entrenched (see the chapters by Pearson and his collaborators, and those by Hoffman, Falk and Salinger, in this volume). Are there lessons to be learned by comparison with these experiences?

One of the problems encountered by the ELMAG team was the absence of any 'visible' testing in a form which would meet lay conceptions of what a test should be (i.e. pencil and paper; worked individually and silently; imposed time limit; objective marking with no scope for teachers to obtain flattering results). Such expectations are too widely prevalent to be ignored. There will be no scope for a new paradigm unless teachers take more control of the old one and are seen to use it alongside whatever other methods they adopt. If teachers for their part were to find the model of assessment acceptable, certain further conditions would have to be met. Most importantly, a choice of materials and themes would have to be offered. The facility to opt out of the exercise when exceptional local conditions made this necessary would also be desirable.

In an ideal world . . .

Could the approach described in this chapter have any role outside national or large-scale mandatory assessment programmes? Assessment and testing have never been a prominent part of the culture of secondary English teaching in the UK, and while it continues to be imposed (in a form which few assessment experts in England regard as valid or reliable) for the prime purpose of establishing national school league tables, this is unlikely to change.

There are always 'niches' which can be proposed for packages of assessment tasks of the type that were developed. For example, as part of a post-training programme, recently qualified teachers might be required to use them as a way of reaching a recognized level of proficiency in assessment. Groups of teachers might agree to operate such assessment tasks over a given period as a way of developing consensus and consistency in their assessment of pupils' work. For purposes of this sort the materials described here would be much enhanced by the inclusion of examples of pupils' performance on the tasks.

More generally, however, the model is relevant to the way a self-regulating profession might operate, for example, to develop greater comparability of standards and expectations across the profession of English teaching and to be seen to self-evaluate and, indeed, to provide an acceptable professional basis on which to inform pupils and their parents about progress and attainment in reading.

References

Department of Education and Science (1989) *English for Ages 5 to 16*. London: HMSO.

East London and Macmillan Assessment Group (1991) 'English Key Stage 3 Report on 1991 Pilot of Standard Assessment Tasks'. Dagenham: East London and Macmillan Assessment Group for the School Examinations and Assessment Council.

Ehri, L. (1995) 'Phases of development in learning to read words by sight'. *Journal of Research in Reading*, 18(2): 118–27.

Gipps, C. and Goldstein, H. (1983) *Monitoring Children: An Evaluation of the Assessment of Performance Unit*. London: Heinemann Educational.

Gipps, C., Steadman, S., Goldstein, H. and Stierer, B. (1983) *Testing Children: Standardised Testing in Schools and LEAs*. London: Heinemann Educational.

Gipps, C., Brown, M., McCallum, B. and McAllister, S. (1995) *Intuition or Evidence?* Buckingham: Open University Press.

Harrison, C. (1995) 'Youth and white paper: the politics of literacy assessment in the United Kingdom'. *English Journal*, 84(2) (February): 115–19.

Task Group on Assessment and Testing (1988) *Report of the Task Group on Assessment and Testing*. London: Department of Education and Science.

Vincent, D. (1996) 'Assessment by classroom teachers'. In J. Beech and C. Singleton, (eds) *Psychological Assessment of Reading*. London: Routledge.

9

TAKING A CLOSER LOOK

A Scottish perspective on reading assessment

Louise Hayward and Ernie Spencer

'One of the very few certainties we have from educational research is that when teachers really believe in something they will make it work.'

J.E. Kemp *Sigma: A Process-Based Approach to Staff Development*

Introduction

During the University of Nottingham seminar 'New Paradigms in Reading Assessment', which was the setting in which this book was conceived, colleagues described the research issues being faced in the assessment of reading in countries such as the USA, Norway, Australia and the countries within the UK. With each presentation the impact of different political and cultural contexts became increasingly clear. It seemed that assessment initiatives in a particular country were influenced significantly by the researchers' perceptions of what was possible and that perceptions of the possible varied quite significantly. In each country projects had been identified from within a fairly narrow band of possibility suggested by culturally influenced definitions of assessment. The predominant assessment model within each project pointed towards differing perceptions of the central purposes of assessment and differing expectations of the role of the teacher. The focus of the seminar was new paradigms in reading assessment: but what would constitute a new paradigm and what might the factors be which could influence whether or not a new paradigm was successful?

While a new paradigm might be conceptualized in a number of different ways, it is likely to be culturally determined. A new paradigm might represent completely new thinking by those working within a culture, significant modification of current assessment purposes, priorities and methods, or the transfer of ideas from one cultural context to another.

What are likely to be important factors in determining whether or not a new paradigm is successful? The cultural context is crucial. Anything which is seen to be too far away from present practice is unlikely to succeed. It would also be important for the new paradigm to meet a perceived need rather than be seen as an additional burden on teachers. It must be credible, practical, 'grounded' in teachers' ideas about learning, teaching and assessment; and yet it must go beyond the level of the 'good idea'.

An important characteristic of a successful new paradigm is that it should extend or expand a particular culture's existing expectations, encourage the belief that the quality of learning experiences can be improved and offer a new vision of the possible. Views about assessment purposes and priorities, such as selection, accountability, support for learning, would be influential in determining the kind of new paradigm appropriate for a particular culture.

A new Scottish paradigm

This chapter describes how the authors have tried to take account of culture and context in their work in Scotland. A number of us, working within higher education and within the Inspectorate have been trying to develop a new paradigm in the assessment of reading by supporting teachers as they 'Take a Closer Look' at children's reading and work with them to identify appropriate 'next steps'. The aim of the programme is to encourage and develop teachers' confidence and professionalism as users of 'assessment as part of teaching'. In terms of the 'postmodernist' ideas about assessment discussed in the opening chapter (Harrison, Bailey and Dewar, this volume), we are seeking to place responsive assessment at the centre of a national assessment system which has as twin central aims support for every pupil and self-referencing by each school against a set of defined levels of attainment. This type of assessment may also provide information which can be used for wider purposes of accountability.

The project was instigated as a Ministerial response to a request made by teachers and brought together policy-makers, researchers, teachers and teacher trainers. As will be discussed in detail below, the Government initiated its Education 5–14 Development Programme in 1989. Critical aspects of these national guidelines were the suggestions that assessment information would come from three main sources:

- from day to day classroom activities; this would be the major source of information;
- from special tasks and tests used occasionally by teachers for specific purposes, e.g., to find out what children know before beginning a topic or, at the end of a topic, to identify what has been learned, and
- from taking a closer look at what pupils are learning and the ways in which they are learning, to identify appropriate next steps.

Although they welcomed these guidelines, recognizing the principles as akin to their own philosophy of teaching, teachers still felt diffident about practical action. They expressed the need for additional advice, especially about the third source of information, 'Taking a Closer Look'.

Further, even though many primary teachers responded positively to the type of assessment proposed in the Assessment 5–14 guidelines, they lacked confidence in the practical application of it and awareness of how assessment information can be obtained in the ordinary course of classwork. There was a tendency to think of assessment and testing as synonymous and to assume that taking a closer look would involve 'diagnostic tests'. This association in teachers' minds of formative assessment and specifically designed tests was one reason for dissatisfaction which arose in relation to the National Tests. Though these tests were intended to serve as confirmation of teachers' occasional summative assessments of pupils' levels of attainment, they were criticized as lacking diagnostic potential.

Acknowledging the fact that National Tests could provide only limited diagnostic information, the Minister for Education responded to teachers' request for help in 'taking a closer look' by establishing a project to take forward diagnostic work in English Language, Mathematics and Science. The Diagnostic Procedures project was a collaborative one, involving the Scottish Office Education Department, represented by Her Majesty's Inspectors of Schools (HMI); the research community, represented principally by the Scottish Council for Research in Education (SCRE), which was already active in the area; and the teaching profession (staff from Colleges of Education and teachers in schools). Thus, teachers' request for additional advice led to the project described in this chapter, the initial intent of which was to develop an initiative which would be part of the government policy framework, informed by findings from reading research and wider educational research, related to teachers' practice, and designed to be used in classrooms.

There are four key elements in the story of the Scottish diagnostic procedures package: (1) the outcome of the project, the package itself; (2) the educational culture into which the ideas would emerge; (3) the numerous research influences on the project; and (4) the significant influence of practical work using the procedures in classrooms. This chapter describes the package itself and the cultural factors surrounding its use, along with a brief discussion of key research and practical influences.

Diagnostic procedures or reading – the package

'Taking a Closer Look at Reading' consists of three parts and a separate booklet of examples of the procedures in practical use. The parts are as follows.

Part 1: Taking a closer look at learning to read

In this first section, diagnostic assessment is established as an aspect assessment as part of teaching, what in the United States is called 'assessment in the service of teaching'. Thus, the procedures are set within the context of learning and teaching. The complexity of the reading process is emphasized, thus reinforcing the need for diagnosis to be a dynamic and interactive process between teacher and learner. Diagnostic Procedures are not context-free but build on teachers' knowledge of the pupils and the pupils' own ideas of what is important. The process relies heavily on teachers' developing professionalism and on raising levels of pupils' awareness of their own learning. Its aim is to take a close look at pupils' learning – at exactly how they are dealing with what they are doing, and at strengths and needs in relation to particular tasks or learning targets. Exploration of pupils' thinking and reactions enables the teacher to tailor teaching to individual needs. Teachers are encouraged to attend to three specific areas: (1) learners' motivation; (2) their previous experiences and present abilities; and (3) effective tasks and flexible teaching methods.

Learners' motivation   The quality of learning will depend on how pupils view themselves as learners. Do students demonstrate confident self-awareness as successful learners or are they not expecting success? The growth of motivation to read, of a desire to 'make the meaning' from what they read, to know 'what it's about', 'what happens next', and 'how to find out' is crucial. Good conditions for effective teaching of reading skills include the provision of attractive books and discussion of its pleasures.

Previous experience and present abilities   Most children already have extensive experience with spoken language, and many have a relatively wide awareness of print before they come to school. Effective teaching of reading, therefore, builds on pre-existing awareness of language and print; it gives pupils the chance to learn with and from others (e.g., through paired reading, home school links) and gradually uses wide reading experience to help pupils become aware of literary genres, structures and styles.

Effective tasks and flexible teaching methods   How pupils interpret and carry out a wide range of reading tasks yields evidence and ideas about next steps. Some evidence will be found in written work, but more will come from observing and discussing with the pupils and from encouraging them to reflect on their work and think about how progress might best be made. It is important that pupils play a role in determining what to read and for what purposes; it is also important that teachers propose purposeful tasks for pupils to engage in and provide guidance as to what to look for in particular texts. Teachers must also recognize that reading at any level of

, the full range of 'literal', 'inferential' and 'evalua-
an integrated process (Lunzer *et al.*, 1979).

art 2: Diagnostic procedures in reading

ie 'Diagnostic Procedures' first seeks to demonstrate that
nent is essentially application of the teachers' professional
1en discusses the nature of evidence to be found in many
day   sroom activities and the identification of areas of exploration
and develop..ent of pupils' 'growth points'. The main focus for the procedures is on how the pupil is interpreting and carrying out a given task and,
while some evidence will be available from the consideration of the finished
'product', more will come from observation of and discussion with the
pupil. Learning to read is a complex process, and because children differ
greatly in their approach to learning to read, it is not possible to propose
a set of specific diagnostic procedures which would always be applied in
the same way and in the same order. Only the teacher, whenever possible
in partnership with the pupil and working from the pupil's own thinking,
can decide how best to gather evidence for a particular pupil, appraise it
and explore what action is most fruitful to pursue. The teacher's goal is to
help the pupils themselves to become more clearly aware of what they are
trying to achieve in a reading task, of their strengths and skills and of
strategies they can use.

Evidence of what is happening during reading may be obtained in a
number of different ways, from the day-to-day activities observing pupils,
considering what they say or write, from questioning, and from special
tasks, including tests. The 'Diagnostic Procedures' manual explains that
one effective way of focusing on something the pupil can deal with is to
observe and discuss with three questions in mind:

- What is being achieved successfully?
  - from the pupil's perspective
  - from the teacher's perspective
- What is being attempted, perhaps without full success?
- What skills does the pupil need?

In addition to questions posed about individual pupils, groups of pupils
working together supportively with clearly defined criteria for success can
also offer helpful insights into 'next steps' for themselves and others. A
crucial element in diagnostic assessment is teachers working with the pupils
to enable them to move on. This involves the identification of the most
helpful next steps and strategies either in continuing work on the current
task or in setting the next tasks. The third section suggests various types
of possible actions to continue pupils' growth.

Part 3: Promoting success in reading: the procedures in practice

This section sets out the Procedures for practical use. They are structured in a way that will enable teachers to internalize them and integrate them into their normal practice. To this end four key Areas for Exploration are suggested, as types of 'advance organizer' for teachers' thinking. These are derived from research and from grounded theory developed by working in classrooms with teachers and learners. The four areas are:

- Attitude and motivation – to reading in general and to the particular task being undertaken.
- Decoding – how the children recognize words and sentences.
- Pursuit of meaning – how the children learn to use prior experience and all the context cues in the text to construct their own perception of what is being communicated.
- Awareness of the author's language use – how the children learn how the author has chosen words, images and their structures to convey meaning, suggest ideas, achieve effects.

Though these four aspects of reading are in practice interrelated, it may be useful to think of them separately in analysing and building on pupils' strengths and in identifying and prioritizing appropriate next steps. All four areas for exploration will be relevant in any kind of reading task. For each there is a continuum of complexity, unfamiliarity and difficulty as the texts become more advanced. Teachers' emphasis, however, should be on improving reading in respect of just one or two aspects of one or two of these areas, identifying 'growth points' which the pupil can develop. Asking pupils to focus on too many areas at once is likely to lead to very little real learning.

Within each area for exploration a number of possible 'questions to consider' have been identified. Appropriate questions can provide a more detailed map of possible aspects to explore in finding out from pupils how they are thinking and what they consider. Sometimes, too, a lot can be learned about pupils' thinking by asking them to identify key questions about a reading task. Linked to the questions to consider are suggestions for helping children to improve their reading. Teachers or, better, teachers and pupils in partnership may wish to consider these as they decide on an appropriate course of action. In the identification of good Next Steps it is important to recognize the pupil as a valuable source of evidence. Which Next Steps does the learner think are likely to be most effective? What does the child think will help him or her to read better? The suggestions for action must be set in the context of each particular pupil's reading development and related to the pupil's other learning experiences. Skills developed in particular tasks will not transfer easily to other contexts unless

141

bridges are built and the learners can not only 'see' them but are able to explain them to themselves and others.

To give some sense of the more specific suggestions provided, Figure 9.1 offers an example of one Question for Consideration and its associated Next Steps for one Area for Exploration. This pattern recurs for each of the questions raised in each broad area.

This, then, gives an outline of the work of the project on 'Taking a Closer Look at Reading'. But how did we come to shape it in this way? What were the cultural features which we had to consider in order to promote the possibility of this becoming a successful new paradigm? How was research to be put to really effective use in classrooms?

Figure 9.1 Area for exploration: awareness of author's use of language

Some Questions for Consideration	Possible Next Steps
• *Are the pupils able to appreciate how the author has used particular language to create particular effects?*	*If you wish to encourage awareness of the effects of particular language use it might be appropriate to:*
	• offer a piece of text where various devices (e.g., italics, bold, print, underlining) have been used and ask pupils to discuss possible reasons for this and whether or not they think that the use of these devices is helpful
	• invite pupils to identify advertisements which they like, to discuss the reasons for their choice, and to describe ways in which the person who created the advertisement tries to encourage people to like it and therefore buy the product
	• ask pupils to choose a piece of text and to account for their reactions by referring to the text – what makes a particular part sad, funny, shocking, tense?
	• ask pupils to identify a story which they would describe as, for example, a ghost story or a love story or a horror story, and to identify the reasons why they would describe the text in this way (perhaps giving headings such as 'choice of words', 'descriptions of characters', 'parts of the story')
	• ask pupils to experiment with the mood or atmosphere of a text by substituting different words (in a 'cloze'-type passage with adverbs and adjectives omitted, for example) to achieve quite different effects

Influences: pedagogical research, reading research and classroom experience

The reality of educational development is that research seldom has a single or even dominant direct influence on schools' practice. It can, however, have significant influence in combination with other critical determinants of what teachers and students do. The story of 'Taking a Closer Look' is one of the development of a context in which practical, day-to-day teaching and assessment can benefit from research and from educational ideas informed by research. Before considering the major factors that influenced the context into which assessment changes were introduced, we will discuss the key research influences on the Diagnostic Procedures.

The content of the Diagnostic Procedures package was shaped by numerous ideas derived from the 'canon of pedagogical research in the last twenty years or so'. Fundamental to the approach taken was research by Vygotsky (1978). Of particular importance is his concept of the 'zone of proximal development', that is, the area in which an individual child's own spontaneous concepts and 'common sense' understanding of the world meet concepts that are presented in school. The development of new learning emerges from the individual's thinking about the world as modified by the new, more comprehensive ideas, and this development of understanding is facilitated by a process of 'internal dialogue' in which the learner mentally compares and 'discusses' his or her 'old' and 'new' knowledge. Teaching can aid understanding by engaging the learner in discussion which makes explicit the links and the differences between 'old' and 'new' concepts and which helps the learner become aware of her or his own learning processes. The emphasis in 'Taking a Closer Look' on dialogue with the pupil, in order to help him or her make explicit how the reading task is being perceived and how it is being addressed, represents an application to the development of reading skills of the concept of the 'zone of proximal development'.

Other key ideas from the whole body of background research also came into play in the Diagnostic Procedures package. These included recognition of the importance of the following:

- Motivating children to attain a higher level of competence (e.g. Bruner, 1983; Entwistle, 1988)
- Students' gaining self-awareness as learners; (e.g. Nisbet and Shucksmith, 1986; Rogers, 1983)
- Teachers' ascertaining how each pupil is understanding the task (s)he is undertaking and of explaining the intended point of it in ways (s)he can grasp (e.g. Donaldson, 1978; Meek, 1988)
- Teachers' awareness of the learners' previous relevant knowledge and experience and of talking with pupils, individually or in groups, to

enable both teacher and pupil to identify any misconceptions and to provide the teacher with the information necessary to modify teaching aims or methods; (e.g. Arnold and Simpson, 1984; Jones, 1992)

• Teachers' suggesting to or negotiating with the learner a limited, manageable number of clear short term aims, which are central to the attainment of key overall learning outcomes; (e.g. Drever, 1987)

• Discussions with pupils to bring to light their ways of thinking and of approaching tasks, and to develop pupils' own awareness of their learning strategies; (e.g. Arnold and Simpson, 1984).

Other significant ideas that influenced the development of the Diagnostic Procedures included the need for teachers to be versatile and to respond to different learning styles and the importance of collaborating with pupils to find the most effective way of progressing (e.g. Entwistle, 1988). Equally powerful was awareness of the importance of providing help to learners where necessary to develop more effective approaches to learning and to building on their preferred styles (e.g. Nisbet and Shucksmith, 1986).

The most powerful influences from reading research came from the University of Nottingham's 'Reading to Learn' work (Lunzer *et al.*, 1984). Several important findings of those studies confirmed the appropriateness of moves which had already been occurring in Scotland in the 1970s to help teachers design school examinations with valid questions about reading. The essence of the advice from the Nottingham work was to ensure that pupils read whatever kind of text with a clear purpose or purposes in mind and to design assessment questions or tasks specifically to test the achievement of the reading purposes. This 'purposes' approach is strongly represented in 'Taking a Closer Look' (1995) as a key element in pupils' and teachers' general orientation to reading and in the form of quite specific purposes for reading. Also influential was the Nottingham critique of reading comprehension 'subskill' hierarchies, which suggested that there is little validity in 'hierarchies' of reading skills in which, for example, inference is a 'higher order' skill than literal comprehension. Our package is based on the assumption that literal, inferential and evaluative interpretations of text can and usually do occur when any reader reads any text.

From Marie Clay's work on reading recovery (1985) we recognized the importance of eclecticism in teacher strategy selection, and that what matters is close individual attention to find whatever approach is best for a particular pupil. As with the strategy adopted in 'Taking a Closer Look', Clay's programme also recognizes the centrality of encouraging development of teachers' own personal reflection about their pupils' reading and about their own teaching.

Another set of powerful influences on 'Taking a Closer Look' came from our classroom based research and subsequent piloting in schools. These valuable experiences reassured the project team that teachers recognized the need for and the validity of 'assessment as part of teaching' and welcomed ideas on how to 'take a closer look'. Our work with teachers in classrooms led to programme modifications as well, such as increasing the extent to which the procedures are constructivist in nature and including within the suggestions for 'next steps' many more suggestions for involving pupils in assessing their own success in tasks and identifying their own proposals for future developments.

Most significantly, classroom work led us to change our original approach, which had involved the development of diagnostic tests intended to indicate whether or not a child had attained a particular target. Changes were made for three reasons. First, although these tests did not seem stressful, they were not effective in encouraging engagement with texts. For example, some pupils were not able to identify the main ideas from a text when responding to test items, but when asked to tell the story to a friend accurately recounted the main ideas. Second, the test information seemed to run counter to one of the central principles of the 5–14 Programme, that teachers should identify pupils' strengths and development needs. The tests focused attention rather on what pupils could not do. Finally, tests appeared to lead teachers towards the collection of information, the completion of the test becoming an end in itself rather than providing evidence to inform action. The development of the procedures as a framework to support teachers' professional judgement with strong emphasis on taking informed action was strongly influenced by classroom experiences.

A receptive context

We come now to the important question of how an initiative incorporating these research influences was to be implemented successfully in the Scottish context. The context is, of course, multi-faceted; but three major factors can be identified: (1) the general professional culture of Scottish teachers; (2) the improvements in assessment practice evidenced over the previous fifteen or so years and occasioned by the requirements of the Scottish Examination Board's (SEB) Standard Grade certification at 16+ (along with advice and exemplification for schools from SEB, the Scottish Consultative Council on the Curriculum and HM Inspectorate); and (3) the current Government policy directing the curriculum and assessment reform, Education 5–14.

The strong professionalism of the teaching force is a crucial factor in Scottish education. It is a highly qualified, wholly graduate body, which has shown itself to be capable of planning and implementing teaching for all the major curricular and assessment policies of recent times. An increasing proportion of teachers possess post-graduate educational qualifications within national and regional frameworks. There is growing awareness among teachers of theory underpinning practice and of the importance of personal and collaborative reflection and planning to help their pupils most effectively, within the framework of national curricular guidance. One particular aspect of teachers' professionalism which is relevant to this initiative is the existence in Scottish schools of increasing numbers of trained Learning Support specialists, whose role includes, as well as interaction with pupils on an individual basis, cooperative teaching and consultation with other teachers about ways of presenting the curriculum and of working with pupils which enable them to understand and learn more effectively. A well planned and fully implemented learning support policy in a school, whether primary or secondary, increases awareness among teaching staff of the importance for each individual pupil's progress of a focus on her/his particular strengths, needs and ways of learning.

Another factor enhancing teachers' concern to develop each individual pupil's potential is the widely held philosophy of primary school teaching stemming from the 'Primary Memorandum' of 1965. This influential national guideline document encouraged primary teachers to provide a broad, balanced and integrated curriculum and to employ teaching approaches which take account of individual pupils' characteristics and potential. Although the quality and range of teaching and assessment approaches vary from school to school, almost all Scottish primary teachers are committed to the philosophy of the Primary Memorandum. They are therefore likely to feel well disposed towards assessment guidance and Diagnostic Procedures which can help them improve individual pupils' ability to progress, whatever their current attainments.

The Scottish Certificate of Education Standard Grade assessment arrangements have enhanced secondary teachers' professionalism in respect of assessment. 'Standard Grade' is the name given to both the courses and the assessment and certification system for pupils aged fourteen to sixteen. This system allows every pupil to obtain a national qualification at one of three levels of award, Foundation, General or Credit. It is a criterion-referenced system: there are 'grade-related criteria', descriptions of expected attainment, for six grades, two for each of the three levels of award. The system also involves a significant amount of internal assessment by teachers, contributing to pupils' certification. One important outcome of the introduction of Standard Grade has been that almost all secondary school teachers are now used to comparing pupils' performance against specified criteria, rather than creating a rank order on a test and allocating grades according to position on such a list. Many teachers use the grade-related criteria formatively, explaining to pupils why their work is attaining a particular grade and discussing with them how they might progress towards the criteria for the next grade above. In many cases, subject departments have extended the Standard Grade type of assessment into the first two years of secondary school (aged twelve to fourteen).

While it cannot be claimed that effective assessment as part of teaching occurs in all secondary schools' courses, there is no doubt that Standard Grade and its associated staff development opportunities have made the concept widely known. Further, they have stimulated a good deal of assessment activity focusing on pupils' strengths and weaknesses, including 'feedback discussions' with individual pupils and often some form of pupil self-assessment.

The third important factor in the creation of a receptive context for Diagnostic Procedures has been the Government's Education 5–14 Development Programme, begun in 1989 and still in progress. Among the concerns which this programme has sought to address were: the varying breadth and quality of the curriculum offered in primary schools (notwithstanding the very good provision in many schools, in accordance with national guidance based on the 1965 Primary Memorandum); differences in the amount and quality of assessment occurring in different schools; the relatively poor quality of information given to parents, both about the curriculum and about their children's progress and attainment; and poor liaison between secondary and primary schools, in relation to both curricular continuity and amount, type and quality of assessment information passed on when pupils transfer to the secondary school at age twelve. The programme also aims to ensure high standards of attainment through effective teaching, including good use of assessment information to take action with the pupil on 'next steps' in learning. Here again a major aim of the programme has been to spread existing good practice across all schools in the country.

The 'Education 5–14' guidelines included the following key elements:

- For each area of the curriculum, a framework of five broad levels of attainment (A to E in ascending order).
- An assessment system incorporating detailed advice and staff development materials on assessment as part of teaching. Teachers are asked to identify what has been attained and strengths and development needs for each pupil. Development needs may include both strengths to be built on or difficulties to be overcome. Teachers are also invited, where possible in collaboration with pupils, to identify specific 'next steps' which offer practical advice as to how progress might be made. In planning a particular block of teaching, teachers and pupils should have a limited number of key learning aims, related to the curriculum requirements, of course, but also addressing needs identified by assessment. These aims should be shared with parents where possible.
- The assessment system also involves occasional (perhaps once or twice a year) summative evaluation by the teacher of the whole body of a pupil's work in a curricular area. This assessment of the level at which a pupil is working should then be confirmed (for English Language and Mathematics only) by a test drawn from the national test bank.

- A system of reporting to parents which identifies the pupil's specific strengths and development needs, proposes 'next steps' in learning and teaching and invites parents to respond, if they wish, and to suggest points to be discussed with the teacher at a meeting.

The national guidelines, 'Assessment 5–14', are structured in a way designed to emphasize the integration of assessment in the complex cycle of learning and teaching. Their sub-title, 'Improving the Quality of Learning and Teaching', further reinforces this idea. As with the earlier guidance on Standard Grade, Assessment 5–14 was, as far as possible, kept free of technical language. Since it was recognized that 'Improving the Quality of Learning and Teaching' depended on developing teachers' professionalism, the documentation drew from research not only on assessment and learning but also on staff development and institutional development.

Teachers, then, were to be active partners in assessment with pupils and parents. For assessment to support pupils' learning it should be recognized as an integral part of teaching and not an adjunct to it, an essential part of an effective teacher's repertoire of skills. Teachers were to be active assessors, taking action on the basis of assessment information from day-to-day work, rather than being mere suppliers and recipients of information about general levels of attainment. The philosophy was clearly stated from the outset:

> Effective teachers will ensure that all pupils are given tasks which are challenging but attainable and that they are given opportunities to assimilate and apply successfully the new concepts, knowledge, skills and attitudes which they are meeting. Good assessment provides the means of judging whether pupils are able to do these things successfully. Assessment and the uses to which it is put cannot be separated from teaching.
>
> (SOED, 1991, Pt 1: 3)

By means of these guidelines and accompanying staff development materials, it was hoped that primary and special school teachers – already committed to a philosophy focusing on the individuality of pupils – and secondary teachers – already familiar with criterion-referenced Standard Grade assessment and associated formative assessment – could be helped to find practical ways of integrating assessment with learning and teaching, building on pupils' current attainments and strengths and thereby ensuring their progress.

Conclusion

The Diagnostic Procedures package was developed from a need identified by teachers, taking into consideration the context within which the procedures would be used and building on teachers' existing professionalism. It was designed to be consistent both with Scottish teachers' values and with existing national assessment frameworks in both primary and secondary schools. The procedures emerged as a synthesis of influences from pedagogical research, reading research and classroom experience: it was recognized that credibility with teachers was likely to depend on attention to both research and classroom theories. The procedures were developed in partnership with teachers, taking into consideration issues of manageability. Finally, when the initial draft of the materials had been developed, the package was piloted in primary and secondary schools in Scotland. Teachers were sent the materials and asked to use and comment on them, to offer advice on how they might be improved. The feedback obtained on the package from all groups consulted has been heartening. The vast majority of teachers who used the materials found them to be useful, practical and consistent with their conceptualization of 'effective practice'. The package was published in 1995 and forms part of the support materials for the national 5–14 Assessment system.

In the context of the analysis presented by Harrison, Bailey and Dewar (this volume) of how postmodernist influences are inevitably changing the ways in which we can conceive of assessment, the Diagnostic Procedures project represents an interesting case study. Several of the points emphasized by the authors – e.g. the elusiveness and dynamic nature of the reading process; the importance of teacher, self- and peer-assessment; the importance of classroom-based assessment activities; the need for eclectic methodologies; the significance of the reader's own understanding of the process of reading and of his or her reconstruction of the text's meaning – all are central principles of the diagnostic procedures. For us, those principles emerged from consideration of effective pedagogy. The perception of Jean François Lyotard, quoted by Harrison and his colleagues, that postmodernism has 'altered the game rules' of assessment seems to be accurate in the case of our particular project. We have arrived at the kind of assessment advocated by our package because it is no longer valid to conceive of effective teaching in terms of generally applicable 'off-the-shelf' practices and solutions. Professional reflection, hypothesis-making, dialogue with students and joint action to try out ways forward are necessary, and are implied both by postmodernist philosophy and by our practical teaching experience.

References

Arnold, B. and Simpson, M. (1982) *Concept Development and Diagnostic Testing. Osmosis in 'O' Grade Biology.* Aberdeen: Northern College.

—— (1984) 'Diagnosis in Action': Occasional Paper No. 1. Aberdeen: Northern College.

Black, H. and Dockrell, W. B. (1984) *Criterion Referenced Assessment in the Classroom.* Edinburgh: Scottish Council for Research in Education.

Bruner, J. (1983) *In Search of Mind: Essays in Autobiography.* London: Harper and Row.

Chambers, A. (1993) *Tell Me: Children Read and Talk.* Stroud: Thimble Press.

Clay, M. (1985) *The Early Detection of Reading Difficulties.* Portsmouth, NH: Heinemann.

Donaldson, M. C. (1978) *Children's Minds.* London: Croom Helm.

Drever, D. (1987) 'Mastery learning in the secondary school: a report of school based research'. Stirling: Stirling University.

Entwistle, N. J. (1988) *Styles in Learning and Teaching: An Integrated Outline of Educational Psychology for Students, Teachers and Lecturers.* London: Fulton.

Fyfe, R. and Mitchell, E. (1983) *Formative Assessment of Reading Strategies in Secondary Schools.* Aberdeen: College of Education.

Godfrey Thomson Unit (1987) *The English Language Skills Profile.* London: Macmillan Educational Ltd.

Great Britain Office (1993) 'Standards in Education HMI: reading recovery in New Zealand: a report from HMI'. London: HMSO.

Harrison, C. and Coles, M. (eds) (1992) *The Reading for Real Handbook.* London: Routledge.

Hayward, L. (1991) 'Research influences on Assessment 5–14'. In SCRE FORUM 'Assessment for the 90s'. Edinburgh: Scottish Council for Research in Education.

Jackson, L. (1984) *Assessment in English in S1/S2.* Dundee: Scottish Consultative Council on the Curriculum.

Jones, Nick (1992) 'Reader, writer, text'. In Ronald Carter (ed.) *Knowledge about Language and the Curriculum.* London: Hodder and Stoughton.

Kemp, J. E. (1986) *Sigma: A Process-Based Approach to Staff Development.* PAVIC.

Lunzer, E. A. and Gardner, K. (1979) *The Effective Use of Reading.* London: Heinemann Educational Books for the School Council.

Lunzer, E. A., Gardner, K,. Davies, F. and Greene, T. (1984) *Learning From the Written Word.* Edinburgh: Oliver and Boyd.

Meek, M. (1988) *How Texts Teach What Readers Learn.* Stroud: Thimble Press.

Millard, E. (1994) *Developing Readers in the Middle Years.* Buckingham: Open University Press.

Morton, T. and Leather, B. (1994) *Readers and Texts in Primary Years.* Buckingham: Open University Press.

Nisbet, J. D. and Shucksmith, J. (1986) *Learning Strategies.* London and Boston: Routledge and Kegan Paul.

Rogers, A. and McDonald, C. (1984) *Writing for Learning.* Edinburgh: SCRE.

Rogers, C. (1983) *Freedom to Learn for the 80's.* Columbus, Ohio: C. E. Merrill Pub. Co.

Scottish Consultative Council on the Curriculum (1990) *Assessment as Part of Teaching in Standard Grade Courses.* Dundee: SCCC.

Scottish Council of Research in Education (1994) *Diagnostic Procedures in Reading – a SCRE Publication.* Edinburgh: SCRE.

Scottish Education Department (1965) *Primary Education in Scotland.* Edinburgh: HMSO.

Scottish Examination Board (1993) *Assessment 5–14: A Teacher's Guide to National Testing in Primary Schools*. Dalkeith: SEB.

Scottish Office Education Department (1991) *'Assessment 5–14 : 'Improving the Quality of Learning and Teaching' National Guidelines'*. Edinburgh: SOED.

Spencer, E. (1979) *Folio Assessment or External Examination?* Dalkeith: SCE Examination Board.

—— (1983) *Writing Matters across the Curriculum*. Sevenoaks, Kent: Hodder and Stoughton for the Scottish Council for Research in Education.

Thompson, G. B. and Brian, G. (1993) *Reading Acquisition Processes*. Clevedon, Avon: Multilingual Matters.

Vygotsky, L. S. (1978) *Mind in Society: the Development of Higher Psychological Processes*. Cambridge, MA: Harvard University Press.

Waterland, E. (1993) *Read with Me: An Apprenticeship Approach to Reading*. Stroud: Thimble Press.

Wray, D. (1992a) *Literacy and Awareness*. London: Hodder and Stoughton.

—— (1992b) *Reading: Beyond the Story*. Widnes: United Kingdom Reading Association.

10

USING DIRECT EVIDENCE TO ASSESS STUDENT PROGRESS

How the Primary Language Record supports
teaching and learning

Beverly Falk

Introduction

Across the USA and in many other nations, educators, parents and policy-makers are pressing for changes in the ways that schools assess and evaluate student learning. Persuaded that traditional standardized tests fail to measure many important aspects of learning and do not support many of the most useful strategies for teaching, practitioners are introducing alternative approaches to assessment into classrooms – approaches that help teachers look more carefully and closely at students, their learning and their work. Indeed, many chapters in this book detail projects in which teachers, administrators and others have worked together to change existing assessment practices.

The Primary Language Record, (PLR) (Barrs, Ellis, Hester and Thomas, 1988), developed in England and increasingly being used in the USA, is one such alternative assessment framework. The PLR involves parents, children and teachers in observing, documenting and analysing literacy development in classrooms. This chapter describes The Primary Language Record, how it operates in practice, and how it provides useful information about students' literacy growth and achievement for teachers, parents, and school systems. Drawing directly upon a series of studies of The Primary Language Record as it is used in New York City public elementary schools (Falk, 1995; Falk and Darling-Hammond, 1993; Falk, MacMurdy and Darling-Hammond, 1995), this chapter examines ways that The Primary Language Record provides supports to teachers as they learn – about their students, their own teaching and literacy learning in general. This chapter is further informed by studies of adaptations to the PLR conducted in

California (Barr and Cheong, 1993; Barr and Syverson, 1994; Miserlis, 1993; Wilson and Adams, 1992) as well as in the United Kingdom (Centre for Language in Primary Education, 1990, 1995; Feeney and Hann, 1991; O'Sullivan, 1995).

What is the Primary Language Record?

The Primary Language Record was conceived in 1985 by educators in England who were searching for a better means of recording and making sense of children's literacy progress. Teachers, school heads, staff developers and local authority representatives collaborated to develop a means for reflecting and supporting existing good teaching practices. The Primary Language Record is a vehicle for systematically observing students in various aspects of their literacy development – reading, writing, speaking and listening. Particular classroom events and samples of work serve as the basis for recording students' progress and interests; recommending strategies for addressing students' needs and building on talents; and discussing ideas and perceptions with students, their parents and other faculty. By virtue of what it asks teachers to observe and record, The Primary Language Record provides a coherent view of what constitutes progress and development in language and literacy learning. Grounded in the philosophy that literacy acquisition progresses in a manner similar to language acquisition, that is, through immersion in meaningful and purposeful activities, the PLR recognizes that developments in language and literacy do not take place in isolation but occur in diverse contexts spanning the entire curriculum. Record keeping for the PLR captures multiple, authentic demonstrations of learning by documenting students at work in natural contexts over extended periods of time. The Primary Language Record encourages teachers to identify children's strengths, to regard errors as information useful to teaching, and to analyse growth patterns in a constructive way; thus, it can support and inform day-to-day teaching and learning in the classroom.

Unlike most traditional tests, the PLR allows students to actively and purposefully construct their own ways of demonstrating what they know and can do rather than placing them in the passive position of demonstrating their understandings by selecting answers from a set of pre-existing responses. In addition to the multiple forms of evidence gathered about each student, a variety of perspectives – those of teachers, families, and students themselves – are included in the assessment data. Clearly, the PLR embodies the principles of responsive assessment delineated by Harrison, Bailey and Dewar earlier in this book.

These ways of providing information about student learning are used to serve multiple purposes simultaneously. The Primary Language Record can be used to:

- inform teachers' instruction in the classroom;
- apprise families about their children's progress;
- provide a continuum of knowledge about students as they pass from teacher to teacher; and
- report to administrators and school systems about individual as well as group progress and achievement.

In contrast to the limited ways in which student progress and achievement are measured through most traditional standardized testing programmes, The Primary Language Record represents a shift in thinking about the purposes and uses of assessment. Rather than measuring student perfor- mance in a decontextualized, snap-shot-like testing situation, it looks at student learning over time in the natural learning context of the classroom. It not only provides summative evaluation (as is the case with most tests), but also provides information that can be used to inform instruction and support student learning through the course of the school year. Assessment through The Primary Language Record is not couched in the secrecy that often surrounds high-stakes testing, but rather is based on clearly articu- lated criteria of what constitutes the continuum of literacy development. And finally, The Primary Language Record is not designed to rank and sort students according to their performance in the way that norm-refer- enced standardized tests are designed to do. Rather, the intention of The Primary Language Record is to provide a variety of audiences with a holistic picture of individual students' progress – as an indicator of the progress the individual has made in regard to the overall literacy learning continuum and as a measure of each individual's own growth (as compared to him/herself) over the year.

This shift in the use and purpose of assessment represented by The Primary Language Record also reflects a shift in stance toward overall thinking about the learning process. The Primary Language Record is based on the premise that good teaching comes not only from knowledge of curriculum and teaching methodologies but also from teachers' knowledge of students. It is grounded in the assumption that teachers need to know their students well in order to shape effective teaching strategies that will support meaningful and lasting learning.

Format of the PLR

The Primary Language Record provides a framework for teachers to observe, document and assess their students' learning. It offers a way of organizing and synthesizing information about individual students' experiences and interests and their approaches to and strategies for reading, writing, listen- ing and speaking in a variety of natural contexts over time. Its format does not mandate a particular time, schedule, or manner of observing and recording but leaves teachers room to decide how, when and where to document information.

The Primary Language Record includes the following components:

Parent interview A record of a meeting between the teacher and the child's family member(s). The purpose of this meeting is to encourage communication and to establish a partnership between home and school. The family shares knowledge about the child as a learner (what language is primarily spoken at home, what the child reads, writes and talks about, changes that have occurred in the child's language and literacy development) as well as observations, concerns, hopes and expectations about the child and his or her experiences of school. The information gained through this discussion supports children's learning at school by providing the teacher with a full picture of the child's development to which the teacher can refer throughout the school year. This information helps teachers understand how much children know and how much they are involved in a range of language and literacy-related activities in their home and community. At the end of the conference, the teacher and family members agree on the points to be recorded in The Primary Language Record. This summary becomes part of the child's permanent record.

Language/literacy conference between the child and teacher A record of a meeting designed to give the student an opportunity to discuss experiences, achievements and interests with the teacher, as well as to provide an opportunity to reflect on his or her reading and writing activities and to assess his or her own progress. For the teacher, the conference reveals the student's interests, preferences for different learning styles and contexts and reasons for making particular choices. It also provides insights into the ways in which the student's language(s) are developing and supporting his or her learning. The conference is a formal opportunity for the student and teacher to develop a joint working plan for the school year.

Narrative report on the child as a language user In this section, the child's strategies, approaches, and behaviours in the areas of talking, listening, reading and writing are all noted and analysed. This section of the report is completed toward the end of the spring term of the school year. It is compiled from concrete evidence – day-to-day teacher observations and samples of student work (book lists, writing, drawing, photos of projects, etc.) collected throughout the course of the school year. Two kinds of entries are made for each area of language development: (1) observations on the child's progress, and (2) a description of any experiences or teaching that have supported the child's development. The child's use of both primary and secondary languages are noted along with any concerns about the child's progress, any ways in which the child's progress is exceptional, or any special educational needs the child may have. Social and curricular contexts of the classroom are also explained and included in this section, matching assessments of the child's progress against descriptions of opportunities provided in the classroom for each of the aspects of literacy to develop.

End of year comments from the child and his/her family   Spring conferences are held with the child individually, as well as with the child's family, to review the child's work over the year and to make a final assessment of progress.

Information for the child's teacher for the following year   This section of the record, filled out by the teacher, is a final assessment of a child's progress in all aspects of language and literacy learning. It provides the next year's teacher with up-to-date information about the child's development. It is a means for current teachers to pass on their experience and understandings of the child and to make suggestions about the kind of supports they think will best benefit the child.

Reading scales   A scoring mechanism that outlines the continuum of literacy development. Based on child development knowledge as well as psycholinguist theories of literacy learning, the scales are designed to describe what a child is able to do, with increasing ease, on the road to developing as a reader. One reading scale for younger children (ages five to seven) charts children's progress as readers on a continuum from *dependence to independence*. Another reading scale for older children (ages six to eight) plots the developing *experience* of readers and describes the ways in which they broaden and deepen their experience of many kinds of texts. Teachers use the scales to help them think about children's progress across a wide age range. They use the evidence gathered through observation and documentation of children's growth during the school year to determine placement of each child on the literacy learning continuum.

The reading scales of the Primary Language Record are useful in several ways. By providing a conceptual framework for understanding students' development, they help teachers to be better observers of children. They serve as a guide to teachers' instruction, pointing out the full range of strategies and skills that encompass literacy proficiency. This helps teachers become more knowledgeable about the different processes and stages involved in literacy development, which, in turn, strengthens their skills in recognizing and responding to the different needs of their students. The scales also provide a shared view and language for student progress among teachers and across grades. They help teachers to talk with and report to parents by providing a meaningful vocabulary and framework based on knowledge of development. This provides continuity in understanding and reporting a child's progress.

In addition, the scales make it feasible to use The Primary Language Record for accountability purposes. The scale numbers assigned to students can be used to monitor the reading levels of individuals and groups. Using the scales in this way can enable schools to obtain an overall picture of their students' reading performance and to report this picture to their communities. Preliminary studies conducted in London, New York City and California are demonstrating that Primary Language Record scale scores are a reliable indicator of literacy proficiency (Barr and Syverson, 1994; Center for Language in Learning, 1995; Feeney and Hann, 1991; Klausner, 1995; Wilson and Adams, 1992).

Using direct evidence to assess student learning

The Primary Language Record relies primarily on direct evidence to assess students' learning. Detailed observations of students at work in a variety of social and curricular contexts in the classroom combined with actual samples of students' work, demonstrate what students know and can do while also revealing students' approaches to their learning. In New York City, where approximately 350 teachers in sixty-two public elementary schools are using The Primary Language Record, many teachers note how this method of keeping track of growth over time in the natural learning context helps them to better understand their students and to use these understandings in their instruction. Primary grade teacher Liz Edelstein expresses their views when she says:

> Without the written record over time I would miss some kids. Only by looking back over this record can you can start to see patterns in what the child is doing – reading, writing, and how it is all connected. All these bits of information come together into a picture that is particularly useful for kids who are struggling in one way or another. Using the PLR has taught me that whatever conclusions I come to about a child or whatever I am going to try to do next has to be grounded in an observation or a piece of work. Observing children closely generally gives me a lot more than a specific recommendation or a particular method or thing to do for a kid. I walk away with some learning that I can apply to all kids.

How the record is actually used to assess and support student learning is demonstrated by the following story of special education teacher Lucy Lopez's experience collecting evidence for the PLR. Lucy's bilingual student, 7-year-old Miguel, was referred to her classroom after being diagnosed as 'learning disabled' with 'Attention Deficit Disorder'. Her early impressions of him were:

He used to jump all over and never focus in. He could never remember what he had learned. He didn't listen and it used to make me mad.

Official school records for Miguel provided Lucy with little information that helped her cope with his behaviour or that provided her with under-standings she could use as she planned instruction for Miguel. They focused almost exclusively on detailed academic sub-skills, noting all the things that Miguel could not do, with no mention of the strategies, approaches, or learning modalities he could employ as a learner:

ACADEMIC

Miguel does not demonstrate strong word-attack skills.
Miguel does not read multi-syllabic words.
Miguel does not recognize content-related vocabulary.
Miguel does not identify and use signal (key) words to increase understanding of a reading selection.
Miguel does not read for a definite purpose: to obtain answers, to obtain general ideas of content, and for enjoyment.
Miguel does not identify the main idea of a passage.
Miguel does not use context clues to define unfamiliar words.
Miguel does not spell words at grade level.
Miguel does not write complete simple sentences.

SPEECH/LANGUAGE AND HEARING

Miguel is not able to use copular and auxiliary verb forms.

When Lucy first received Miguel's records she noticed that the phrase 'Miguel does not' was used in almost every sentence. She was not surprised, therefore, that after presenting Miguel in the light of such deficits, the description of him concluded with the following:

SOCIAL/EMOTIONAL DESCRIPTION

Miguel has a negative self-concept.

As Lucy used The Primary Language Record as a guide to observe Miguel and to keep track of his progress, she began to see him differently. She began to identify his learning strategies, the specific competencies he was mastering in reading and writing, as well as areas in which he demonstrated strength. This helped her to focus on what Miguel *could* do, rather than dwelling only on his problems and what he was *not* able to do. The following entries from Miguel's PLR demonstrate how Lucy's documented observations provided her with information about his learning strategies and behaviours that were useful guides to teaching:

> Miguel enjoys looking at books and can retell stories. He memorized most of his favorite nursery rhymes with intonation and sang some of them. When reading he points to each word as he reads. He runs his fingers across the page when reading unfamiliar texts and uses picture clues to read unknown words. His sight vocabulary is developing through the use of 'key words' [a personal word bank developed from the child's own interests].

This description of Miguel's reading reveals that despite his lack of fluency in English and his inability to decode precisely, he was able to gain meaning when reading from texts. Among Miguel's reading strategies, the observation notes that he relies on pictures to help him figure out the words, suggesting to Lucy that she provide him with books containing lots of pictures to assist him. The observation also reveals information about Miguel's interests, guiding Lucy in her selection of books for him to read and prompting her to encourage the development of Miguel's sight vocabulary by enlarging his collection of 'key words.' In a similar way, Lucy's recorded observations of Miguel also note that he is developing a wide range of writing and spelling strategies:

> Miguel is developing interest in written expression in English. He enjoys writing on a variety of topics. He draws illustrations to go with his writing. At times he uses inventive spelling and is beginning to use sound/symbol relationships to spell unknown words. He also refers to his 'key words' for correct spelling, looks around the classroom for words, or will ask a classmate to spell a word.

Lucy used what she learned from this observation to encourage Miguel's social interest in writing and to support his efforts to use his classmates as both idea and spelling resources.

In these ways the PLR helped Lucy to see beyond the problems presented by Miguel's behaviour; to see that he was indeed making progress as a learner. As Lucy noted Miguel's strengths across the curriculum, she became more able to plan instruction that built on his interests and that met his specific learning needs. The PLR guided her planning by including in its final section the question, 'What experiences and teaching have helped/would help development?' The following recommendations for how to further support Miguel's learning demonstrate how Lucy's earlier observations and documentation laid the groundwork for her teaching strategies:

Provide him with familiar texts and simple pattern language books around themes that will capture his interest.

Make copies of these books in both Spanish and English for Miguel to take home to read to his mother.

Support Miguel's interest in developing a sight vocabulary by encouraging him to build up a collection of personally meaningful 'key words' that can become both spelling and reading resources.

Encourage Miguel's social interest in writing by supporting his efforts to use his classmates as learning resources and supports.

Provide opportunities for involvement in class plays and presentations to foster Miguel's spoken language development.

These suggestions were passed on to Miguel's subsequent teacher, making it possible to provide continuity in the school's approach to his instruction.

Changing the way teachers teach

Lucy, and other teachers like her, have had considerable support as they have learned how to use the Primary Language Record. In the New York City Primary Language Record Project consultants are employed to work directly on-site with PLR teachers in classrooms, encouraging teacher change by modelling instructional practices, offering feedback, providing information about learning theory and literacy development, as well as facilitating meetings with teachers across classrooms. In addition, during after-school hours, at universities and out-of-school sites, consultants host study groups and graduate courses where teachers share their ideas and their work with other professionals from across the city. Many teachers attribute a new sense of professional growth to their participation in these activities. Liz Edelstein, now in her fourth year of attending a PLR study group, explains how her participation in it has helped her to develop as a reflective practitioner:

> We read articles, talk about our reading, our work in the classroom, and about using the PLR. As we discuss what we notice about children, we also begin to notice what we are noticing. We become more reflective about our own practice and more conscious about what we are learning.

As teachers have learned about literacy development and students' literacy learning through their exposure to the PLR and its accompanying professional development activities, they have changed their teaching in a variety of ways. Participants in an interview study of twenty-two New York City teachers using the PLR (who represent varying stages of professional experience – from novice to veteran teacher) all credited the PLR with significantly influencing their instruction (Falk, MacMurdy and Darling-Hammond, 1995). These comments from one teacher are reflective of their experience:

> The way I teach and assess children is different from the way I taught and thought about it before. I started using the PLR because I was looking for some way to make my hunches about children more concrete. Before I had ideas about kids but no evidence. I felt like there must be a better way to do this. I found it with the PLR. For me it is an instructional tool. Based on what I see the child doing, and what the child and parents tell me, I now have information on what I can do to work together with them and to help the child. Sometimes it's as small a thing as knowing the kind of book a child likes to read so that I can suggest what to read next; or it's knowing that a child likes to reread so I know to be sure to do that with her. Having the PLR evidence gives me more confidence in myself as a teacher because I have a real basis for my decisions.

Eighteen of the twenty-two teachers interviewed in the same study pointed to PLR use as enhancing their abilities to individualize instruction. Iliana Ordonez, who teaches eight/nine year olds in a dual language classroom, typifies their views on this issue:

> Keeping the observational records of the PLR has helped me to gear my work to each child, individualizing and giving children the support they need. I've become aware that each child is learning at her own pace and that each child knows something and is good at something. The children know that I see that and it makes them feel secure. All of this has come to me through my work with the PLR.

Many of the teachers interviewed – nineteen of the twenty-two – described how using the PLR to observe has helped them to better identify students' interests and strengths and to subsequently use these understandings to provide more effective instruction. Janet Chan, a teacher of eight/nine year olds in Brooklyn, New York, explains how the PLR helps her to uncover the differing capabilities and strengths of her students:

> Before I started using the Primary Language Record, reading for me was two-dimensional – you either could read an unfamiliar text or you couldn't. I had previously relied mainly on phonics to teach reading and had used books whose only purpose was to teach children to read. Through the PLR I learned about all the strategies

– semantic, syntactic and phonetic cues – that go into reading. As I learned about all these components of the reading process, I began to realize all the things that my kids could actually do. Even if kids couldn't independently read an unfamiliar text, they could still do a lot of the behaviors that constitute reading. The way that the PLR asked me to observe and record gave opportunities for kids to show their strengths so that I could build on them for future instruction.

Because the PLR's definition of literacy encompasses reading, writing, listening and speaking and because it clearly articulates that learning is most successful when embedded in meaningful, purposeful and real-life experiences, many teachers have found that PLR use has led them to expand the range of their instructional strategies and transform their classrooms so that they can offer opportunities for students to engage in the kinds of behaviours that support this broader vision of literacy and learning. Janet Chan explains:

> The PLR format made me set up times to converse with parents and kids. The observation guidelines asked me to observe kids while they were reading so I had to set up a structure in my classroom where kids had time to read independently and where they were engaged enough in the process that I could conference with them individually. The PLR asked me to look at their writing. Before the PLR I never had opportunities for writing in my classroom. Now I make writing a big thing.

Other teachers describe still other changes in their teaching that have evolved from PLR use. Teachers report that they provide more opportunities for peer learning and collaboration and more choices for students in the learning environment; they teach in more integrated, interdisciplinary ways and utilize learning contexts that stretch beyond the walls of the school. Still other changes involve adopting literacy strategies that are well recognized as effective – using children's literature rather than basal readers as the primary source for instruction; making classroom libraries a central aspect of the learning environment; providing regular opportunities for teachers to read aloud to their students; creating classroom environments that are rich with print; and using a range of media as vehicles for students' literacy expression.

Promoting teacher collaboration and ongoing inquiry

Teachers involved in the PLR project are as diverse a group in their thinking and experience as the children they are teaching. Nevertheless the PLR has

supported and challenged a variety of teachers in their views of what constitutes effective teaching, and has provided them with a range of entry points
for their learning. Teacher collaboration and communication have increased
as a result of PLR work. Many PLR teachers frequently gather together
during their lunch or preparation periods to hold conversations about children and to use each other to problem-solve about their work. Participation
in the conversations of PLR study groups has also led many of the teachers
involved to consider a host of questions and issues that tap into deeply
rooted values that influence their teaching. The following story from a PLR
study group demonstrates the power that reflection can have in shaping
and reshaping teachers' beliefs, attitudes and practices related to diversity.

One teacher of eight and nine year olds raised a concern with her
colleagues at a study group meeting about a group of boys in her class who
read science books and talked together everyday during language arts time.
Although this was a time when the teacher encouraged children to read
and write and talk together, she was particularly concerned about one boy
in this group who still struggled to achieve fluency in his reading. She was
concerned that he was spending too much time talking and not enough
time practising his reading. In relating her concern to her colleagues, she
realized that although she openly encouraged the stronger readers to
converse, the very same process of chatting with others made her nervous
if it was being done by weaker readers. She began to question whether it
was fair to hold different standards of behaviour for different kinds of
students:

> Does that mean that a struggling reader shouldn't talk as much as
> a competent reader? I thought about the role of practice in learning
> to read and how I know that practice is very important. But I also
> thought about the role of choice in learning and how important
> it is for learner motivation. I thought about the relation between
> teacher choice and student choice. Classrooms generally are struc-
> tured around teacher choice. I want to support and encourage
> student choice but if I decide this boy needs to practice his reading
> more, and all the while he wants to talk about books, I am taking
> away his right to make his own choice. And I never do this to
> competent readers. They get to choose what they want to do because
> their choices generally coincide with mine.

The implications of the tension this teacher felt are subtle but powerful;
they have to do with issues of standards, autonomy, empowerment and
equity. Liz was torn between her responsibility to have all students achieve
high standards, and the importance of providing them with equitable
learning opportunities. Having the opportunity to make choices – in this
case, talking with others – is part of students' opportunity to learn, yet Liz

was concerned that spending time talking would take away too much of the time that the weaker students needed to focus on reading if they were to achieve high standards.

Liz eventually resolved this tension by structuring a time in her classroom when *all* students were required to engage in quiet, independent reading.

> I played around with ways to make that more appealing. And in fact, after a while, what I did worked! They all did settle into reading independently – to the extent that they were able. They all were willing to engage in doing what readers do – choose a book, sit and give it the attention it requires, trust that something is going to happen that is worthwhile. They all got over the hump of the resistance to reading – everybody would sit or lie on the floor and read. I looked up one day and said, 'Wow, everybody's reading!' I know not everybody was reading the way a reading test would measure. But everybody was engaged with a book and this to me is an important measure of reading.

Liz is quick to point out that if she hadn't been looking at children in her classroom so closely and if she hadn't had the opportunity to discuss these issues in her study group, she most likely would not have noticed what these children were doing and would not have contemplated the important issues that were raised by the situation.

> What I came to realize when I was looking at this is that we put so much emphasis on reading and skills development in school we don't nurture other things that need to be nurtured in order for skills to develop. I really want to learn how to do this so that I can help all kinds of learners learn better.

Is this not the goal of professional (indeed, any kind of) learning – to help individuals reach the point of questioning, searching and seeking opportunities to reflect on and change what they do? Many teachers who use The Primary Language Record, through learning how to observe and keep track of their students, learn how to bring their students to this juncture. They also come to this juncture themselves. Documenting and reflecting on student work helps teachers better support student learning while, at the same time, it also supports teachers as they engage in their *own* knowledge development. Teachers experience firsthand what they come to understand is essential for all students' learning: each individual requires a different look and a different pathway to growth. Lucy Lopez expresses this in a poem inspired by her PLR work with her students and her colleagues:

I AM SPECIAL

Teacher, I may not follow
directions as clearly
as you want me to.
I may not speak as clearly as you.
I may not read as fluently as you.
I may not express my ideas in writing as clearly as you.
But, I am learning at my own pace.
Can you see that?!!

References

Barr, M. and Cheong, J. (1993) 'Achieving equity: counting on the classroom'. Paper presented on 12 March 1993 at a symposium held in Washington DC on 'Equity and Educational Testing and Assessment', sponsored by the Ford Foundation.

Barr, M. and Syverson, M. (1994) *Overview of the* California Learning Record: *Report on Regional Moderation Readings*. La Jolla, CA: The Center for Language in Learning.

Barrs, M., Ellis, S., Hester, H. and Thomas A. (1988) The Primary Language Record. London: ILEA/Centre for Language in Primary Education.

Center for Language in Learning. (1995) *Connecting Classroom and Large Scale Assessment: The CLR Moderation Process*. El Cajon, California.

Centre for Language in Learning (1990) *The Reading Book*. London: ILEA.

—— (1995) *Language Matters, No. 2/3*. London.

Falk, B. (1995) 'Authentic assessment as a catalyst for learning: An inquiry model of professional development'. Paper presented at the Annual Meeting of the American Educational Research Association, San Francisco, California.

Falk, B. and Darling-Hammond, L. (1993) The Primary Language Record *at P.S. 261: How Assessment Transforms Teaching and Learning*. New York: National Center for Restructuring Education Schools and Teaching.

Falk, B., MacMurdy, S. and Darling-Hammond, L. (1995) *Taking a Different Look: How* The Primary Language Record *Supports Teaching for Diverse Learners*. New York: National Center for Restructuring Education Schools and Teaching.

Feeney, K., and Hann, P. (1991) 'Survey of reading performance in year 2: Summer 1991'. London: Lewisham Education.

Goodman, K. (ed.) (1979) *Miscue Analysis: Applications to Reading Instruction*. Urbana, Ill.: National Council of Teachers of English.

Klausner, E. (1995) 'The Primary Language Record as a reliable option for assessing children's literacy: Report of the initial phase of development of a process for moderation'. Unpublished paper.

Miserlis, S. (1993) 'The classroom as an anthropological dig: Using the California Learning Record (CLR) as a framework for assessment and instruction'. Unpublished paper.

O'Sullivan, O. (1995) The Primary Language Record *in Use*. London: Centre for Language in Primary Education.

Wilson, M. and Adams, R. (1992) 'Evaluating progress with alternative assessments: A model for Chapter 1'. Unpublished paper.

11

CHALLENGING THE ASSESSMENT CONTEXT FOR LITERACY INSTRUCTION IN FIRST GRADE

A collaborative study

James Hoffman, Nancy Roser and Jo Worthy

Former Student: 'I'll be moving back to town soon. Do you know of any positions available for teachers in area schools?'
University Professor: 'What grade level are you interested in teaching?'
Former Student: 'Even'.

'Even'? In Texas, a teaching assignment in an even-numbered level means one's students will not have to take the statewide assessments that are given only in odd-numbered Grades – 3, 5, 7, etc. This young teacher seeking employment had decided views about testing. Like most of us in the USA, those attitudes stem from when we were 'tested' as elementary students. We associated those tests with springtime, 'number two' pencils, and the curious ceremonies of our teachers – from hanging the 'Testing' sign on the classroom door to breaking the seals of the test packets. The teacher's seriousness of tone and attention to the exact wording of test directions meant the activity wasn't business as usual. Instead, the regular school schedule was set aside, and the whole school hushed. Although everyone sensed that something really important was going on, the exact nature of that importance was never fully revealed. Testing time went away as quickly as it had arrived. Ironically, these tests were about the only work we ever did in schools that didn't get handed back the next day with a grade attached.

Although times change, today's schools are still deluged with tests. Perhaps the tests are not the kind of continuous 'micro' inspections that were part of the mastery learning curriculum movement of the 1960s, such as the Wisconsin Design, Fountain Valley, or other versions of skills-based management systems. Rather, current testing programmes seem to be of the 'high-stakes' variety, often with dramatic consequences for individual students (e.g. promotion, graduation), for teachers (e.g. salaries, reward, career advancement), for schools (e.g. resource allocations, administrative reassignments), and for districts (e.g. accreditation, status, rewards). Over the last two decades, approximately 80 per cent of the states in the USA have implemented large-scale assessment plans, in addition to any local level testing requirements.

The impact of these high-stakes testing schemes on classroom teaching seems much greater than in the past. Pressures within the system to get students to perform well fall directly on the shoulders of teachers – those on the 'front line', those 'in the trenches'. Not surprisingly, teachers are spending enormous amounts of time preparing students for tests. More importantly, the content of the tests and the format of test items seem to be shaping the curriculum (see, for example, Stephens, *et al.*, 1995; Tirozzi *et al.*, 1985; Turlington, 1985). The classic instructional design principle that assumes the primacy of instruction and only then considers assessment has given way to a new paradigm. The new frame begins with teachers deciding *what* to teach and *how* to teach it based on what is going to be tested and how it will be tested. For example, when students' writing will be assessed by having them write in a specified mode, it is that mode of writing that teachers stress in class instruction, activities and homework. Does anyone doubt that the students in classrooms where teachers adapt their curriculum to the test and its format achieve higher test scores? Because of the enormity of the pressure, many excellent teachers have selected themselves out of the classroom altogether, or, as in the case of the young teacher above mentioned, have begun to seek out those teaching contexts that are least affected by testing.

The current educational enterprise accepts a business/factory metaphor for teaching and learning (i.e., maximizing 'outputs' while minimizing resource allocations). Roles and responsibilities are distributed across many different groups or management teams. To make defensible decisions, the various stakeholders in the educational process (parents, teachers, administrators and policy-makers) require different sorts of information about the amount and kinds of student learning. As a result, the large-scale assessment plans instituted by administrators and policy-makers are often viewed by teachers as both invalid and intrusive. Conversely, the assessments teachers themselves plan and conduct to inform their teaching are sometimes viewed by administrators and policy-makers as suspect – both subjective and unscientific. The two perspectives on assessment often seem to operate totally independently of one another. For example, administrators and policy-makers require classroom, schoolwide and district data, and interpret these data for their own purposes; teachers need to know about students' progress, strengths and needs. Wixson, Valencia, and Lipson (1994) describe these distinctions as the 'separate' arrangement of internal and external assessments.

There is an alternative. Collaborators in varying sites have designed single assessment plans that encompass shared goals and address the legitimate needs of all stakeholders (see, for example, Salinger and Chittenden, 1994; Salinger, this volume). Ideally, these assessment plans provide valid, reliable data that are useful to teachers in making instructional decisions, to administrators and policy-makers who must monitor student progress on a broader scale, and to other audiences such as parents.

In this report, we describe the experiences of a group of Texas first grade teachers who have been striving to develop such an assessment plan. Although this project was initiated by teachers, over time it has become a broader collaborative endeavour involving central administration as well as a team of university-based teacher educators. The project has been existence less time than the one reported by Salinger (this volume), but it bears similarities in the ways in which teachers and 'outsiders' have collaborated to bring about change in early literacy assessment practices. The chapter reports the effort in three sections. In the first section, we describe the context for the development of the assessment model, which we named *Primary Assessment of Language Arts and Mathematics* (PALM). In the second section, we describe the features of PALM, as devised by the development team. Finally, we describe the design, execution, and results of an evaluation study of the PALM model.

The PALM initiative: a chronology

Located in south-central Texas, the Austin Independent serves a diverse community of close to one million citizens with sixty-two elementary schools. For the past several years, the district has been involved in a state-mandated movement toward site-based management, in which instructional programmes are determined by each school and may, therefore, vary substantially from one school site to the next. In the primary grades, however, all schools administer a formal assessment – a norm-referenced achievement test (i.e. the *Iowa Test of Basic Skills* or ITBS) each spring to students in odd-numbered grades. Testing typically involves the dedication of three full days, with one or two additional days of 'practice testing' to acclimatize students to item-type, test format and testing procedures. The results of the norm-referenced test are used by the district's Board of Trustees as the primary data source for monitoring school quality. Informal assessments are at the discretion of individual teachers of the norm-referenced tests.

The PALM project developed as a possible alternative to the norm-referenced standardized tests administered in the early grades. The plan and a chronological summary are presented below:

Autumn, 1993 First grade teachers in several schools raised questions on their local campuses regarding the value of the ITBS as a measure of young children's literacy. They expressed concerns related to issues of validity ('The tests do not really measure what we are teaching or what the students are learning') as well as utility ('The results are not helpful in making instructional decisions').

Spring, 1994 Through informal networks, a small group of first grade teachers from several elementary schools met to discuss their concerns over the norm-referenced test and to propose a plan of action. They approached the district's central administration with a request for a waiver from standardized testing for first graders, presenting their proposal to the Associate Superintendent for Curriculum. New to the district, the Associate Superintendent expressed support for the initiative, and recommended that the group prepare a plan for an alternative assessment to replace the ITBS. Toward that end, the teachers first adapted a developmental checklist from another district, making minor modifications to suit local needs. The Associate Superintendent arranged for the group to meet with the district's Board of Trustees to present their request for a waiver. The presentation to the Board was effective and a waiver was granted. As a result of concerns expressed by some Board members, however, an evaluation study was mandated for the 1994–5 school year. An alternative assessment system was informally piloted by six teachers during the Spring term, 1994. Planning for a full-scale evaluation study for the forthcoming school year was also initiated.

Summer, 1994 A planning team consisting of six first grade teachers and two university-based teacher educators worked to refine the PALM model and to formulate plans for the evaluation study. An overarching goal was to develop an assessment plan to address the needs of teachers, as well as parents, administrators, policy-makers and students. In late summer, during the district's inservice for first grade teachers, an information session was offered explaining the PALM initiative. All teachers (over 120) who attended the meeting were invited to join in the development project, as well as the evaluation study. A total of twenty-two teachers from thirteen different schools, including several of those from the original group of teachers, volunteered to participate in the evaluation study.

Autumn/Spring, 1994–5 The group of teachers and university-based teacher educators met four times over the academic year in all-day, inservice sessions. Each session was focused on refining the PALM model and planning for data collection for the evaluation study. The district's research and evaluation division identified a group of comparison teachers to be included in the PALM evaluation study (matched to PALM teachers based on years teaching experience and school contexts). The comparison teachers, along with the PALM teachers, participated in extensive interviews regarding their perspectives on and experiences with assessment strategies.

Summer, 1995   The volunteer group, now consisting of classroom teachers, school administrators and teacher educators, met over several days to complete data analysis and to begin interpreting findings from the assessment. Because of the varied perspectives of the group members, the task of data analysis became as much a time for negotiating views on assessment as it was a time for scoring, recording, and analysing data.

The chonology of the initial stages of the project suggest the extent to which the teachers acted out of frustration with the existing standardized test and the gratifying way in which their requests for change were welcomed by their school administrators.

The PALM model: description of an alternative assessment plan

This section describes the features of the PALM model as implemented during the 1994–5 academic year. As designed, the PALM model draws on a 'performance assessment' perspective and emphasizes the use of 'authentic' assessment strategies (Guthrie, Van Meter, Mitchell and Reed, 1994). The PALM model has been developed in consideration of the principles and guidelines advanced by Harrison, Bailey, and Dewar (this volume) regarding 'responsive assessment'. In the model, emphasis is placed on the classroom and classroom practices with increased attention to teacher assessments, student self assessments and peer assessments. A wide range of methodologies is drawn upon, including readers' responses to literature.

Data gathered through the initial PALM effort that are reported here were collected in one of two contexts: as part of ongoing instruction or, alternatively, in a context that reflects 'typical' instruction. Thus, the model adheres to usual definitions of 'authentic' assessment. Three types of performance assessment opportunities are included in the PALM model: (1) curriculum embedded assessments; (2) 'taking a closer look' assessments; and (3) on demand assessments. Each of these strategies is described in some detail below.

Curriculum embedded assessments

Curriculum embedded assessment refers to the data gathering for instructional planning or assessment that teachers may do in conjunction with their routine, ongoing instruction. For example, effective teachers constantly observe their students as they engage in learning activities, continuously monitoring students for the quality of their work, adapting instruction in response to these observations. In addition, they make long-term instructional decisions based on their students' performances. The PALM model affirms the common-sense practice of skilful observation as a worthwhile, trustworthy, and significant part of an assessment scheme. The PALM model also requires that teachers take time periodically to document their observations in a systematic way, such as collecting samples of student work accompanied by notes from the teacher (or student) explaining why this work is important evidence of learning. Documentation may also take the form of anecdotal notes of student engagement in various learning activities. The PALM model asks that teachers become somewhat disciplined in collecting their observations of all students on a regular basis.

'Taking a Closer Look' assessments (see Hayward and Spencer, this volume)

The second type of performance assessment in the PALM model refers to gathering data that is part of teachers' in-depth study of individual learners. Close-up inspection of particular skills is and has been a part of the entrenched practice of most effective teachers, but from time to time, individual students may present their teachers with greater challenge. Teachers must learn to ask and gather data that help them decide: Where is *this* student in his/her development? What does he/she need? Why is she/he performing in the way(s) I have observed? The toughest challenges don't all arise at the same time, and they don't always involve the same children. Nevertheless, the puzzles are there because all children are different and respond in different ways. Good teaching (and good assessment) demands adjustment for those individual differences.

Within the PALM model, the 'taking a closer look' assessments provide all teachers with the tools and methodologies for the kinds of systematic observation that the most effective teachers already use. Strategies useful in this type of assessment are quite familiar to most teachers, and the list is always expanding. They include collecting running records; conducting interest inventories; engaging in interviews and conversations with students about what they are thinking, learning, questioning, understanding; administering and interpreting informal reading inventories; providing opportunities for problem solving: using miscue analysis procedures, and think-alouds, etc.; and varying instructional conditions to determine how students respond to different kinds and levels of support.

These are just a few of the many ways in which teachers can 'take a closer look'. They are not typically done with all students at the same time; rather, they are seen as strategies to be applied selectively on an 'as needed' basis. The PALM model suggests teachers incorporate these strategies to record and interpret performance as a supplement/complement to their continuous curriculum-embedded assessment strategies. With evidence collected through these means, teachers are able to set the most appropriate learning goals for all students.

On demand assessments

On demand assessments involve data gathering within a particular time frame and under prescribed, more standardized conditions. Typically, on demand assessments document and interpret student performance on specific learning tasks. These tasks are designed to be authentic in the sense that they reflect the kinds of learning activities that the students are familiar with in their classroom instruction. They are controlled in terms of certain key variables (e.g. materials or topic of a writing task) to permit comparisons over time for individual children, as well as comparisons of individuals with peers.

The specifics of the on demand assessments may vary from one year to the next because tasks are designed to mirror the kinds of classroom activities that are part of the 'typical' instructional routines. The on demand assessments for the 1994–5 PALM evaluation study were designed to occur over one week and were scheduled for the first week in May. In order to insure commonalty and comparability across sites, a guide for teachers described how the on demand assessment tasks were to be conducted. The tasks for language arts on demand assessments included the following:

* *A Personal Journal.* All students participating in the project worked in specially designed response journals for the week of the on demand assessments. Students were given time each day to write in their journals. The teacher discussed and modelled entries. Sharing (reading from and talking about the journal entry) was a part of the classroom routine.
* *Literature Response Journal: Read Aloud* (responding in writing to a story read aloud by the teacher). Children wrote their thoughts and responses to a chapter book read aloud each day by the teacher. After each chapter was read aloud, the students wrote in their response journals. Again, sharing of journal entries was encouraged.
* *Literature Response Journal: Free Choice* (writing in response to self-selected books). The reading libraries set up in each classroom were similar across all sites in terms of the number of books and the types of selections available. The students were given time each day to do free choice reading in addition to responding in their journals.
* *Learning from Text Experience.* An informational trade-book, *Snakes* by Seymour Simon, was the focus for this assessment. Before reading the book aloud to the class, teachers directed the students to write in their journals everything they knew about snakes and what they wanted to learn. After the read-aloud, the students were given an opportunity to write about what they had learned that was new to them from the book. Discussion followed.
* *An Oral Reading/Shared Reading Exercise.* The book *The Chick and the Duckling* had been read during the year as a part of the students'

reading series. Following an oral review of the book, the students individually read the book aloud to the teacher. In addition, the children read a second book of comparable difficulty they had not seen before. Oral reading was tape recorded to determine accuracy and rate. Teachers rated the fluency of both read-aloud performances, and analysed student performance using quantitative and qualitative techniques.

• *An Interview/Inventory.* Each student met with his or her teacher individually to discuss reading habits, attitudes, and sense of self as a reader/writer. The discussion was organized around a series of probes requiring a Likert-like scaled response.

The intent in designing these tasks for the language arts on demand assessment has been that each would reflect typical instruction so closely that students would not notice any major disruptions to normal learning routines. For the 1994–5 academic year, on demand assessments were developed for the areas of reading and writing. Planning for on demand assessments for mathematics and speaking/listening is under way.

Record keeping and interpretation

These three types of performance assessments (curriculum embedded, 'taking a closer look', and on demand) yield an enormous amount of data on learners. The PALM model recommends that a portfolio strategy be used for collecting and organizing the data from individual students. The concept of portfolio assessment as it is applied within the PALM model can be understood in terms of three dimensions. The first is *portfolios as a place* for gathering documentation of students' progress and interpretations of the data that are collected during the assessment process. In this case, portfolios reflect the work of the individual learners. Secondly, portfolios can be thought of *as a process* in which the data or information have been selected for inclusion because of their informative value. Portfolios may sometimes include samples that students (and/or teachers) view as representing the students' best work in a particular area or may show work in progress, such as rough drafts. In whatever form, portfolios present work across different areas of learning and performance, and are not limited to one particular type of work. Portfolios may also include information on why each piece was selected for inclusion in portfolio (e.g. students' reflections). Portfolios may also be thought of *as documentation* or a way to gather evidence to support decision-making at varying levels.

The PALM developmental profile

As the project progressed, teachers needed a way to aggregate data. Thus, the PALM developmental profile was devised to represent some of the

173

indicators of children's increasing proficiency with language and literacy. The profile is neither the assessment system nor the data that have been gathered, but instead a record of judgements/interpretations about the data that have been collected using the performance assessment strategies. The documentation in the portfolio informs and supports the judgements that are recorded on the profile.

The PALM profile requires that the teacher monitor development. The absence of any teacher 'mark' on the profile form communicates that a child has not demonstrated the behaviour, strategy, or skill in question. A 'check' indicates that the behaviour has been observed on occasion, but not consistently. A 'plus' mark is used to indicate behaviours that students consistently demonstrate. [A revised version of the profile uses the mark 'S' in place of the check mark to indicate the behaviours that are observed in a supported context, while an 'I' indicates that the student demonstrates this behaviour working independently.]

The PALM profile is intended to be particularly useful when communicating with parents and receiving teachers (the developmental profile is passed on from one year to the next). In addition, continuous revisions in the form and its content will ensure its alignment with reporting procedures, and with the developing curricular frameworks in the district.

The PALM evaluation study

The PALM evaluation study that had been required by the Board of Trustees was designed to address the following questions:

1   Can the PALM alternative assessment model be implemented successfully in first grade classrooms that serve a wide variety of student populations and with teachers representing a wide variety of instructional philosophies and experience?
2   Does the PALM model contribute to more informed teaching and testing in a way that standardized, norm-referenced testing does not?
3   Does the PALM model yield data for other audiences (e.g. administrators) that are comparable to or more informing than the data generated though the Iowa Test of Basic Skills?

The participants in the evaluation study were the twenty teachers involved in the PALM project for the entire 1994–5 academic year and their students (N = 342). Data were also gathered from twenty comparison teachers and their students (N = 312). As part of their inservice meetings, the PALM teachers discussed and addressed implementation issues. Classroom observations/visits were conducted by the university-based teacher educators to verify use of the model, as well as offer support. In addition, the university educators conducted a structured end-of-year interview with both the

PALM and comparison teachers designed to capture the teachers' impressions, reactions, insights and change. All students in both PALM and comparison classrooms took the ITBS components focused on language arts, reading and mathematics. All teachers were asked to rank their students, based on perceived skill level, from highest to lowest. A survey/questionnaire was sent home to the parents of all of the students in both the PALM and comparison classrooms. The questionnaire focused on the parents' judgements of the quality (accuracy, frequency and clarity) of the feedback they had received on their child's progress.

The results related to the first two questions are drawn from an analysis of the interview data, as well as classroom visits by the university-based teacher educators. The results related to the third question draw on a statistical analysis of the data gathered through PALM scores and students' ITBS scores.

1 Can the PALM model be implemented successfully in first grade classrooms that serve a wide variety of student populations and represent teachers from a wide variety of instructional philosophies and experience?

Of the twenty-two teachers who volunteered to participate in the PALM project in late summer, 1994, twenty successfully implemented the evaluation plan in their classrooms. Three data sources determined teachers' successful participation in the evaluation study: (1) teacher self-reports of successful implementation during the final interviews; (2) artifacts and documentation collected from each of the classrooms (e.g. completed developmental profiles, on demand assessment journals for each student); and (3) confirming observations by the university-based teacher educators. Over half of the teachers participating in the project were teaching in schools that serve students from economically disadvantaged communities. Several of the classrooms served students who were bilingual or 'limited English proficient'. No differences were detected in teachers' successful implementation as a function of the student population served. The participating teachers varied in terms of teaching experience (from a first year teacher to a teacher with over twenty-five years experience in the district). The teachers also represented a broad range of instructional philosophies and approaches. Several teachers described themselves as subscribing to 'whole language' philosophy, while other teachers described their teaching as very 'code' focused because 'that's what our students need'. No differences were detected in the success of the implementation as a function of either length or nature of teachers' experience or of their instructional philosophy.

Some components of the model presented a greater challenge to teachers than others. Most teachers described the difficulty they had with the actual documentation of student behaviours. In the interviews, teachers shared some of the different strategies they used in making observations, keeping anecdotal records, collecting work samples and organizing portfolios. The degree of support offered through the four inservice days and the informal networking that occurred across the PALM sites were viewed by the participants as critical to its successful implementation. All of the PALM teachers reported that the use of the model required a greater investment of time and energy than simply administering the norm-referenced test. Of the eight comparison teachers who attended the one day inservice, none reported implementation of the PALM model in their classrooms. Several of these teachers commented that the model appeared too complicated to implement on their own.

2 Does the PALM model contribute to more informed teaching and testing in a way that standardized testing does not?

We examined the data from our teacher interviews to address this question from an interpretive perspective. In terms of self-reports, all of the PALM-implementing teachers described their teaching as more effective as a result of using the new assessment model. They commented that the model helped focus their attention more sharply on indicators of development, and that as a result, their instructional decisions were enhanced.

- 'I didn't assess as often until I used the Developmental Indicator Profile. I'm more focused now.'
- 'The kids enjoyed it; we actually spent more than a week so it gave a better assessment of student performance.'
- 'This helps me rethink.'

They described the model as improving their skills, in helping them organize information for students in a meaningful way and commented on its value for communicating with parents regarding individual student progress. They also reported positive feelings about what they would be able to pass on to their students' future teachers that would assure continuous progress. Finally, they felt affirmed in the fact that the assessment strategies associated with PALM reflected their teaching efforts.

- 'This is my own philosophy. This is what ought to be done.'

No teacher in either the PALM group or in the comparison group viewed the ITBS norm-referenced testing or its results as a positive influence on their teaching ('I learn nothing from the test. I never see it again.'). In fact, the vast majority of the teachers in both groups viewed the ITBS as worse than a waste of time. Many teachers saw the test experience itself as defeating to children ['I only had two cry today'] and inappropriate to measure the teaching and learning that is part of the district's curriculum. The interviews with the comparison teachers (i.e. those not participating in the PALM training or implementation) revealed a combination of confusion and concern over assessment in the district. When asked about the district's policy in regard to assessment of children's basic understandings, nearly all of the comparison teachers responded that they were uncertain. Most assumed that there were no expectations/requirements for assessment at Grade 1, and thus teachers were free to do whatever they wanted to do (including nothing). Most of the teachers reported relying on informal measures to track student progress.

We also addressed this question from a different perspective by using the database we collected from both teachers and students. Specifically, we compared the correlations of teacher's rankings of students (i.e., on perceived skill level in reading) with the students' performance on the ITBS reading test. The teachers were asked to rank their students (from highest to lowest) the week prior to the ITBS testing. The overall correlation between the teachers' rankings and the ITBS total reading score was $r = 0.58$. Separating out the correlations for the PALM teachers and the comparison teachers, we found the PALM teachers' rankings to be correlated with the ITBS performance at the $r = 0.62$ level, while the comparison teachers' rankings were at the $r = 0.38$ level. These correlations are somewhat difficult to interpret because the rankings are relative to the class/school context. In some cases, a child ranked by the teacher in the top 5 per cent of his class may have had a lower ITBS score than a child ranked in the bottom 5 per cent of another class in another school. Therefore, we ran correlations within classes, relating rankings to ITBS scores. The average correlation across all teachers was $r = 0.75$. Twelve of the seventeen teachers in the PALM group had correlations higher than this mean. Only six of the fourteen teachers in the comparison group had correlations higher than the mean. We interpret these patterns to mean that the PALM teachers, based on their intensive involvement in performance assessment over an entire year, were more sensitized to students' differences and strengths. This interpretation is consistent with Wolf's (1993) notion that participation in performance assessment leads to more informed assessment overall. We have no direct evidence that teachers' instructional decision-making was better as a result, but clearly the awareness of performance levels was higher.

3 Does the PALM model yield data for other audiences (e.g., administrators) that is comparable to or better than the data generated though typical ITBS testing?

To address this question, we compiled the data from several sources: the developmental indicator profile, the ITBS, teacher ratings (e.g. of children's oral reading fluency), teacher rankings of student performance and the results of on demand assessments (e.g. writing in response to a story read aloud). A quantitative score from the developmental profile was derived by calculating the number of indicators. Those behaviours that were occasionally in evidence scored one-half point, while those consistently evident received one point. These indicators were calculated separately for the three periods in which the developmental profile was applied (i.e., after the first nine weeks of school; just before the on demand assessment week; and just after the on demand assessment week).

A scoring rubric was developed for the student journals completed as part of the on demand assessments. Each journal was scored on a five point scale – from 1 (low) to 5 (high). The journals were scored holistically for overall quality, as well as analytically for accessibility, spelling, other writing conventions, sentence fluency, word choice, voice, and response/comprehension; thus, the scoring of journals yielded eight scores (one overall and seven analytic) for each of the students. Raters were trained to the following criterion levels: 80 per cent or better agreement on the holistic scale; 65 per cent or better exact agreement on the analytic scales; and 90 per cent agreement or better on all scales within a plus or minus range of one point. All journals were scored independently by two raters. The final score assigned to a student on a scale was either the agreed – on score or the mid-point between the two raters – if the raters disagreed by only one rating point. Thus, if one rater assigned a score of 3 to a student's journal on sentence fluency and the other rater assigned a 4 for that same trait, the student received the average of the two ratings, or 3.5. If the two raters disagreed by more than one point on the scale, a third rater was brought in to arbitrate. In only thirteen cases of over 7000 rating decisions made in the scoring of the journals did the two raters disagree by more than one point on any scale. Three scores were derived from the oral reading sample (familiar text and unfamiliar text). These included: accuracy of word recognition, number of self-corrections and a teacher rating of student fluency. Three scores were also derived from the inventory of beliefs, attitudes and habits. These scores represented the average rating of students on the questions that probed their viewpoints regarding reading.

As a first step in the data analysis, descriptive statistics were calculated for each of the measures used in this study (across the twenty participating teachers). As a second step in the data analysis, interrelations were calculated that related key sets of data. Next, a regression analysis was performed using variables representing the key elements of the PALM model to predict the reading score derived from the ITBS. Based on the conceptual structure of the PALM model and the findings from the intercorrelational analysis, the following variables were included: (1) the total score from the third and final developmental profile rating; (2) the score from the holistic rating of the journal used in the on demand assessment; and (3) the fluency rating for the oral reading of the unfamiliar text.

The multiple regression analysis produced an R value of 0.86 for this model, which suggests a strong relationship with the results of the ITBS for reading. All three of the variables included in the PALM model contribute significantly to the prediction. This suggests that the properties of the PALM model for gauging the development of reading abilities and skills in a normative sense are quite strong. These data provide comparable performance ratings to the ITBS and should, therefore, be as useful as the norm-referenced test scores in making policy decisions regarding the extent of learning. This analysis also suggests that all aspects of the PALM model (curriculum embedded assessments, 'taking-a-closer-look' assessments and on demand assessments) are essential to its success.

The data from the parent survey regarding the quality of the information received on student progress did not reveal any major differences in opinions between the parents of children in the PALM group and the parents of the children in the comparison group. The interviews with the PALM teachers suggest that this absence of difference may be the result of misalignment of the PALM model with existing report cards and other reporting methods. The PALM teachers would like to see reporting aligned more closely with assessment so that the information gathered through PALM could be shared in more meaningful ways. Several teachers in the PALM group interviewed their students regarding the forms of assessment. These teachers reported that all of the students favoured the PALM assessment over the ITBS. The comment of one first grade student is particularly revealing:

'On the ITBS test they only know if you bubbled in the right answer or the wrong answer. On the journal (PALM) test, they know what you are thinking.'

Conclusions

The PALM model, when implemented fully, provides teachers with information they view as informative to instructional decision-making. Although we have no data that reflect specific changes in decision-making, our findings suggest that participation in performance assessment led to increased awareness of students' skill/proficiency levels. None of the teachers, whether in the PALM group or in the comparison group, found the results of the standardized tests to be useful to them. This finding regarding the utility of standardized tests results is consistent with others who have conducted investigations in this area (e.g., Carey, 1985). The PALM model yields data on students from a performance assessment perspective that is consistent and converging. In this sense the PALM evaluation study affirms findings from other systematic investigations of performance assessment in reading (e.g., Paris, Calfee, Filby, Hiebert, Pearson, Valencia and Wolf,

1992; Valencia and Place, 1994). In addition, we have demonstrated that the psychometric properties of the PALM model are at least as strong as those of the standardized test, and provided data that are equally informative to a wide variety of external audiences.

Beyond the local audience for the evaluation study, the PALM initiative has implications for the broader educational community. First, the initiative demonstrates that it is possible to design an assessment plan for the primary grades that is responsive and considerate of the learner. In addition, this initiative demonstrates that it is possible to design an assessment plan that can satisfy both teacher needs and the needs of those who deal directly with administrative and policy level decision-making. A comprehensive performance assessment model can provide a normative database that has solid reliability and validity features. In considering the findings from this PALM evaluation study, it is important to note that it focused on early primary, in contrast with most of the studies of performance assessment that have tended to focus on the middle grades. The results of this study are consistent with the suggestion of Wixson, Valencia and Lipson (1994) that we must seek out ways to embed the assessments conducted for external purposes and audiences within assessments conducted for internal uses.

Through the collaborative development effort (including scoring the assessments together) we have been successful in building greater trust among the constituencies regarding the quality of the assessments (Wiggins, 1993). Through the development, implementation, and ongoing studies of alternative assessment plans like PALM, we may begin to reduce the tension and strife that has become a part of the assessment context. We can, in the process, discover positive ways in which the stakeholders in education can work together toward their shared goals.

There are challenges ahead for both teachers and the district as they look toward the future of this project. Performance assessment requires an enormous investment of effort on the part of the teacher. Will teachers continue to see the value of PALM when the evaluation study suggests that the external audiences can be satisfied with the administration of a norm-referenced test? Will the district offer the support needed to inservice teachers in the model as well as provide the resources necessary for the data collection and analysis associated with the on demand assessments? The literature on performance assessment suggests that the initial enthusiasm and energy associated with the implementation of the model may wear off (Calfee and Perfumo, 1993). Only with the commitment of all concerned is there any likelihood that the strategies will become practice *and* policy.

References

Calfee, R. C. and Perfumo, P. (1993) 'Student portfolios: Opportunities for a revolution in assessment'. *The Journal of Reading*, 36, 532–7.

Carey, R. F. (1985) *Program Evaluation as Ethnographic Research*. Providence, RI: Department of Education (mimeo).

Guthrie, J. T., Van Meter, P., Mitchell, A. and Reed, C. T. (1994) 'Performance assessments in reading and language arts'. *The Reading Teacher*, 48, 266–71.

Paris, S. G., Calfee, R. C., Filby, N., Hiebert, E. H., Pearson, P. D., Valencia, S. W., and Wolf, D. P. (1992) 'A framework for authentic literacy assessment'. *The Reading Teacher*, 46, 88–98.

Salinger, T. (1997) 'Consequential validity of a district-wide portfolio assessment program: Some would call it backwash'. In C. Harrison and T. Salinger (eds) *International Perspectives on Reading Assessment: Theory and Practice*. London: Routledge.

Salinger, T. and Chittenden, E. (1994) 'Focus on research: Analysis of an early literacy portfolio: Consequences for instruction'. *Language Arts*, 71, 446–52.

Stephens, D., Pearson, P. D., Gilrane, C., Rowe, M., Stallman, A. C., Shelton, J., Weinzierl, J., Rodriguez, A. and Commeyras, M. (1995) 'Assessment and decision making in schools: A cross-site analysis'. *Reading Research Quarterly*, 30, 478–99.

Tirozzi, G. N., Baron, J. B., Forgione, P. D. and Rindone, D. A. (1985) 'How testing is changing education in Connecticut'. *Educational Measurement Issues and Practice*, 4, 12–16.

Turlington, R. D. (1985) 'How testing is changing education in Florida'. *Educational Measurement Issues and Practices*, 4, 9–11.

Valencia, S. W. and Place, N. A. (1994) 'Literacy portfolios for teaching, learning, and accountability: The Bellevue Literacy Assessment Project'. In Sheila W. Valencia, Elfrieda H. Hiebert and Peter P. Afflerbach (eds), *Authentic Reading Assessment: Practices and Possibilities*. Newark, DE.: International Reading Association, 134–56.

Wiggins, G. P. (1993) *Assessing Student Performance*. San Francisco: Jossey-Bass.

Wixson, K. K., Valencia, S. W. and Lipson, M. Y. (1994) 'Issues in literacy assessment: Facing the realities of internal and external assessment'. *Journal of Reading Behavior*, 26, 315–37.

Wolf, D. P. (1993) 'From informal to informed assessment: Recognizing the role of the classroom teacher'. *The Journal of Reading*, 36, 518–23.

12

CONSEQUENTIAL VALIDITY OF AN EARLY LITERACY PORTFOLIO

The 'backwash' of reform

Terry Salinger

Introduction

Critics of testing practices abound in the USA and become especially vocal when they discuss tests and assessments used in the early childhood grades. Many early childhood educators and assessment experts contend that too much testing is done and too many erroneous decisions about young learners are made because of test data that have been gathered with inappropriate, faulty, culturally insensitive, or poorly administered instruments (see *Young Children*, July, 1993; Meisels, 1985, 1987; NAEYC, 1988; Pearson and Stallman, 1994). Other critics point out that even in early childhood classes, tests can actually determine instruction through teachers' tendency to 'teach to the tests' their students will take, whether they are tests to determine how 'ready' they are for instruction or whether or not they 'qualify' for 'special' enrichment or remedial services (Brandt, 1989; Koretz, 1988; Shephard and Smith, 1990).

To remedy the problems, some critics argue that no child should be tested with standardized instruments prior to at least fourth grade. Others suggest that teacher observation and analysis of student work should be used to keep data from traditional tests in their proper perspective. In addition to moderating the incorrect inferences that can often be drawn from standardized test data, this alternative would afford appropriate levels of credibility to classroom teachers as reliable assessors of young children's learning (Hills, 1993; Pearson and Valencia, 1987). These two points – the accuracy of inferences made about students and teachers' credibility as assessors – are critically linked at all levels of schooling but perhaps nowhere more intimately than during children's first few years in school. Understanding children's learning during these initial years in school requires high levels of inference on the part of teachers; they must be able to observe and understand students' behaviours on several levels. Essentially, they must bring to bear on their observations and subsequent decision-making their knowledge of child development, the structure of the disciplines students are striving to learn and the pedagogic options that will best facilitate individual students' intellectual and emotional growth. Well-trained, knowledgeable teachers keep all these data sources in their heads, and apply them as needed in thousands of interactions with children and decisions made each day. It is by no means inappropriate to expect that when teachers are supported in collating and externalizing their under-standings about students' learning, the results will provide useful and reliable assessment data (Chittenden, 1991).

From both a policy and a practical perspective, assessment and testing can readily be seen as aspects of a dynamic system within schools. Realization of this systemic effect has played a central role in the movement away from dependence upon external testing instruments and toward 'alterna-tive', 'authentic', 'performance-based', or 'authentic' assessment, as charted in many of the chapters within this book (see also Stiggins, 1994; Valencia, Hiebert, and Afflerbach, 1994). These classroom-based forms of assessment place teachers and students firmly in the centre of the assessment calculus; they capitalize on the work that students actually do every day and provide direct indicators of performance.

Especially in the language arts, development of these newer assessments often represents attempts to align a student-centred curriculum and the means by which student progress is measured. Sheingold and Frederiksen (1995) suggest, 'As with tasks or activities we carry out in the real world, performance assessment . . . emphasize[s] extended activities that allow for multiple approaches, as well as a range of acceptable products and results' (2). Unlike traditional multiple-choice testing, which is conducted on a single occasion, newer assessment procedures imply an ongoing process that results in more useful and more varied information about students. The ultimate purpose of performance assessments is to present a cumula-tive, rich portrait of learners' strengths, weaknesses and capabilities, thereby enabling teachers to help each student learn more effectively.

Performance assessments can take many forms, including complex tasks students carry out over several days and collections of work samples that become tangible artifacts to document students' learning. No matter the form, assessment methodologies are contextualized within the fabric of the classroom. For example, students may read an unfamiliar book aloud, while their teacher records deviations from text and notes apparent strategic reading behaviour, producing data that will be analysed later and will contribute to instructional decisions about students. Students may also keep portfolios of work collected over time that are analysed according to specific rubrics or guidelines.

Interest in performance assessment is widespread in the USA, and many teachers have adopted alternative assessments for classroom use. Often, projects to develop primary portfolios or performance assessment tasks parallel attempts to enhance instruction and to involve teachers actively in instructional and evaluation decision-making processes. While definitions and interpretations of alternative assessment methods differ from location to location, the central purposes seem to be to support instruction and to align assessment with the curriculum.

Few school districts, however, have actually undertaken the massive job of moving toward systemic use of alternatives to standardized, multiple-choice tests; they remain instead at the exploratory stage, trying to determine how and if to proceed. There is much to learn from districts that have worked toward wider assessment reform (Gomez, Graue and Bloch, 1991; Lamme and Hysmith, 1991; Valencia, Hiebert and Afflerbach, 1994). One such district, whose efforts are discussed in this chapter, has made tremendous strides in reforming its assessment practices. Almost ten years ago, the district began what has become a massive reform effort.

The development and implementation of an early literacy portfolio in the district's early childhood programme has been the linchpin of change, ultimately motivating new assessments in upper grades and in mathematics (Mitchell, 1992). The portfolio has emerged slowly, the result of several years' work. In this way, it is not unlike portfolio assessment approaches introduced into numerous districts; but this portfolio programme differs from many such efforts in that its development has been grounded in current research and theory and its use has been investigated empirically. Because the district as a whole had adopted an attitude of reform toward its assessment practices, it has been an excellent locale in which to investigate the long-term effects of change.

This chapter begins by describing the district and its reform efforts and then discusses one part of the empirical investigation of uses of the early literacy portfolio. Specifically, it discusses an attempt to identify any changes in instructional practice and in teachers' attitudes toward teaching, learning and early literacy content that have resulted from using the portfolio. In the USA, this effect is often referred to as the 'consequential validity of assessment', the changes that result as a consequence of new assessment models. In the UK, the term used for this phenomenon is 'backwash', a rather nice way of thinking about the effects of reform.

The district

The district is relatively typical of the Mid-Atlantic region of the USA. It is medium in size, with a population that is ethnically, racially and economically diverse. Total enrolment is approximately 4600 students. Many children qualify for instruction in English as a second language, and for free lunches, the usual indicator of lower socio-economic status. As New York City sprawl has extended farther out from the city limits, the rural nature of the district has changed gradually to semi-rural and suburban. The district supports seven elementary schools, each of which has some degree of autonomy in its decision-making process. The student population and teaching staff are relatively stable, and teachers in the early childhood and elementary grades are primarily seasoned professionals.

Background

Movement in the early childhood grades toward instruction that would be less didactic and more attuned to children's capabilities and needs provided the impetus for assessment change. Before work on the portfolio began, teachers in the kindergarten, first and second grades had undertaken the task of reforming their curriculum. With the enthusiastic support of the district administration, teachers moved from a traditional approach based on the concept that students needed extensive amounts of drill and practice prior to actual literacy instruction toward one that was more 'developmentally appropriate' (NAEYC, 1986a, 1986b). The desired approach would emphasize identification of the skills, strategies and background experiences students brought to school and build upon these strengths. Children entering the schools would not be tracked or grouped according to artificial criteria or screening tests, and teachers would be expected to deal with diversity of talent, background experiences and languages. Essentially, schools would be 'ready' for students, rather than expecting students to come to school 'ready' for a predetermined sequence of activities and experiences.

As they planned their new curriculum, teachers met in study groups, read a lot, talked among themselves and discussed ideas with researchers from Educational Testing Service (ETS), the test development company whose headquarters were nearby. These researchers served as 'critical friends' throughout the change process, talking with teachers, asking questions, probing assumptions and occasionally making suggestions. A large library of current books was set up and together teachers analysed and discussed current theoretical advances in early literacy. They thought about invented spelling, children's writing and storybook retelling; they gave students journals and expanded their classroom libraries. They stopped depending on a basal reader series and spent more time reading to and with the children. Over time, instruction became child- and project-centred.

It was within this context of change that plans for the early literacy portfolio were initiated. Writing about the district's portfolio development process, Mitchell (1992) has said, 'As a natural consequence of [the teachers'] new approach to teaching, a new assessment was needed. Since all testing exercises an influence on what is taught and how, it was clear that developmentally appropriate teaching could be thwarted by an emphasis on the discrete knowledge and skills required to succeed on machine-scorable, multiple-choice tests' (155). Teachers themselves requested elimination of the standardized test that was administered to all first graders; they had worked hard to understand the research base for their emergent literacy curriculum and wanted assessments aligned with the theoretical assumptions shaping their programme. Additionally, teachers thought that the standardized test failed to reflect the full extent of their students' literacy accomplishments. The standardized test for first graders was administered because of district, not state, requirements, although some form of valid measurement was necessary for all students who were referred to special services such as special education classes or Title I assistance programmes. Administrative response to teachers' request that the standardized test be suspended was a challenge: if teachers could devise an alternative that would have strong enough psychometric integrity to be used for accountability purposes outside individual classrooms, the test would be eliminated.

As in many districts, work on the portfolio was carried out by teams of teachers who invested emotionally and intellectually in the changes they sought to bring about; but in this district, teachers were supported by their administrators and worked in collaboration with their ETS 'critical friends'. The processes of development, evaluation and revision of the portfolio required that the teachers attend to various aspects of their current classroom practices and assessment needs. They considered practical matters such as collecting and storing student work and the thorny issue of evaluating or scoring assessment data.

Even from the beginning stage of the pilot testing phase, the portfolio was intended for use and interpretation across classrooms in the district. As the teachers decided the components of the portfolio – the work samples and other materials to be included – a set of procedures was developed; and staff were given training in their meaning and use. Wherever possible, all teachers who would implement the portfolio were helped to understand the underlying theoretical base of instruments such as a running record, or the word awareness writing activity during which students spell a series of words using whatever level of invented spelling they can use. A schedule for collection of specific documents was determined, but teachers were encouraged to adapt their own classroom management styles to best accomplish the collection process. Some work is collected yearly, although procedures change as students gain more proficiency. For example, children provide story retellings orally, but when they are able to write their retellings, the collection mode changes. The *Concepts about Print* test, however, is collected only during kindergarten and the beginning months of first grade.

The core contents of the portfolios are the same district-wide so that teachers can reliably recognize and understand documents in any portfolio from any school in the district. Nevertheless, teachers have considerable flexibility in determining other documentation that goes into the portfolios to enrich the portrait of each student. Teachers have also suggested additional documentation over the years, especially as they have identified aspects of literacy not fully captured by the core components of the portfolio. For example, second grade teachers have included more assessments of students' critical reading and higher order thinking. The contents of the portfolio that all teachers use are:

- *Concepts about Print* test (Clay, 1979) for kindergarten and beginning first grade students
- writing samples drawn from students' daily writing or journal entries
- story retellings (Morrow, 1988)
- oral reading records (running records) (Clay, 1985)
- an invented spelling activity in which students spell twelve words 'as best they can'
- sight word inventories
- interviews with parents and students
- yearly self-portrait
- higher order thinking/comprehension inventory
- 'optional' forms that are supposed to be used to document students perceived as having difficulty acquiring literacy

In no way did the portfolio 'drive' district instructional reforms; rather, the early childhood assessment initiatives have been intended to sustain and strengthen improvements in classroom practice. This has not been an overnight process; consider the benchmarks presented in Figure 12.1. There has been strong support for the portfolio. The district did its work well in explaining the portfolio and featured it in a booklet given to every parent of children in early childhood classes. The booklet stresses that

> the portfolio gives substance to our contention that we take children wherever they are when they enter our program and move them forward as they become competent readers and writers.
> (South Brunswick, 1991)

The portfolio has been allowed to change over time but to change in a systematic way that reflects efforts to validate the methodology and investigate its effectiveness as a replacement for a commercial, standardized test. As Figure 12.1 suggests, the portfolio was phased in over three years, with adjustments made periodically during the first round of implementation. Development and introduction of a scale to evaluate the portfolio contents represented instantiated use of the portfolio as the major assessment method for students in kindergarten through to Grade 2. The scale is discussed below.

Figure 12.1 Chronology: early literacy portfolio

School Year	
1987–8	• Recognition of need for curriculum change.
1988–9	• Study groups established and in-service opportunities provided for interested teachers.
	• New early childhood curriculum is developed and implemented.
	• Summer 'Lab school' established for teachers to build their understanding of new methodologies, including strategies such as story retellings that would be critical to the portfolio system.
	• First draft of portfolio developed.
1989–90	• Use of portfolio is initiated in small sample of kindergarten classes.
	• Second draft of portfolio developed.
	• Summer 'Lab school' again provided.
1990–1	• Portfolio used in all kindergarten classes.

The emergent literacy scale

A critical issue confronting the portfolio project concerned the credibility and uses of portfolio evidence beyond the classroom. There is a fundamental tension between the teachers' and students' needs for data expansion or elaboration and parental and administrative needs for data reduction and summary. The theoretical question is: how can rich, qualitative evidence be reduced or aggregated to meet accountability concerns without trivializing, distorting, or undercutting the instructional value of such evidence? The practical question is: how is each child doing in comparison to the others in the class? The tensions surrounding these questions were certainly not unique to this district. Wixson, Valencia and Lipson (1994) state, 'There have always been multiple purposes for literacy and there have always been differences in the information needed for various purposes. . . . External assessment purposes almost always involve monitoring of educational programs and/or large numbers of students. . . . In contrast, literacy assessments for internal purposes are primarily concerned with instructional decision-making whether within the regular classroom or special setting' (315–16).

Answering questions about internal and external use of the portfolio required that some sort of score be assigned to each student's collection of work; and because the district 'administration is characterized not only by its visionary dedication to teachers but also by its hard-headedness about evaluation' (Mitchell, 1992, 160), the score had to represent a rigorous and valid analysis of portfolio contents. Teachers and their researcher/consultant 'critical friends' began to design a scale of early literacy development, an instrument that could be used as a metric against which to measure students' portfolios. Drawing on the work of Don Holdaway (1979) and Marie Clay (1985), the *Primary Language Record* (Barrs, Ellis, Hester and Thomas, 1989; see also Falk's chapter in this volume), methodology used at Manhattan's Central Park East elementary school, and other descriptions of early literacy growth, the teachers drafted behavioural anchors for a six-point scale. *The Primary Language Record* served an especially important purpose for the teachers because it showed them how an assessment could combine observational records, work samples and a rating scale.

The resulting scale, which is presented in Figure 12.2, is a developmental instrument referenced directly to contemporary research and practice, not a checklist of specific behaviours. Use of the scale requires a holistic stance about literacy acquisition and child development. The scale describes the progression of development of children's abilities to make sense of and with print and is couched in terms of what a child *knows and can do* at each phase of that progression. Descriptors presume that children understand the cognitive and linguistic resources they draw upon as they begin to make sense of print.

Children's strategies and abilities for making sense of print are the primary focus of the scale; broader dimensions of literacy, such as interest in reading or general language proficiency are not considered. A caveat to the scale clearly states: 'The scale does not attempt to rate children's interests or attitudes regarding reading, nor does it attempt to summarize what literature may mean to the child. Such aspects of children's literacy development are summarized in other forms.' One can, of course, deduce many of these aspects of literacy development by reading across some of the documentation included in most portfolios. The parent and student interviews often provide very relevant information.

The intent of the scale is to span development from a level typical of most children at kindergarten entry through to achievement at the completion of second grade. District expectations are that most children will progress through two Emergent stages, two Beginning stages and two Independent stages during this period. The scale is used for district-wide accountability as the official metric for summarizing students' literacy growth. The official status afforded to the scale means that it essentially states the district's standards of performance for the early childhood programme and allows teachers to monitor their results in relationship to those standards.

Teachers use the scale at the middle and end of each school year to evaluate the contents of their students' portfolios; they assign a rating to each portfolio and supply these data to the district to monitor general student progress and to meet state and local evaluation requirements. Teachers can apply the scale in half-point increments when students possess characteristics expressed in both the upper and lower scale point, thus producing a full range of eleven score points.

Figure 12.2 Early literacy scale, version in sixth draft

---

1 EARLY EMERGENT

Displays an awareness of some conventions of reading, such as front/back of books, distinctions between print and pictures. Sees the construction of meaning from text as 'magical' or exterior to the print. While the child may be interested in the contents of books, there is as yet little apparent attention to turning written marks into language. Is beginning to notice environmental print.

2 ADVANCED EMERGENT

Engages in pretend reading and writing. Uses reading-like ways that clearly approximate book language. Demonstrates a sense of the story being 'read', using picture clues and recall of story line. May draw upon predictable language patterns in anticipating (and recalling) the story. Attempts to use letters in writing, sometimes in random or scribble fashion.

3 EARLY BEGINNING READING

Attempts to 'really read'. Indicates beginning sense of one-to-one correspondence and concept of word. Predicts actively in new material, using syntax and story line. Small, stable sight vocabulary is becoming established. Evidence of initial awareness of beginning and ending sounds, especially in invented spelling.

4 ADVANCED BEGINNING READER

Starts to draw on major cue systems: self-corrects or identifies words through use of letter-sound patterns, sense of story, or syntax. Reading may be laborious, especially with new material, requiring considerable effort and some support. Writing and spelling reveal awareness of letter patterns. Conventions of writing such as capitalization and full stops are beginning to appear.

5 EARLY INDEPENDENT READER

Handles familiar material on own, but still needs some support with unfamiliar material. Figures out words and self-corrects by drawing on a combination of letter–sound relationships, word structure, story line and syntax. Strategies of rereading or of guessing from larger chunks of text are becoming well established. Has a large, stable, sight vocabulary. Conventions of writing are understood.

6 ADVANCED INDEPENDENT READER

Reads independently, using multiple strategies flexibly. Monitors and self-corrects for meaning. Can read and understand when the content is appropriate. Conventions of writing and spelling are – for the most part – under control.

Notes on the scale: The scale focuses on development of children's strategies for making sense of print. Evidence concerning children's strategies and knowledge about print may be revealed in both their reading and writing activities.

The scale does not attempt to rate children's interests or attitudes regarding reading, nor does it attempt to summarize what literature may mean to the child. Such aspects of children's literacy development are summarized in other forms.

At mid-year, a sample of each teacher's portfolios is sent to a district-wide moderation (calibration) meeting, where teachers from across the district read, discuss and rate their colleagues' portfolios. The teachers work in pairs to evaluate portfolios of children whom they do know only through the evidence in the portfolios. The pairs assign a rating to each portfolio, which is then compared to the rating that had been assigned by the classroom teacher. Agreement coefficients have ranged from mid 0.80s to low 0.90s (Bridgeman, Chittenden and Cline, in press).

A critique of the Emergent Literacy Scale

The early literacy scale has been an important component of the success of the portfolio assessment system, and as will be discussed below, teachers in the district are enthusiastic about its use. Without detracting from its significance, it may be interesting to step back and analyse the scale and its implications.

The terminology used on the scale – progressing from 'Early Emergent' to 'Advanced Independent Reader' – derives mostly from Holdaway (1979). Sulzby (1994) has pointed out the dangers inherent in the term 'independent' used in this way, stating that equally well 'one could say that children "independently" render their emergent reading attempts' (278). She would prefer the term 'conventional reading' for the end point of a scale such as this because the acquisition of literacy implies being able to demonstrate certain linguistic behaviours that have been socially – or conventionally – recognized as markers of 'real' reading and writing.

To Sulzby, children demonstrate conventional literacy when they can 'read from unfamiliar (or familiar) text and move flexibly and in a coordinated fashion across all aspects of reading to interpret a text. . . . and [can] produce a text another conventionally-literate person can read conventionally and that the child also reads conventionally' (278). Words such as 'multiple strategies' and 'under control' in the descriptors for an 'Advanced Independent Reader' (Figure 12.2) capture at least some of the intent of Sulzby's definition of a child who can be considered conventionally literate.

The scale may, however, too strongly imply a sequence of six distinct stages in children's progression toward 'Advanced Independent Reading.' The teachers may indeed have initially thought of the scale in this way, believing that they could actually find discrete evidence in student work of each of the score points they wished to define. However, as Sulzby and others point out, children do move along a progression as they seek literacy, but the concept of fixed, clearly-defined stages cannot be fully supported (Kamberelis and Sulzby, 1988; Pappas and Brown, 1988; Sulzby and Teale, 1991). Instead, children seem to gather strategies and information together into a kind of repertoire of knowledge, strategies and skills that they add to and adjust with each new piece of experience they garner. Children may, for example, know a lot about reading and less about writing at any one time, but still be progressing toward conventional literacy in quite satisfactory ways.

For a rating scale to be substantively better – that is truer, more sensitive and more accurate – than standardized tests scores, it has to be flexible enough to accommodate the idea of students amassing a potentially mixed repertoire of information about reading and writing. As the teachers used their early literacy scale, they did indeed find this to be true. Initially, portfolios were to be assigned a rank of 1–6; early in the use of the scale, teachers began to assign half points as well, thereby expanding the range of scores that could be assigned to eleven. In the interviews described next, numerous teachers commented that the scale simply was not rich enough, did not fully evoke the breadth of ways in which students demonstrate their progression toward literacy.

Assessing the portfolio

After three full years of implementation of the assessment, two of the district's 'critical friends' undertook an empirical study to investigate the consequential validity of the portfolio, that is, the extent to which the portfolio system in general and especially use of the scale had actually influenced teachers' thought and practice (Jones and Chittenden, in press; Salinger and Chittenden, 1994). The purpose was not to find out whether teachers liked the portfolio, but how the portfolio had changed their practice. At the onset of the study, certain data had already been collected. For example, statistical analyses comparing the portfolio and the first grade standardized test had shown that the scale provided greater sensitivity to early indicators of literacy development than did the test scores that had been collected yearly. That is, assigning students to points on the scale gave a more accurate picture of their literacy development than the reports generated at the same time of the year by the standardized test. Additionally, the high inter-rater reliabilities from the moderation meetings indicated that the teachers could use the scale accurately.

The study consisted of developing and field-testing a questionnaire that was administered to sixty-three of the sixty-four primary teachers in the district's seven elementary schools. At the time of the interview, 17 per cent of the teachers were in their first or second year of teaching; 40 per cent had three to nine years of experience; and 43 per cent had been teaching ten or more years. Questions concerned:

- teachers' methods for collecting, storing, and organizing portfolio data
- the pieces of evidence they have found most and least useful for instructional decision-making
- the mechanics of scoring portfolios and moderating scores
- usefulness of the portfolio in conferring with parents
- the extent to which portfolio data reflect students and the dimensions of literacy instruction within each class and within the district.

About a third of the questions and issues put before the teachers concerned the scale. Of specific interest were teachers' opinions about the scale itself, the rating process and the benefits of the district moderation meetings. Teachers were also asked how they had learned to use the scale.

Each interview took thirty to forty-five minutes. The teachers were familiar with the interviewers, and the interviewers had spent time in many of the teachers' classrooms. Teachers started with a 'walk through' of a 'typical' portfolio of their own selection; they explained what the portfolio could show them about the students' strengths and weaknesses. Teachers then rated each piece of portfolio documentation according to their sense of its usefulness for assessment and answered questions about management of the portfolio and about the scale and related procedures.

Two types of data were available for analysis: answers to specific questions and teachers' comments about the portfolio and work samples themselves. All questions asked of teachers had been open-ended, and teachers' spontaneous comments had been noted as much as possible in their own language. Immediately after each interview, time was set aside for the interviewers to complete notes taken as the teachers spoke. These notes were systematically analysed by independent investigators (Jones and Chittenden, in press; Salinger, 1995). A framework for coding and analysing the teachers' responses was developed through a study of a sub-sample of interview protocols stratified to ensure representation of grade levels, schools within the district and teachers' years of experience; the revised framework was then applied to a new sample of interviews to ensure sufficient reliability for use with the entire sample.

Consequential validity: backwash of the assessment

One of the district goals for the portfolio has been to give teachers a mechanism to 'document progress of every child [and] provide data to support and inform decisions about daily teaching'. Analysis of teachers' responses in the interviews suggest that the portfolio achieves this goal in both direct and indirect ways.

Almost all teachers stated or implied that the portfolio helped them monitor and evaluate children's progress, often through confirmation of hunches or the provision of specific evidence about students' performance. This function of the portfolio resembles that of traditional testing and classroom workbook activities to the extent that the assessment procedures become a kind of template for evaluating learning. The portfolio also seemed to give teachers a way of keeping track of students' progress over time. Changes in literacy learning can occur rapidly and dramatically, and samples in the portfolio collected at specific intervals during the year helped teachers understand changes in specific students and to perceive those patterns that seemed to be most prevalent among young learners in general. This understanding seemed critical in helping teachers recognize those students who needed extra help and those who were just slower in the process one teacher described as 'getting their acts together'.

Analysis of the data that focused on teachers' perceptions of the scale sought to uncover changes in instruction and decision-making that accrued from using the scale; it also sought limitations that teachers saw in the scale, the portfolio and assessment procedures in general. As independent analyses were conducted, four specific categories of responses seemed to emerge. Teachers viewed the scale as serving the following functions:

- supporting instructional decision
- enhancing communication with others
- confirming or enhancing the review process
- indicating patterns of literacy development.

The functional category termed *supporting instructional decisions* was the least prevalent, and this is quite surprising. Proponents of classroom-based alternative assessments like to talk about 'assessment in the service of instruction'. They mean that newer forms of assessment give teachers more information about each student and enable them to make better decisions, to tailor instruction more finely and to motivate students more effectively than they could without this information.

Remarkably few (only about 10 per cent) of the comments could be construed as falling into this category. Some teachers did say that the scale alerted them to *things I need to work on* for certain students or instruction that should be *fine tuned*; but this was not common. A few teachers mentioned that students' point on the scale played a role in decisions about grouping, but these comments too were rare. One example was the teacher who found the scale useful 'for conferencing [i.e., setting up conferences with students], placement of groups, and who to partner children with'.

It was unclear from the few teacher comments whether teachers were referring to the numbers assigned to the students or to descriptive aspects of the scale. Obviously, if they were taking their cues from the wording of the behavioural anchors of each scale point, they were depending on a richer understanding of emergent literacy than the rather static concept represented by the numerical scores alone.

Because there were so few comments that could be categorized here, generalizations are risky; but the very fact that there were so few is definitely significant in terms of the portfolio system itself. Teachers seemed not to view the portfolio as a 'service to instruction'; it seemed to serve another function. This does not mean that instruction did not benefit from the portfolio approach; but the connection was at a more systemic level in that the entire process of developing the portfolio, changing instructional emphasis, collecting portfolio documentation and then evaluating the contents of the portfolio periodically had brought about a change in teachers' way of 'doing school', rather than in the process of making discrete, individual decisions.

Communicating with others

Approximately 22 per cent of the teachers made comments that could be coded as stating or implying that the scale score enabled them to *communicate with others in specific ways*. Teachers said that contents of the portfolio provided concrete evidence of students' performance and were therefore often more valuable than their own summaries or observations when they needed to discuss or communicate about a student.

The most common recipient of these communications was students' next teacher, as most teachers seemed reluctant to talk about the scale score *per se* with parents. Some teachers contended that to do so would be foolhardy because parents would not understand the underlying theoretical base and would simply consider it 'another number.' Rather than suggesting that the teachers were condescending toward the parents, these sentiments seem to point to three things. First, the teachers were realistic about parents' expectations, needs and potential misinterpretations, although they consistently reported that the portfolio itself was invaluable for explaining students' progress during parent conferences.

Second, teachers may have felt that to designate a number for a child to someone who lacked insight into the scale's developmental nature would misrepresent the complex nature of early literacy acquisition. In this way, they were beginning to realize that the scale served a valuable assessment purpose but also had limitations, because it implied that the dynamic, iterative process of learning to read and write could be divided into distinct, identifiable stages.

Third, comments about the value of the scale for communicating to others seem to indicate that teachers sensed that they, the professionals, shared a special language and set of understandings about the scale. Teachers who had been involved in the portfolio development teams would obviously feel this way, but even those who were new to the portfolio and moderation process – some of whom were still grappling with procedures – recognized that the scale represented a somewhat 'technical' and 'professional' aspect of 'doing school'. The scale enhanced communication among knowledgeable professionals:

- '[The scale is] most useful as something to pass on to the next teacher to provide a context for the work samples.'
- 'The scale is for the next teacher.'
- '[The scores] at least give you a point at which to start.' [That is, at the beginning of each school year – note perspective of receiving teacher.]
- 'I look at where they were at the end of kindergarten.'
- '[It's] useful when looking at other portfolios, and to talk to other teachers.'
- '[It] was an eye opener, because we're isolated. [Looking at the scale,] you find people who agree with you and have common consensus.'
- '[During the moderation meeting,] we had a wide discrepancy on one [student's portfolio]. Then we say that writing was being rated too low.'

Confirming or enhancing review

Twenty-three per cent of the teachers made comments which suggested that they had come to depend on the scale to *confirm or enhance their review process*. The tone of comments categorized thus suggested a higher level of professionalism than the relatively generic comments teachers had made about work in the sample portfolio used in the 'walk through' that began each interview. The difference was subtle but clear. Teachers realized that the scale provided a systematic, almost standardized way, of evaluating the evidence in the portfolio. Key words here are *systematic, standardized* and *evidence*. While obviously some of the information teachers gathered in the process of reviewing the portfolios had immediate impact on instruction, this category of comments is qualitatively different from the few comments suggesting support for instructional decision making. Teachers really seemed to see themselves assuming the role of data analyst, an essential shift in self-concept if teachers are to assume the responsibilities inherent in classroom-based assessment.

- 'It's useful. . . . it makes me think about what this child did in all areas. . . . A good review process.'
- 'It makes me look at everything in the folder. . . . puts meaning to the folder when I scale it.'
- 'It more or less confirms what I thought . . . very few surprises.'

- 'Some kids are very easy to place and I don't need to look closely at the portfolio.'
- 'For other children, I have to really analyze the portfolio.'
- 'It is helpful . . . when I sit down with the scale, I see how young they are and see how little they [kindergarten children] have accomplished.'
- 'Yes, [it's useful] but not with those who are doing well, with those who are not progressing.'
- 'It's a natural way of evaluating children – not tests! [It is] assessment without pressure, very individualistic.'
- 'I pretty much know where children are, but I do go through the folders to recheck.'
- 'If you don't have evidence [in the portfolio], you can't rate [a student].'
- 'You find out if you are really indeed using the [portfolio] material versus your [everyday] knowledge.'

Indicating patterns

Most frequently, teachers alluded to the benefits of the scale for providing *indications of patterns of literacy development.* More than 25 per cent of the comments could be thus categorized. Teachers maintained that they could see progress in children's work as they reviewed the contents of the portfolio and referenced the work against the scale. It was especially interesting to hear teachers talk about looking back over the accumulated work from previous years as a way of seeing 'real progress' over time; this was interesting because during the planning stage discussions about what should go into the portfolio teachers had resisted the idea of carrying any work over from year to year. They had maintained quite emphatically that first grade 'just wouldn't want to see that kindergarten stuff', and it might as well just be discarded after scoring each year.

Comments that suggest this searching for patterns include:

- '[The scale] lets me focus on progress.'
- 'I find it interesting that the children have really grown.'
- I like the scale because when I look at my class I can see the children's levels . . . [the scale] lets me see the range.'
- 'It's helpful with younger children, but with independent readers – what's next [in their development]? I have struggles [assigning students] between levels 3.5 and 4.5 and then some children achieve a 6 in first grade.'
- 'The child I mentioned [previously in the interview] clearly is a visual learner, doesn't use invented spelling, phonics, remembers words and uses them – his results [on the scale] are skewed.'
- '[The scale is] useful. . . . you get an overall picture of where the class is.'

Some teachers reported that the scale also helped them identify children who were not making progress:

- 'The scale serves as a red flag for at risk children.'

In some ways, it is not at all surprising that this is the most common category of comment about the scale. The entire process of reviewing and revising the early childhood curriculum had sought classrooms that were more child-centred, with teachers more focused on identifying and building upon what children bring to school with them. The teachers had indeed embraced a way of thinking about students, instruction and assessment that was different from their previous perspective, and the portfolio helped them operationalize their new view.

Other findings

Teachers made some additional comments about the scale in response to other interview questions, especially those about the moderation/calibration meetings.

- '[The meetings] make teachers realize how important it is to label and date things for others [to maintain the developmental flow].'

In total, only three (5 per cent) of the teachers said that they found the scale of little or no use. Nine teachers (18 per cent) offered recommendations or technical limitations of the scale, in comments that showed the extent of their thinking about the entire process:

- 'I think there's a point missing between 3 and 4 – a big jump.'
- 'There should be a separate scale for reading and writing.'
- 'There's a problem when kids top out a 6 very early. All 6's are not the same.'

As suggested before, comments such as these hint at teachers' uneasiness with the scale as a finite measure of students' progression toward literacy. It is entirely possible that the process of applying the scale to students' work was even more illuminating to the teachers than their struggle to define and refine the descriptors for the six points. As they compared work against the scale, they sought to match student performance against the rich but relatively static descriptors and could often identify what was missing in the descriptors. They saw the subtle aspects of literacy development they had failed to capture in their verbal descriptions, the 'missing points', the 'big jumps' that students demonstrate as they progress in individualistic ways toward reading and writing.

Many teachers talked positively about the moderation/calibration meetings and several said that they *'come too late in the year'* or were too short for the kinds of professional interchange and growth teachers experienced as they ranked and discussed portfolios. Teachers again seemed to suggest that the scale did not quite capture what they were seeing in students' work; one stated that she had 'wanted to have more time to find out where discrepancies in scores existed [during the calibration meeting].'

It was somewhat surprising to find few teachers suggesting that they had adopted a more reflective stance toward their students or their decision-making because of the portfolio. On the whole, they were very task-driven rather than inquiring beyond students' attainment of specific strategies of levels of development. One teacher did show considerable evidence of reflection as she talked about material in the portfolio. For example, she said that information about out-of-school activities collected on the parent interviews 'helped me determine novels I might use with the children for reading, since I do not have reading groups'. Referring to a writing sample, she said, 'It's hard to interpret [because of invented spelling] and I should have put in some notes at the time to make this sample more interpretable; its from 4 months ago. It's my fault; I was just learning how to manage the portfolio.' About retellings as indication of comprehension, she stated, 'this child needs work on details. I chose to have her write her retelling instead of oral mode because I felt she was just at the point where she could begin to handle writing. . . . Retellings give me some idea of comprehension, but not enough. We need a piece on comprehension. I include my own task, which is a narrative passage with comprehension questions, to be answered in writing.' Finally, when asked what she can glean in general from the portfolio documents, she answered, 'At the beginning of the year, it helps me get to know the kids. At midyear with some children, it forces them to show me strategies I otherwise didn't know they had. . . . [It] makes me shut up and listen. And that's hard for a teacher to do.'

Issues raised by teachers

Even though the majority of the teachers expressed very positive views about the portfolio assessment, the teachers also raised many issues and offered recommendations for modifications. As with most portfolio projects, teachers were concerned about management of the portfolio and its component parts. They said that the process of compiling multiple documents and collecting individual records of reading and story retelling for each child at intervals throughout the school year requires considerable organization and time. Accommodating this demand had necessitated their rethinking many of their classroom routines, the level of direct supervision young learners needed, and the actual arrangement of furniture in their rooms. Many teachers had woven the portfolio activities into their classroom routines and on the whole felt that the assessment blended well with every-day practice. Some pointed out, for example, that collecting writing samples, listening to children read, or asking them about sight words, were a part of ongoing instruction; the requirement of periodically documenting such activities was not seen as especially complicated. One teacher said that she had not found the 'portfolio much work – it just kind of happens [because] it's just what you're doing anyway'. She stated that she 'integrates the port-folio collection into daily routines [and] makes copies of many pieces' that she thinks might be good documentation for the portfolio. Another teacher reported that she had her part-time aide take over the class so that she could administer instruments such as the Concepts about Print test on a one-to-one basis; she has also developed a system of reading a story to small groups of students who then in rapid succession are taken from the class individu-ally for the story-retelling aspect of the assessment. Most of the positive com-ments stressed the value of the portfolio for the teachers themselves, but one teacher said, 'It's a very nonthreatening way to test a kid. Some kids coming to this school are so uptight, and this is good because they don't even know they're being assessed.'

Another issue raised by teachers concerned the *scope* of literacy assess-ment and the adequacy of the portfolio in meeting their assessment needs. Thus, a number of kindergarten teachers were concerned about an emphasis on reading and writing, to the neglect of language development and chil-dren's emerging interests in literature. Second grade teachers, by contrast, wanted more sensitive indicators of reading comprehension, and many, like the one quoted above, had added a measure of higher order thinking and comprehension. Some noted the importance of the personal dimension and individuality of each child. Thus, the self-portraits were valued by a number of teachers, for, as one said, 'they remind me that there's a child inside the portfolio!' Overall, the majority viewed the portfolio as meeting their literacy assessment needs, with the mesh between assessment and instruction being most complete at the first grade level.

Shifting paradigms

What I think is most striking in the teachers' comments is a real shift from a traditional way of thinking about students' learning and develop-ment to a less traditional one. I hesitate to invoke the overused term 'para-digm shift', but it does seem to fit here. In the USA, when the term paradigm shift is used, it frequently refers to change from dependence on multiple-choice tests to more open-ended performance assessments that are often developed, scored and interpreted by classroom teachers themselves. For there to be a real paradigm shift, however, change has to be much deeper than instituting new forms of assessment; and unfortunately, in a lot of places, changes are superficial at best.

What went on in this district was real systemic reform – deep-seated, intense change among the early childhood teachers and the administrators who oversee their work. The effects of change could be seen at numerous levels: instantiation of a child-centred instructional approach, reliance upon and validation of teacher-controlled assessment procedures and an emergent sense of professionalism among teachers. Change came about for many reasons, but among them was the level to which teachers took control of the change process, worked to understand what they wanted, articulated their vision and were given time to work out the details of that vision. The scale was very much a part of the vision, the real technical glue, as it were, that sets this assessment reform apart from many other reform efforts.

In developing the scale, teachers articulated their ideas about what young students should know and be able to do in reading and writing. The teachers had depended on their own experiential base and on actual student work as verification of what they wanted to include. If they felt they needed more documentation to substantiate the anchors for each scale point, they changed the contents of the portfolio to provide more information. The process was iterative and dynamic; the scale is now in the sixth version and may well change again in the near future.

During this process of reforming instruction and assessment, the teachers seemed to have shifted in their thinking about student learning and about ways to assess it. Their comments indicate that they have taken responsibility for evaluating their students, for making decisions and for substantiating their assessments of students' growth. Even more significantly, the teachers seem to have moved away from ranking and comparing students to thinking about growth in terms of each student's progress along a developmental continuum that is illustrated by specific kinds of work. They believed all students could learn, realized that traditional means of testing would not measure academic growth as they construed it and set about changing the metric applied to their students. Shephard has expressed quite succinctly what the teachers felt intuitively: 'Traditional psychometrics was developed in the context of individual differences in psychology [that is, the trait theory premise that assessment should result in comparisons] and focused on static assessment of differences rather than the assessment of changes due to learning' (1991, 6). Again, teachers' comments illustrate:

- 'I know where the kids are, but I don't think of them as numbers.'
- 'Yes, [the scale is helpful], but we don't group by levels.'
- '[The scale is] useful, but you can't just look at the scale. You need to go back to the [work in the] folder.'

This continuum of learning, expressed in terms of the anchors on the scale, represents collaboratively constructed, publicly stated, and widely understood standards. Thus, placing students 'on the scale' means more than change in assessment procedures; it represents a change in the way teachers think about students and by extension about the very act of teaching.

References

Barrs, M., Ellis, S., Hester, H. and Thomas, A. (1989) *Primary Language Record Handbook.* Portsmouth, NH: Heinemann.

Brandt, R. (1989) 'On misuse of testing: A conversation with George Madaus'. *Educational Leadership,* 46(7): 26–9.

Bridgeman, B., Chittenden, E. and Cline, F. (In press) 'Characteristics of a portfolio scale for rating early literacy'. Princeton, NJ: Educational Testing Service Center for Performance Assessment.

Chittenden, E. (1991) 'Authentic assessment, evaluation, and documentation of student performance'. In V. Perrone (ed.) *Expanding Student Assessment* Alexandria, VA: Association for Supervision and Curriculum Development, 22–31.

Chittenden, E. and Courtney, R. (1989) 'Assessment of young children's reading: Documentation as an alternative to testing'. In D. S. Strickland and L. M. Morrow (eds), *Emerging Literacy: Young Children Learn to Read and Write.* Newark, DE: International Reading Association, 107–20.

Clay, M. M. (1979) *Reading: The Patterning of Complex Behaviour.* Portsmouth, NH: Heinemann.

—— (1985) *The Early Detection of Reading Difficulties,* 3rd edn, Auckland, NZ: Heinemann.

Gomez, M. L., Graue, M. E. and Bloch, M. N. (1991) 'Reassessing portfolio assessment: Rhetoric and reality'. *Language Arts,* 68: 620–8.

Jones, J. and Chittenden, E. (in press.) 'Teachers' perceptions of rating an early literacy portfolio'. Princeton, NJ: Educational Testing Service Center for Performance Assessment.

Koretz, D. (1988) 'Arriving in Lake Wobegon: Are standardized tests exaggerating achievement and distorting instruction?' *American Educator,* 12(2): 8–15, 47–52.

Hills, T. (1993) 'Assessment in context: Teachers and children at work'. *Young Children,* 48: 20–8.

Holdaway, D. (1979) *The Foundations of Literacy.* New York: Ashton Scholastic.

Kamberelis G. and Sulzby, E. (1988) 'Transitional knowledge in emergent literacy'. In J. E. Readence and R. S. Baldwin (eds), *Dialogues in Literacy Research.* Chicago, IL: National Reading Conference, 95–105.

Lamme, L. L. and Hysmith, C. (1991) 'One school's adventure into portfolio assessment'. *Language Arts,* 68: 629–40.

Meisels, S. J. (1985) *Developmental Screening in Early Childhood: A Guide,* rev. edn. Washington, DC: National Association for the Education of Young Children.

—— (1987) 'Uses and abuses of developmental screening and school readiness testing'. *Young Children,* 42(2): 4–9, 68–73.

Mitchell, R. (1992) *Testing for learning: How new approaches to evaluation can improve American schools.* New York: Free Press.

Morrow, L. M. (1988) 'Retelling stories as a diagnostic tool'. In S. M. Glazer, L. W. Searfoss and L. M. Gentile (eds). *Reexamining Reading Diagnosis: New Trends and Procedures.* Newark, DE: International Reading Association, 128–49.

National Association for the Education of Young Children (NAEYC) (1986a) *Good Teaching Practices for 4- and 4-year olds*. Washington, DC: Author.

—— (1986b) *Position Statement on Developmentally Appropriate Practice in Early Childhood Programs Servicing Children from Birth Through Age 8*. Washington, DC: Author.

—— (1988) *Testing of Young Children: Concerns and Cautions*. Washington, DC: Author.

Pappas, C. C. and Brown, E. (1988) 'The development of children's sense of the written story language register: An analysis of the texture of "pretend reading"'. *Linguistics and Education*, 1: 45–79.

Pearson, P. D. and Stallman, A. (1994) 'Resistance, complacency, and reform in reading assessment'. In F. Lehr and J. Osborn (eds) *Reading, Language, and Literacy: Instruction for the Twenty-first Century*. Hillsdale, NJ: Lawrence Erlbaum Associates, 239–52.

Pearson, P. D. and Valencia, S. W. (1987) 'Assessment, accountability, and professional prerogative'. In J. E. Readence and R. S. Baldwin (eds), *Research in Literacy: Merging Perspectives*. Rochester, NY: National Reading Conference, 3–16.

Salinger, T. (1995) 'In England they call it "backwash": Consequential validity of an early literacy portfolio'. Presentation, University of Delaware Colloquium Series.

Salinger, T. and Chittenden, E. (1994) 'Analysis of an early literacy portfolio: Consequences for instruction'. *Language Arts*, 71: 446–52.

Shephard, L. (1991) 'Psychometricians' beliefs about learning influence testing'. *Educational Researcher*, 20(7): 2–16.

Shephard, L. A. and Smith, M. L. (1988) 'Flunking kindergarten: Escalating curriculum leaves many behind'. *American Educator*, 12(2): 34–8.

Sheingold, K. and Frederiksen, J. (1995) 'Linking assessment with reform: Technologies that support conversations about student work'. Princeton, NJ: Educational Testing Service Center for Performance Assessment.

South Brunswick Board of Education. (1992) *Early Childhood Education: A Guide for Parents and Children*. South Brunswick, NJ: Author.

Stiggins, R. J. (1994) *Student-Centered Classroom Assessment*. Columbus, OH: Merrill.

Sulzby, E. (1994) 'Children's emergent reading of favorite storybooks: A developmental study'. In R. B. Ruddell, M. R. Ruddell and H. Singer *Theoretical Models and Processes of Reading*, 4th edn. Newark, DE: International Reading Association, 244–80.

Sulzby, E. and Teale, W.H. (1991) 'Emergent literacy'. In R. Barr, M. L. Kamil, P. Mosenthal and P. D. Pearson (eds) *Handbook of Reading Research*: Volume II. White Plains, NY: Longman, 175–213.

Valencia, S. W., Hiebert, E. H. and Afflerbach, P. P. (1994) *Authentic Reading Assessment: Practices and Possibilities*. Newark, DE: International Reading Association.

Wiggins, G. (1993) *Assessing Student Performance: Exploring the Purpose and Limits of Testing*. San Francisco: Jossey-Bass.

Wixson, K. K., Valencia, S. W. and Lipson, M. Y. (1994) 'Issues in literacy assessment: Facing the realities of internal and external assessment'. *JRB: A Journal of Literacy*, 26: 315–38.

INDEX